The Vogue for Russia

To Ben, Gwen and Henry

The Vogue for Russia

Modernism and the Unseen in Britain 1900–1930

Caroline Maclean

EDINBURGH
University Press

© Caroline Maclean, 2015

Edinburgh University Press Ltd
The Tun – Holyrood Road, 12(2f) Jackson's Entry, Edinburgh EH8 8PJ

www.euppublishing.com

Typeset in Minion by
Servis Filmsetting Ltd, Stockport, Cheshire,
and printed and bound in Great Britain by
CPI Group (UK) Ltd, Croydon CR0 4YY

A CIP record for this book is available from the British Library

ISBN 978 0 7486 4729 3 (hardback)
ISBN 978 0 7486 4730 9 (webready PDF)
ISBN 978 1 4744 0350 4 (epub)

Contents

Note on Transliteration

The main text and the bibliographical references conform to the Library of Congress transliteration system, omitting diacritics and ligatures. Certain familiar names – for example, Eisenstein, Tolstoy, Dostoevsky – are spelled as they customarily appear in English, with -*y* used for final ий and ый. In quoted material the form given in the originals is preserved. This scheme of transliteration means that in some cases Russian names are not immediately familiar: for example, Nijinsky becomes Nizhinsky.

Acknowledgements

For permission to quote from unpublished materials I am grateful to the Beinecke Rare Book and Manuscript Library at Yale University; the Harry Ransom Center at the University of Texas at Austin; King's College Archive Centre, Cambridge; the National Art Library, Great Britain; the Special Collections at the British Film Institute National Archive; and the Tate Gallery Archive, London. I am also grateful to Annabel Cole for granting permission to quote from the unpublished papers of Roger Fry, and to Rogers, Coleridge and White for permission to quote from Frances Partridge's unpublished memoir of Boris Anrep. Despite my efforts, some copyright holders remain untraced or have not replied to correspondence at the time of going to press. Please contact the publisher if you hold copyright for any of the material published here and any changes or omissions will be corrected in subsequent editions.

I have received a great deal of support throughout the period of writing the book. My first thanks go to Rebecca Beasley, who supervised my doctoral thesis at Birkbeck, where this book began. Her intellect, support and friendship over the years have been very important and I am grateful for all her help and advice. I would like to thank Laura Marcus and Tim Armstrong for their expert comments and support, and also the readers at Edinburgh University Press, whose comments have undoubtedly improved the current book. I am grateful to Linda Dalrymple Henderson and Bruce Clarke for their comments on my work on the fourth dimension, and to Aimée Brown Price for introducing me to them. And thanks to Laura Salisbury and Andrew Shail, whose suggestions helped shape earlier drafts of Chapters 3 and 4. Other friends and colleagues have read portions of the book, or have contributed and supported me, and made research days in the British Library a pleasure: in particular, Corinna Csáky, Sam van Schaik, Eliane Glaser, Chris Tayler, Ophelia Field, Lara Feigel, Matthew

Taunton, Reina van der Weil, Justin Sausman and Chloë Houston Mandy. I would also like to thank all at Edinburgh University Press, especially Jackie Jones, Jenny Daly and Dhara Patel, and to my copy-editor, Wendy Lee. Thanks too to Maria Starkova-Vindman for her help with the transliteration.

During the course of my research, librarians and archivists at several institutions have been of enormous help, especially at the Beinecke Rare Book and Manuscript Library, the Harry Ransom Humanities Research Center, the Houghton Library, the National Art Library, the Tate Gallery Archive, King's College Archive Centre, the British Film Institute Special Collections and the British Library. One year of research was spent in Boston and I would like to thank Elaine Scarry and William Todd for sponsoring me at Harvard and the Harvard Society of Fellows for giving me a room to work in. And thank you to Julia Markovits for organising it all. I am also grateful to the members of the British Literature Colloquium at Harvard for feedback on my first chapter.

And finally, thanks to my family for their continued love and support, to my parents Mavis and Robert Maclean, and to my sister Sarah and her family, Geoff, Edie and Arthur. And to my extended family – the Markovitses and Bilstons who have supported me from near and far. And most importantly I want to thank Ben, Gwen and Henry, who make it all possible. I dedicate the book to them, with love.

An earlier version of Chapter 4 appeared in *Literature and History* (Manchester University Press, spring 2012) and an earlier version of Chapter 2 appeared in *Russia in Britain, 1880–1940: From Melodrama to Modernism*, edited by Rebecca Beasley and Philip Ross Bullock (Oxford University Press, 2013) and are reproduced here by kind permission of the publishers. The unpublished memoir of Boris Anrep held at the National Art Library, copyright © Frances Partridge, is reproduced here by kind permission of the author, c/o Rogers, Coleridge & White Ltd, 20 Powis Mews, London W11 1JN.

Introduction

On 21 June 1911 Sergei Diagilev's Ballets Russes gave their premiere performance at the Royal Opera House as part of the celebrations for the coronation of George V. Leonard Woolf described the Ballets Russes in his diary: 'I have never seen anything more perfect, nor more exciting, on any stage.'[1] Alexandra, the Queen Mother, apparently moved from the Royal box to an orchestra seat for performances of *Le Spectre de la rose* to get a better view of Vatslav Nizhinsky's final leap.[2] Rupert Brooke wrote that in the summer of 1911 he 'alternated between seeing the Russian Ballet at Covent Garden and writing sonnets on the lawn' at Cambridge. John Maynard Keynes made a number of trips to 'view Mr Nijinsky's legs' during the same summer.[3] In 1912 Constance Garnett published her first translation of Fedor Dostoevsky's *The Brothers Karamazov* and went on to translate almost his entire works over the next nine years. On honeymoon in Italy in the same year, Virginia Woolf read Dostoevsky's *Crime and Punishment* in French and wrote to Lytton Strachey: 'It is directly obvious that he is the greatest writer ever born: and if he chooses to become horrible what will happen to us? Honeymoon completely dashed.'[4] Earlier that year, in March 1912, Katherine Mansfield used her Russian alias, Boris Petrovsky, for the first time in the journal *Rhythm*. In the same issue, aspiring art critic Michael Sadleir introduced the British public to the spiritualist aesthetics of Vasily Kandinsky for the first time.[5] In October 1912 Roger Fry hung thirty-five Russian paintings, most of which had never been seen before in Britain, in his 'Second Post-Impressionist Exhibition'.[6]

The vogue for Russian literature, politics, dance, music and the visual arts in Britain grew steadily in the nineteenth century and reached its height in the 1910s and 1920s. Samuel Hynes noted that Russianness alone sometimes 'seemed a measure of value'.[7] But it was not always a measure of value during this period. On 16 December

1910 a group of Latvian 'revolutionary expropriators' murdered three policemen in Houndsditch, East London, triggering a press campaign against 'foreign aliens' and a false accusation of the revolutionary and founder of the Free Russian Library in Whitechapel, Aleksei L'vovich Teplov.[8] The relationship between Russia and Britain in the nineteenth and twentieth centuries is a richly diverse and expanding field of scholarship, as two recent publications demonstrate: *A People Passing Rude: British Responses to Russian Culture* (2012), edited by Anthony Cross, and *Russia in Britain, 1880–1940: From Melodrama to Modernism* (2013), edited by Rebecca Beasley and Philip Ross Bullock.[9] The focus on the institutions ('libraries, periodicals, government agencies, concert halls, universities, publishing houses, theatres and film societies') as opposed to the individuals who disseminated Russian culture in *Russia in Britain*, has informed my approach in this study. However, certain individuals do emerge from an institutional basis, including Boris Anrep, Vasily Kandinsky, Petr Ouspensky and Sergei Eisenstein.[10] Other recent scholarship on Russian culture in Britain that has informed this research includes Peter Kaye's analysis of the reception of Dostoevsky in England; Ol'ga Kaznina's work on Russian exiles in England; Laura Marcus's work on Soviet cinema and the Russian translations published by the Hogarth Press; and the wealth of scholarship on the Ballets Russes, Russian theatre and visual arts in early twentieth-century Britain.[11]

The impact of particular Russian writers in Britain has a long history, from Helen Muchnic's early investigation in *Dostoevsky's English Reputation* (1939) and Royal Gettmann's *Turgenev in England and America* (1941), to broader accounts found in Dorothy Brewster's survey of critical literature in *East–West Passage: A Study in Literary Relationships* (1954) and Gilbert Phelps's *The Russian Novel in English Fiction* (1956). More recent accounts of the impact of individual Russian authors in Britain include *Dostoevskii and Britain* (ed. W. J. Leatherbarrow, 1995), *Tolstoi and Britain* (ed. W. Gareth Jones, 1995), *Ivan Turgenev and Britain* (ed. Patrick Waddington, 1995) and Glyn Turton's *Turgenev and the Context of English Literature, 1850–1900* (1992). And the field now includes studies on individual modernists and their engagement with Russian culture, including Roberta Rubenstein's *Virginia Woolf and the Russian Point of View* (2009), Joanna Woods's work on Katherine Mansfield and Neil Cornwell's book on Joyce. Also relevant to this study is Rachel May's account of British translations and transformations of Russian literature.

My research adds to this growing body of scholarship by offering a sustained study into the overlap between the vogue for Russia and the vogue for the unseen in modernist Britain. 'Unseen' in this context captures a range of occult activities, beliefs and organisations that include, at different points, spiritualism, magic, theosophy and mysticism. Arguably, 'unseen' could have been replaced by 'magic', 'spirituality', 'uncanny', 'occultism' or 'enchantment', but it was chosen because it captures the way that science and occultism co-existed on the same spectrum, from the magic rituals practised by members of the Hermetic Order of the Golden Dawn to the scientific experiments conducted by the Society of Psychical Research. To quote from Janet Oppenheim's seminal *The Other World* (1985):

> The quest for a hidden pattern, a unifying framework, a fundamental theory, to bring together every diverse particle and force in the cosmos, was intrinsically the same, whether one stressed the links between heat, electricity, magnetism, and light, or looked for connections between mind, spirit, and matter.[12]

I will offer brief, by no means exhaustive, overviews of the vogue for Russia and the vogue for the unseen in Britain, and also the evolution of theosophy and occultism in Russia, later in this introduction, before considering the spaces where they co-exist and overlap in individual chapters.

The Vogue for Russia concentrates on the exchange and interchange of ideas about art and the unseen circulating between Russia and England during the period from about 1900 until about 1930. The importance of the Russian radical philosophy of Petr Ouspensky to the British novelist Mary Butts, for example, was complicated by the work of the British mathematician and philosopher Charles Howard Hinton, who influenced Ouspensky; and Kandinsky's spiritual aesthetics expressed in *Über das Geistige in der Kunst* (1912) were underpinned by a wide range of material, including that of British theosophists Annie Besant and Charles Leadbeater in *Thought-Forms* (1905). In other words, cultural exchange is not simple; theories of art are absorbed across cultures but are transformed in the process. To quote Stephen Hutchings: 'cultures develop as *organic wholes*' and when external influences are absorbed they are subject to '*structural transformation*'.[13] Rather than map one set of cultural ideas on to another, this study seeks to peel back layers and think through the structural transformations that occur along the way.

The majority of the book questions how and why Russian aesthetics contributed to British modernism rather than the other way round. Generalisations about British Russophilia swiftly run into a circular argument: Russian aesthetics were appealing because they were Russian. To begin elsewhere, the traditional chronology of modernist scholarship narrates a progression from nineteenth-century realism to modernist abstraction. And yet, to take an iconic example, after Kazimir Malevich painted 'Black Square' in 1915, he returned to figurative painting in the 1920s and 1930s. The study of the unseen in the modernist period complicates the trajectory of realism to abstraction, or symbolism to formalism by thinking through abstraction as another form of realism.

Four of the key figures associated with the birth of abstraction in the visual arts, Kazimir Malevich, Piet Mondrian, František Kupka and Vasily Kandinsky, moved towards abstraction through their engagement with theosophical, mystical and spiritual theories and beliefs, as opposed to through a rejection of mimetic realism. Malevich presented his 'Black Square' as the formula for universal feeling and 'the nonrepresentational and cosmic quality of Being'.[14] Kandinsky argued in 1911 that a general interest in abstraction was being reborn 'in the forms of occultism, spiritualism, monism, the "new" Christianity, theosophy, and religion in its broadest sense'.[15] Even the establishment of the Bauhaus, the new school for the arts in Weimar Germany, now regarded as the epitome of simplified form and function, caused a stir in the press in early 1920 when its founder, Walter Gropius, was accused of being 'full of philosophical, metaphysical, and mystical thoughts'.[16] Steven Marks has quipped that Russian constructivism had a 'spiritual intensity that almost seems to have negated their professions of atheism and materialism'.[17] The move to abstraction in the early twentieth century, then, could be characterised as a move towards a different form of realism, a realism of the unseen. As David Shields puts it, rather bluntly, in his opening to *Reality Hunger*, 'every artistic movement from the beginning of time is an attempt to figure out a way to smuggle more of what the artist thinks is reality into the work of art'.[18] Leigh Wilson has expertly argued that magic reconceptualised the mimetic for modernists by offering the possibility of animated as opposed to inert copy.[19] My argument here runs in parallel to Wilson's, that Russian aesthetics of the unseen, whether it be Dostoevsky's world of inner psyches, the spiritual synaesthesia of Kandinsky's colour system or Ouspensky's theory of a fourth-dimensional space, contributed to the move amongst British modernists to find ways to formulate this new, authentic, unseen experience. The resulting emphasis on form over mimesis was, in some ways, a byproduct.

Hutchings's model has informed my approach. He tracks the relationship between art and the everyday (the 'virtually untranslatable phenomenon of *byt*') in Russian modernist fiction, and argues that, rather than acting as mutual reinforcement (as they do in *Madame Bovary*, for example), they undermine each other and act as mutual contamination, so that in Chekhov's 'The Kiss', provincial life 'acquires the features of a pointless anecdote' and art 'adopts the humdrum inconsequentiality of provincial life'. He argues that the term '*byt*' itself connotes negativity, but through dialogue with the Eastern Church's 'Orthodox trinitarian thought with its urge to resist the hierarchies of the particular and universal, flesh and spirit' Russian modernists (including Andrei Belyi, Vasily Rozanov and Aleksei Remizov) reconfigure the relationship between art, life and narrative. They transfer and mix up the human and the divine, the 'everyday' or humdrum ('*byt*') and 'true' life ('*zhizn*'), and dissolve narrative frames in the process. Although Hutchings asserts that British modernists like Woolf and Joyce differ from their Russian counterparts because they see a pattern underlying the 'dank stench of *byt*', one of the ways to account for the reception and transformation of Russian aesthetics in Britain is to think through the separation of *byt* and *zhizn* in British modernism.[20] *The Vogue for Russia* tells the story of some of the ways in which Russian aesthetics turned the insides out of British modernism, bringing together formalism and occultism, art and the unseen, *byt* and *zhizn*.

The vogue for Russia

In 1887 Matthew Arnold declared that the 'Russian novel now has the vogue, and deserves to have it', but Russomania, and indeed Russophobia, in Britain began much earlier than that.[21] Laurence Senelick has described how Russomania 'overwhelmed the streets and salons in the years 1812 and 1813' when Britain became an ally of Russia in the Napoleonic wars.[22] The Crimean War (1853–6) stirred curiosity amongst the British and Russians about their enemy, leading to an increase in translations of Russian texts into English, usually from French or German, as well as several plays being produced about the war.[23] In fact, the bilateral relationship between Russia and Britain has not been straightforward since the sixteenth century, when Richard Chancellor arrived in Arkhangelst in 1553 at the court of Ivan the Terrible. Fluctuating between allies and enemies over the centuries, the Anglo-Russian entente of 1907 brought Russia and Britain into the Triple Entente with France, contributing to the enthusiasm for Russian culture in the early 1900s, which only grew with the revolutionary period. This was accompanied, as Philip Bullock notes, by ideological distaste, 'where Britain was a parliamentary democracy with a constitutional monarchy, Russia was an autocracy' and where Britain claimed to 'espouse free trade' Russia only abandoned feudalism in 1861.[24] The build-up of support for the first stage of the revolution in February 1917 grew in some quarters: for example, with Sidney Webb's establishment of advisory committees to prepare the working classes for power or Leonard Woolf's establishment of the 1917 Club, a mixture of artists, writers and 'politicals', who formed 'something like an intelligentsia'.[25]

In her lively survey of the history of translations of Russian texts into English, *East–West Passage* (1954), Dorothy Brewster chronicled the publication of critical works on Russian literature from Charles Turner's *Studies in Russian Literature* (1882) to Maurice Baring's *Landmarks of Russian Literature* (1910) and beyond. Political exiles living in Britain, including Petr Kropotkin, Sergei Stepniak-Kravchinsky and Feliks Volkhovsky, were important conduits for Russian politics and culture during the period. Stepnyak-Kravchinsky and Volkhovsky were responsible for introducing Russian literature and language to Constance Garnett (she recorded that Volkhovsky 'suggested my learning Russian and gave me a grammar and a dictionary'), prompting her comprehensive translations of the work of Turgenev, Tolstoy, Dostoevsky, Chekhov and Aleksandr Gerzen (Herzen).[26] Other important translators in the early twentieth century were Maurice Baring, Stephen Graham, John Cournos, Aylmer Maude and Louise Maude.[27] Few people spoke Russian in Britain at the start of the twentieth century and it was not an established subject in universities. Bernard Pares established the first School of Russian Studies at Liverpool University in 1907, and the School of Slavonic Studies was set up at King's College, London, in 1915, although Russian had been taught at King's since 1899. Beasley has thoroughly documented the history of Russian studies in early twentieth-century Britain, and so it is sufficient here to note that by the outbreak of the First World War Russian could be studied at university level at five institutions: Manchester, London, Oxford, Cambridge and Liverpool.[28]

From the time of the earliest translations of Russian literature into English, its spiritual, as opposed to its material qualities, were emphasised. Arthur Quiller-Couch wrote in *Pall Mall Magazine* in February

1901 that Tolstoy and Turgenev 'vindicate and establish the truth that the concern of [Russian] fiction is with things spiritual, intimate, deep; not with things material, external, shallow; with interpreting the hearts of men, not with counting their buttons'.[29] Although there are quite a few buttons in Tolstoy and Turgenev that one could count, the connection to Woolf's 'Character in Fiction' (1924) is compelling. Woolf differentiates between the Russian novelist who would 'pierce through the flesh' to 'reveal the soul – the soul alone, wandering out into the Waterloo Road, asking of life some tremendous question which would sound on and on in our ears after the book was finished', and the English novelist who would bring out the 'buttons and wrinkles; her ribbons and warts' (and the French novelist who would offer a 'general view of human nature').[30] The fascination with the hearts and not the buttons of men grew steadily with, in Dmitry Mirsky's phrase, 'the cult of Dostoievsky' between 1912 and 1920, the period of Garnett's translations of Dostoevsky.[31] Gordon Campbell referred to 'great Dostoevsky nights' at the Lawrences and John Middleton Murry declared that 'the objective "pattern" of Dostoevsky had declared itself, through me as instrument'.[32] Maurice Baring's influential *Landmarks of Russian Literature* declared that Dostoevsky's genius 'soars higher and dives deeper than that of any other novelist, Russian or European'.[33]

The emphasis on the spiritual was part of the stereotype of the Russian soul, still prevalent today, which was, amongst other things, romantic, exotic, enigmatic, authentic, strong and sensitive. Anthropologist Dale Pesmen notes that the 'Russian soul is what, in Russian and Soviet books, films and folklore, idiotically romantic foreigners write about', but it is also a 'trope of romantic national self-definition' that was vital to a 'changing repertoire of options and practices that evoked and mediated actions, interpretations, and change' in the 1990s.[34] The ethnography of the Russian soul is beyond the scope of this project but the proliferation of the myth is apparent in early twentieth-century Britain, as three publications from 1916 alone demonstrate: *A Slav Soul and Other Stories* by Aleksandr Kuprin, selected and edited by Stephen Graham; The *Soul of the Russian* by Marjorie and Alan Lethbridge; and *The Soul of Russia*, edited by Winifred Stephens.

The *Soul of the Russian* declared that 'the Slav' moves in a different world from ours, a 'world of dreams', 'a world of the intangible, of the speculative': in fact, in a 'world as far removed from the precision of the scientist as is the furthest star from this earth'.[35] *The Soul of Russia* offers a slightly less homogenised and intellectually demeaning overview, consisting of a collection of articles by Russian as well as

British writers, poems and prints on a range of topics including the Ballets Russes, Natal'ia Goncharova, Dostoevsky, Russian folklore, and international relations. It was published in aid of Russian refugees and distributed by the General Committee of the All Russian Union of Zemstvos (local government). In her introduction Stephens hoped that the book might provide the 'merest glimpse' into Russia's 'noble, but sometimes unfathomable soul' to 'knit more closely those bonds of mutual interest and friendship which unite us to our heroic Ally'.[36] The soul here, then, serves as political currency. The spiritual and the political are brought together in an article in the same collection by the history professor N. I. Kareev (translated by Adeline Lister Kaye), called 'How Far Russia Knows England' in which he hoped both nations would arrive at a point where they have an 'unprejudiced and sympathetic regard for the spiritual world of each other's national ego, to the benefit of both nations and of all mankind'.[37]

Earlier during the war, thirty-four 'Russophiles', including Edward and Constance Garnett, Henry James, H. G. Wells, Arnold Bennett, John Galsworthy and Jane Harrison, came together to shift the public perception of Russia as ruthless and barbaric. They signed a declaration called 'Russia in Literature: Tribute by British Men of Letters', in which they referred to the 'ever-present sense of spiritual values, behind the material' that enabled Russian literature to 'move so naturally in a world of the spirit'.[38] Grammar and the spiritual form an unlikely alliance in Jane Ellen Harrison's *Russia and the Russian Verb* (1915), in which she stated her 'need' for the 'imperfective aspects' of Russian verbs that 'feed me spiritually'.[39] As Rachel May concluded in her book on Russian translations, the period from 1910 to 1925 were the years of the 'Russian craze' in Britain.[40]

The idealisation of the Russian soul was also a result of misgivings about England and appealed to those reacting against a modern industrialised Britain. Stephen Graham's popular books on Russia substituted a romantic, mystical version of Russia for the lost conservative utopia of rural England, apparent in, for example, *A Tramp's Sketches* (1912), *Undiscovered Russia With 26 Illustrations and 3 Maps* (1912) and *With the Russian Pilgrims to Jerusalem* (1913).[41] In 1905 Edward Garnett described the 'profound abyss' that separates the 'national life and moral ideals of the Anglo-Saxon and the Slav'. The Englishman seeks worldly success and righteousness, and from this springs 'our lack of charity, our hard superiority to the "sinner", our open or secret self-complacency, and also – what is perhaps even more insidiously narrowing – our distrust of our own human impulses, our dislike of letting our emotions go'. We find 'perpetually in Russian literature', continues Garnett, that the 'Russian soul is deepened, made tender, lovable, and broadly human by recognising unflinchingly all the darkest and saddest strands of human life'.[42] Helen Smith points out that Garnett had set himself the task of explaining the 'unfamiliar mental habits and emotional colouring' behind the Russian fiction translated by his wife.[43] Tolstoy, for Garnett, was the 'strength of the national soul incarnate in one strong man'. This national soul, continued Garnett, with 'its hatred of *nuances, delicatesse,* rhetoric and sentimentality', was combined with its 'tenderness, its pity, its true love and charity for its brothers'.[44] In 1925 Roger Fry recorded a conversation he had with Dmitry Mirsky when they bumped into each other at the Hôtel de l'Étoile in Chablis. Presumably 'well-oiled', according to G. S. Smith, Fry supposed Mirsky was 'preoccupied with your soul. All Russians seem to me to suffer from hypertrophy of the soul.' Mirsky apparently replied, 'No, I don't know at all that I have a soul.'[45] It was perhaps Fry and his contemporaries who were suffering from hypertrophy of the Russian soul.

The vogue for Russia in early twentieth-century Britain cannot be separated from the vogue for the Ballets Russes. In June 1911 the Russian Ballet, directed by Sergei Diagilev, arrived in London with Tamara Karsavina and Vatslav Nizhinsky as the lead dancers and sets and costumes designed by, amongst others, Nikolai Rerikh (Roerich), Leon Bakst and Aleksandr Benua (Benois).[46] It is possible that Anrep chose Rerikh as one of the exhibitors in Fry's 'Second Post-Impressionist Exhibition' in 1912 as a result of seeing his set and costume designs for the Polovtsian dances. Leonard Woolf captured the spirit of excitement in his diary: 'The Russian Ballet became for a time a curious centre for both fashionable and intellectual London. It was the great days of Diaghilev with Nijinsky.' He continued: 'night after night one could go to Covent Garden and find all round one one's friends, the people whom one liked best in the world, moved and excited as one was oneself'.[47] Lyn Garafola has highlighted the gap between the memories and the reality of the social makeup of the audience, noting that during the pre-war seasons the audience largely consisted of the British ruling class, rather than the 'intelligentsia'. And yet, Diagilev 'touched the Bloomsbury imagination, animating its fantasies with movement', as is evident in Duncan Grant's *Queen of Sheba* (1912) and Vanessa Bell's panels for the Omega room at the Ideal Home Exhibition in 1913.[48] The *Daily News* referred to *Le Pavillon d'Armide* as 'sumptuous and magnificent entertainment' and to the 'exquisite colouring, graceful movement' and 'sprightly' music that 'made a spectacle surpassing in artistic feeling and charm anything yet seen in this country'.[49]

Although Diagilev's first season offered little that was new in terms of ballet scenarios, the Ballets Russes came to represent an exotic Eastern otherness for British audiences.[50] *The Times* praised and bestialised the 'savage-joyful panther-leaping of the men' in *Prince Igor* (*The Polovtsian Dances*), and Frank Swinnerton wrote in his book on the Georgian cultural scene that the 'English public' were 'longing for whatever was savage and untamed, the wildnesses of "Scheherazade" and "Tamar" were like firewater to the innocent native'.[51] *Vogue* claimed that the English wanted to know the 'truth about these semi-Asiatic and semi-European people', as though they were a new species to analyse.[52] The Russian diplomat Petr Aleksandrovich Liven (Lieven) wrote in 1936 that the 'West expected from Diaghilev not only Russian national colour, but something like Eastern Asiatic exoticism which the Press and public demanded of anything Russian'.[53] Dar'ia Protopopova has argued that the fascination with 'the East and the archaic' triggered the fashion in Britain for all things Russian in the early twentieth century.[54] The combination of apparently Eastern primitivism and Western fauvism, enigmatic spiritualism and heady materialism was certainly an enticing mix for British audiences.

The vogue for the unseen

Spiritualism, occultism, theosophy, magic and mysticism are not discrete movements. They are defined by mystery and the unknown, and so it is worth setting out some distinctions. The following brief survey draws on the early pioneering *Encyclopaedia of Occultism* by Lewis Spence in 1920 and on more recent histories of occultism and esotericism by Antoine Faivre, Wouter Hanegraaff, Nicholas Goodrick-Clarke and Maria Carlson, as well as the recent modernist scholarship of Mark Morrisson, Alex Owen, Leon Surrette, Timothy Materer, Roger Luckhurst, Pamela Thurschwell, Marina Warner and Leigh Wilson.[55]

The year 1848 tends to mark the starting point of spiritualism because of the famous table rappings allegedly experienced by sisters Catherine and Margaretta Fox in New York. The movement expanded rapidly and included séances, automatic writing, levitation, clairvoyance, telepathy and ectoplasmic materialisation, a process by which a physical substance is claimed to be produced, as a result of spiritual energy. Historian Alex Owen asserts that in America the number of spiritualist believers might have reached between one and two million during the height of the craze in the 1850s. In Britain the figure has been put at somewhere between 10,000 and 100,000.[56] Famous British converts to spiritualism include Arthur Conan Doyle, Elizabeth Barrett Browning and Queen Victoria. Spiritualism, unlike occultism, was not concerned with knowledge and explanation. Whereas members of occult sects went through initiation ceremonies, spirit mediums required no training.

The Society for Psychical Research (SPR) was set up in 1882 in Britain to investigate spiritualism using scientific methods with Henry Sidgwick, Professor of Moral Philosophy at Cambridge, as President. Members included the physicists Oliver Lodge, William Barrett and Lord Raleigh, the classical scholar Frederic Myers and the psychologist William James. Other prominent members included Arthur Balfour, Prime Minister (1902–5), and his younger brother, the classical scholar Gerald Balfour, who was President of the Apostles (the Cambridge Conversazione Society) when Roger Fry gave his first speech as Vice-President. Roger Fry attended meetings of the SPR during his time at Cambridge and, according to Virginia Woolf, he 'visited haunted houses in a vain pursuit of ghosts'.[57] By the 1880s spiritualism had come under considerable attack in both America and Britain, but it became popular again after the First World War, when families wanted to contact their deceased loved ones. Owen describes the prominent part played by women as practising spiritualists between the 1860s and 1880s, and Joy Dixon positions spiritualism and theosophy in relation to the English feminist movement in her book *Divine Feminine* (2001).[58] Spiritualism and (as will be discussed) theosophy are movements that were set up by women, and there is scope for further research on gender and Russian aesthetics in relation to the unseen, but gender is not significantly marked in the discussion here.

There are clear distinctions to be drawn between spiritualism and occultism. Broadly speaking, spiritualism is based on the idea that the dead can communicate with the living through an untrained human medium, and so is available to all classes and beliefs. By contrast, occultism is concerned with hidden or secret esoteric knowledge that is available only to a select few initiates. The idea that objects held 'occult' properties that were unseen can be tracked back to the medieval period, and the idea of an occult force became popular in the eighteenth century when Franz Anton Mesmer (1734–1815) borrowed it to describe the 'fluid' that he believed connected all beings and things to each other. This formed the basis of his theory of 'animal magnetism', a popular vitalist theory in the eighteenth century. The first use of the term 'occultism' is believed to have appeared in Jean-Baptiste Richard de Randonvillier's *Dictionnaire des mots nouveaux* (1842). Éliphas Lévi popularised the term in his *Dogme et rituel de la haute magie* (1856), and Helena Blavatsky introduced the term to the English-speaking world in the weekly journal *Spiritual Scientist* in 1875. In *Isis Unveiled* (1877), she defined occultism as 'the whole range of psychological, physiological, cosmical, physical, and spiritual phenomena'.[59] To paraphrase Hanegraaff: current scholarly use of the term 'occultism' tends to refer to the nineteenth-century developments within Western esotericism, including spiritualism and modern theosophy, comprising 'all attempts by esotericists to come to terms with a disenchanted world'.[60]

One of the most famous organisations of the 'unseen' from the modernist period is the Hermetic Order of the Golden Dawn. Founded in 1888 to teach occult science through ritual magic, it used Éliphas Lévi's work as its foundation and sought to establish order from an array of occultist activities, including Christian mysticism, Cabala, alchemy, Freemasonry and theosophy.[61] W. B. Yeats was one of its most high-profile members and his interest in an eclectic range of mysticism and magic has been fully explored. The use of 'the occult' with the definite article was a late twentieth-century development, which, according to James Webb, has come to mean anything that cannot be explained, or 'rejected knowledge', as popularised by Colin Wilson's *The Occult* (1971).[62] Scholarship on modernism and occultism began in the 1970s with work on Henry James and W. B. Yeats, and within art history with Sixten Ringbom's work on Kandinsky and theosophy.[63] Demetres Tryphonopoulos opened up scholarship on Pound and his interest in 'metaphysical occultism' and Leon Surette elevated the importance of mysticism and occultism over materialism and positivism in Pound, Eliot and Yeats. Timothy Materer has described the importance of 'occult lore and ritual' for a coterie of modernists, including Yeats, Pound, Eliot, H.D., Robert Duncan, Sylvia Plath and Ted Hughes.[64]

Recent research into science and occult discourses in the modernist period has focused on the importance of energy and thermodynamics as a framework to connect science and literature (Bruce Clarke, *Energy Forms: Allegory and Science in the Era of Classical Thermodynamics*, 2001); the idea of telepathy and its 'fugitive leap across distance' and 'the rich analogic potential of occulted connection' (Roger Luckhurst, *The Invention of Telepathy*, 2002); and Mark Morrisson's 'alchemical renaissance' of the 1880s (*Modern Alchemy*, 2007).[65] The revolutionary impact of non-Euclidean geometry and *n*-dimensional theories of space on modernist artists and writers has been thoroughly documented in the work of Linda Dalrymple Henderson, which will inform the chapters on the fourth dimension in this study, and more recently Miranda Hickman's work on geometry and modernism.[66] And in Tim Armstrong's *Modernism, Technology and the Body*, the body becomes a site of corporeal occultism, or of 'obscurity and experiment'.[67] In her biography of the latter part of Yeats's life, Brenda Maddox wrote that the 'academic world is less embarrassed by the paranormal than it used to be'.[68] It is now possible, as this study demonstrates, to analyse the contribution of mysticism, spiritualism, theosophy and occultism, grouped here as the unseen, to the aesthetic forms of British modernism.

Although spiritualism and occultism had obvious differences in terms of practice and clientele in Britain, the two movements converged at the end of the nineteenth century. Hanegraaff argues that recent scholarship is responsible for a lazy convergence of terms but Owen's definition of a 'new spiritualism' that included occult elements and an elite version of Victorian spiritualism is compelling. What we could call an 'occultist spiritualism' was concerned with questions about the spiritual dimensions of the universe; it drew on medieval and Renaissance Christian mysticism, neo-Christianity and Eastern religions. The widespread popularity of this occultist spiritualism is clear from the range of books, journals and organisations that proliferated during the first decade of the twentieth century. Owen rightly points out that historians have been 'off-beam' in ignoring a phenomenon that was 'so obviously remarked upon and important at the time'.[69] Owen appropriates 'enchantment' as a way to describe 'the sense of the magical, the numinous, and a state of mind seemingly at odds with the modern outlook'.[70]

Russia and the unseen

As in Europe and North America, spiritualism was popular in Russia during the second half of the nineteenth century. Maria Carlson's history of the theosophical movement in Russia reveals that civil servants and members of the military formed the largest groups of adherents.[71] Educated Russians spoke French and so the 'spiritisme' of Allan Kardec (Hippolyte Léon Denizard Rivail, 1804–69) was initially more popular than Anglo-American scientific spiritualism, although this changed through the efforts of Aleksandr Nikolaevich Aksadov, a self-defined scientific spiritualist. Facing the censorship of the church, Aksadov founded the journal *Psychische Studien* in Leipzig in 1874 and, with two university professors from the Imperial University in St Petersburg, formed a Scientific Commission for the Study of Mediumistic Phenomena in 1875–6, headed by the chemist Dmitry Mendeleev (1834–1907). Mendeleev was accused of attempting to sabotage the research by publishing negative results before the experiments had begun, and the ensuing press coverage only served to increase the popularity of the spiritualists. The Manifesto of 17 October 1905 eased censorship restrictions, allowing the widespread publication of occult material, and Carlson notes that more than thirty occult titles were published in Russia between 1881 and 1918, at which point many of them were banned.[72] One of the more popular publications, *Rebus* (1881–1917), had more than 16,000 subscribers in 1905, and in 1906 reported that 'all of Petersburg is caught up in an unusually powerful mystical movement' and 'a veritable maelstrom of little religions, cults, and sects has taken shape there'. The Russian Spiritualist Society for Study in the Areas of Experimental Psychology, Psychic Phenomena and Spiritualism was established in 1906 and the first Congress of Spiritualists in October 1906 was attended by more than 400 people.[73]

The widespread interest in occultism in nineteenth-century Russia has been loosely connected to Russia's defeat in the Crimean War (1853–6), the abolition of serfdom in 1861, the industrialisation of the 1890s and the European-wide decline of organised Christianity. In the early twentieth century, the unexpected defeat in the Russo-Japanese War (1904–5), followed by the 1905 Revolution, the assassination of the Prime Minister Petr Stolypin in 1911, the suffering and social unrest caused by the Great War, and the 1917 Revolution have all been cited as triggers for the revival of occultism. Social upheaval and political unrest clearly played a huge part, but the ideas emerging in Russian theosophy and occultism were also rooted in Russian symbolism, French decadent literature and German idealist philosophy, and therefore held appeal for educated Russians. Andrei Belyi, for example, defined the symbolist worldview as synthetic in nature and based on idealist, religious and occult philosophies.[74]

Russian occultist organisations may have borrowed their structures from the West, but they also drew on indigenous cultural, religious and pre-Christian heritage. Carlson points to the long tradition of witchcraft and sorcery as well as mystical sectarianism in Russia, as shown by the earliest Russian magic books, which date back to the seventeenth century.[75] The Orthodox Russian Church held its own Gnostic traditions, including those of Boehme's mysticism and mystical Freemasonry, but in 1822 the Church convinced Tsar Alexander I to confiscate occult books and to ban all mystical and secret societies. In response, Russian presses were set up elsewhere, notably in Warsaw and Leipzig, and occult books were either imported or smuggled across the borders. In the 1840s the Slavophile movement declared that Western ideas and institutions were not suited to Russia. Slavophiles turned instead to Russian folktales, myths and legends, many of which featured supernatural beings and forces that derived from the 'peasant *dvoeverie* (dual faith)' which had co-existed happily with Christianity. Even in the 1920s, Bernice Rosenthal argues, the occult themes of Soviet literature 'were transformed into the magical or fantastic elements that observers have noted in Socialist Realism'.[76]

French occult classics were important in Russia, as they were across Europe. The works of Lévi were widely read, and in particular *Dogme et rituel de la haute magie* (1856), *Histoire de la magie* (1860) and *La Clef des grands mystères* (1861). After the relaxation of censorship in 1905, Russians had access to texts translated by the Russian Symbolists Bal'mont and Briusov, including work by St Yves d'Alveydre, the German philosopher Karl DuPrel, Camille Fammarion, Allan Kardec and Paul Sédir. The French occult revival triggered a renewed interest across Europe and Russia in medieval mysticism, alchemy, Cabalism, Rosicrucianism, Gnosticism and ancient Hermeticism.

Theosophy

Theosophy was a highly intellectual movement that appealed to writers and artists in Russia, Europe, North America and beyond. Holbrook Jackson noted in 1913 that the 'revival of mysticism' in Britain 'revealed itself in the Theosophical movement' and Carlson writes that theosophy found its niche in the Russian Silver Age because it shared the 'major concerns and vocabulary of the creative and God-seeking intelligentsia'. Modern theosophy (as opposed to the Christian theosophical writings of the seventeenth century) was established with the founding of the Theosophical Society in 1875 and became a 'universal, cosmopolitan phenomenon'.[77] Spiritualism may have had more adherents but theosophy had 'greater influence on art and thought'.[78] The Society was set up by the Ukrainian Helena Petrovna Blavatsky (1831–91) and the American Colonel Henry Steel Olcott (1832–1907) in New York. The original aim of the Society was to 'draw together men of goodwill whatsoever their religious opinions, and by their desire to study religious truths and to share the results of their studies with others'. The Society sought to form a Universal Brotherhood of Humanity and emphasised the study of religions and philosophies, including neo-Platonism, Swedenborg and the Cabala, that may have expressed the 'Divine Wisdom'.[79]

In its first year, members of the Theosophical Society were concerned with experiments in psychometry, thought reading and mesmerism. A year later, it turned its attentions to psychic experiments, including attempts to achieve out-of-body experiences. In 1879 Olcott and Blavatsky travelled to India, and the work of the Society became closely associated with Eastern esotericism. In 1880 Olcott and Blavatsky moved to Sri Lanka (then Ceylon) and became involved in the revival of Buddhism there. Blavatsky's teachers, Mahatmas Morya and Koot Hoomi Lal Sing, were purportedly living hidden in the Himalayas. However, when they began to communicate by letters that mysteriously dropped from the ceiling of the 'Occult Room' of the headquarters in Adyar, Blavatsky's followers became suspicious, particularly when one letter included a quotation from a volume of essays by Frederic Myers. In 1884 Blavatsky's friend, Emma Coulomb, announced that 'Madame Blavatsky was a fraud' and that she had forced her husband to 'build a trapdoor to deliver Mahatma letters and trick apparatus in the Occult Room'.[80] Richard Hodgson, a member of the Society for Psychical Research, was sent to India to investigate the activities of the Theosophical Society. Hodgson concluded that the letters had been written by Blavatsky or her assistant, and wrote in his report that he had

> no doubt whatever that the phenomena connected with the Theosophical Society were part of a huge fraudulent system worked by Madame Blavatsky with the assistance of the Coulombs and several other confederates, and that not a single genuine phenomenon could be found among them all.[81]

A previous report in the published proceedings of the Society for Psychical Research described Blavatsky as 'neither the mouthpiece of hidden seers, nor as a mere vulgar adventuress; we think that she has achieved a title to permanent remembrance as one of the most accomplished, ingenious, and interesting imposters in history'.[82] Blavatsky returned to England after the scandal and completed her second major work, *The Secret Doctrine* (1888), to accompany *Isis Unveiled* (1877).

Her home in Lansdowne Road became a place of pilgrimage for undeterred writers, artists and scholars in London.

The Secret Doctrine claimed that the object of a human's existence was the return to a single divine source (known variously as the Original Creative Impulse, One Unity or Divine Thought), through repeated incarnations, and to seek one eternal truth that had become obscured over time. Theosophists were encouraged to believe in seven planes of existence – physical, astral, mental, intuitional, spiritual, monadic and divine – and that humans perceive the first three or four planes, but in time will develop the ability to perceive all seven planes and reach perfection. Perception in (or on) the astral plane was connected to the fourth dimension, asserted the theosophists, because objects were perceived from all directions at once, an idea that had obvious appeal to cubists. If space was not strictly three-dimensional, claimed theosophists, time was also considered illusory, given its bond with the material world. The disruptions of, and liberations from, space and time, and theories of new powers of perception are not new in discussions of modernism but their theosophical Russian heritage offers an alternative narrative.

Blavatsky's emphasis on synthesis in the *Secret Doctrine*, subtitled *The Synthesis of Science, Religion and Philosophy*, appealed to people's sense of order and also catered to eclectic tastes. Theosophy, as an international organisation, offered a synthesis of East and West, science and religion, a unity of the arts, 'a global utopia' and a kind of 'spiritual Darwinism'.[83] After Blavatsky's death in 1891 and Olcott's in 1907, Annie Besant became President of the Theosophical Society and, with Charles Webster Leadbeater, established what became known as 'second-generation Theosophy'. In addition to Besant's role as an educational and social reformer, she and Leadbeater introduced Catholicism into the society, as well as a focus on the practice of psychic or occult powers, as opposed to a theoretical understanding of occultism.[84] However, Besant's leadership lost members of the Society, including the scholar G. R. S. Mead, who had been Blavatsky's private secretary. Mead and 700 British members separated themselves and formed the Quest Society. Despite this, theosophy, argues Goodrick-Clarke, was 'perhaps the single most important factor in the modern occult revival'.[85] Undoubtedly, theosophy appealed to intellectuals as an alternative to spiritualism and as a bridge between religion and science. The Theosophical Society's influence and international reach are evident today in the Anthroposophical Society, established in 1913 by the German theosophist Rudolf Steiner (1861–1925), which remains active; the remaining 'Theosophical Society – Adyar', still active in India; and the 'Theosophical Society', which refers to itself as the sucessor organisation to the original Society and is based in Pasadena, California.

Spiritualism in Russia may have had a more public profile, but, as in Britain, theosophy was more influential for artists, writers and philosophers. Theosophy appealed to the educated Russian elite because it offered an alternative to the industrialised world of strikes, social unrest and a growing middle class. Theosophy provided a reality 'of mind and art where absolute aesthetic and spiritual values still held'. However, Blavatsky's reputation suffered in Russia, largely due to the publication of Vsevolod Solov'ev's book *Zhritsa* (1904), a damning account of her excesses and scandals.[86] Anna Kamenskaia (1867–1952) became head of the newly formed Russian Theosophical Society in 1908. She was active in social work and the Women's Movement in Russia and became a personal friend and follower of Annie Besant after hearing her speak for the first time in England in 1902. Back in Russia, Kamenskaia set up a small theosophical group, which proliferated into more unofficial groups, encouraged by the participation of Anna Pavlovna Filosofova (1837–1912), mother of the writer and philosopher Dmitry Filosofov and aunt of Sergei Diagilev. With the censorship law relaxation of 1905, the journal *Vestnik Teosofii* was set up in January 1908, based on the *Theosophical Review* in London, and it included an artistic and literary section on the spiritual in art. The Russian Theosophical Society was established in November of that year. The inaugural meeting was held on 17 November 1908 in St Petersburg and Kamenskaia was elected General Secretary.

Carlson suggests that by 1910 there were probably several thousand (mostly female) Russian theosophists, although only 300 were registered officially in St Petersburg in 1913. Members of the Russian Theosophical Society were involved in numerous philanthropic activities, including working in food kitchens and hospitals, and running nurseries and day care for children, and they had a pedagogical circle that met regularly, as well as being involved in arts and crafts, believing that people were happier if using their hands. Famous Russian theosophists include symbolist writer Andrei Belyi, scholar, writer and critic Viacheslav Ivanov, composer Aleksandr Skryabin, poet Maksimilian Voloshin, the painters Nikolai Rerikh and Vasily Kandinsky, and the philosopher Petr Ouspensky, whom Carlson calls the 'most important and visible Theosophical thinker in Russia'.[87] Ouspensky wrote:

In 1907 I found the Theosophical literature, which was prohibited in Russia – Blavatsky, Olcott, Annie Besant, Sinnett, etc. It produced a very strong impression on me although I at once saw its weak side. [. . .] it opened doors for me into a new and bigger world. I discovered the idea of esotericism, found a possible approach for the study of religion and mysticism, and received a new impulse for the study of 'higher dimensions'.[88]

Although Ouspensky left the Russian Theosophical Society in 1914, much of his subsequent philosophy had its roots in theosophy's attempt to unite science, philosophy and religion. His work was indebted to the idea that time and space are non-linear and his mystical mathematics influenced a number of Russian abstract artists, including Matiushin and Malevich. In 1915 Ouspensky met Gurdzhiev and decided to follow his teachings. Having met A. R. Orage on a brief visit to London before the war, Ouspensky wrote a series of articles in 1919 for *The New Age* called 'Letters from Russia', in which he concluded that Bolshevism was 'a catastrophe, a shipwreck'.[89] When the White Army was being evacuated to Turkey by the British, Ouspensky was helped by Orage's former Russian correspondent, Carl Bechhofer Roberts, to escape to Constantinople, where he met Gurdzhiev again. In 1921 he went to London and lectured at the Quest Society, organised by G. R. S. Mead. The war gradually led to the demise of *Vestnik Teosofii* and after the Bolshevik revolution in 1917, occult societies were persecuted and later closed by official decree in 1922.

Politics and aesthetics cannot be artificially separated. John Rodkers's 'Russian Impressions', written after a trip to the Soviet Union in 1933, demonstrate this well; to quote Ken Hirschkop, they were 'Soviet', rather than 'Russian' impressions or 'evaluations of the success or failure of the communist enterprise'.[90] This is not a book about the response of British modernists to Russian politics, but the interrelationship between politics, aesthetics and the unseen certainly deserves further attention. For example, we might contrast Woolf's engagement with the 1917 Club, her 'plod[ding] off in the foggy cold to address the Guild upon the Russian revolution' and correcting Meriel Buchanan's account of the Kornilov affair in *The Times Literary Supplement*, with Butts's anti-Bolshevism and her fascination with Ouspensky and exiled 'White' Russians.[91] There is scope to explore further the ways in which the interest in the unseen might be considered as a form of denial, or as a way to avoid the political. But, as in any scholarly work, there are omissions to account for, and the majority of the book remains within the world of British aesthetics.[92] Also beyond the scope of the book are the various other 'unseens' that permeated modernist Britain, but it is worth mentioning, for example, the Catholic mysticism of Friedrich von Hügel and his tripartite theological structure involving mysticism, history and science – an important influence on the Christian mysticism of Evelyn Underhill.

Chapter 1 asks why Roger Fry included a room full of Russian artworks in his 'Second Post-Impressionist Exhibition', alongside the British and French artworks (as opposed to, say, Italian futurism or German expressionism), and why scholars have, to a great extent, ignored the Russian pictures. In answering this, the Russian artist Boris Anrep emerges as a significant figure for Bloomsbury aesthetics. Anrep's choice of largely spiritually inspired Russian artworks and his ideas about Byzantine mosaics and his sympathies for the Slavophile movement are read alongside the Bloomsbury aesthetics in which he was immersed. In her work on Bloomsbury and the philosophy of Bertrand Russell and G. E. Moore, Ann Banfield hints at the importance of mysticism in discussions in Cambridge and Bloomsbury around the time of Russell's 'Mysticism and Logic' (1914), and Jane Goldman refers to the 'spiritual dimension of significant form'.[93] Building on these nuggets, the chapter returns to Fry's interest in Byzantium and mysticism in his early career and offers a spiritually inflected, mosaicist reading of *The Waves* (1931) via the prism of Anrep's aesthetics. Also relevant to this chapter are Woolf's collaborative translations of Russian texts with the Ukrainian émigré Samuel S. Kotelyansky and her numerous reviews of Russian literature.

Chapter 2 examines Russian aesthetics within British modernist magazines. It begins with the moment when Kandinsky's aesthetics were first introduced to the British public in 1912, in an article by Michael Sadleir in *Rhythm*. I trace the emphasis on the unseen within the Bergsonian philosophy of the journal. The chapter broadens out into a consideration of the aesthetics of the journal's editors, John Middleton Murry and Katherine Mansfield. Murry's early aesthetics were closely aligned with a Bergsonian concept of rhythm, which evolved into a more overtly mystical and, ultimately, religious concept of harmony during the course of his career. By contrast, despite the circumstances of Mansfield's death at Georgy Ivanovich Gurdzhiev's 'Institute for the Harmonious Development of Man' in Fontainebleau, the relationship between art and the unseen remains complicated, an opacity visible in Mansfield's work.

Chapter 3 turns to the mathematical theory of the fourth dimension as mediated via the Russian radical philosopher, Petr Ouspensky.

Widely read in Britain, Ouspensky's *Tertium Organum* was of particular significance to British novelist Mary Butts, whose work serves as a case study here for the fourth dimension in British modernism. The idea of a fourth-dimensional space originated in non-Euclidean geometry and became popular amongst theosophists and spiritualists in Europe, America and Russia. It was taken up as an aesthetic device by writers and artists of the modernist period, as in Max Weber's *Interior of the Fourth Dimension* (1913) and Ford Madox Ford and Joseph Conrad's collaborative novel, *The Inheritors* (1901). Perception of the fourth dimension required a new way of thinking and looking, a delayed perception, like Viktor Shklovsky's theory of *ostranenie* (estrangement). New modes of perception triggered new modes of expression, which are discussed in relation to Butts's *Taverner* novels, *Armed with Madness* (1928) and *Death of Felicity Taverner* (1932), as well as her published and unpublished journals.

Chapter 4 reconsiders the importance of Russian montage to British modernism via Sergei Eisenstein's theory of 'overtonal' montage, a theory he aligned to a fourth dimension of space. Eisenstein's theories of film were published in Britain in *Close Up* (1927–33), the first British journal to 'approach films from the angles of art, experiment and possibility'.[94] The chapter analyses the rhetoric surrounding early photography and film before moving on to Eisenstein's overtonal montage as he described it in 'The Fourth Dimension in the Kino' (1930).[95] Eisenstein's theories are used to analyse Kenneth Macpherson's film *Borderline* (1930) and to investigate H.D.'s (Hilda Doolittle) later work, contributing to an emerging body of work that situates her aesthetics within the context of her interest in Russian aesthetics and film.

Susan Stanford Friedman's narratives of 'modernisms' reveal the contradictions between the understanding of modernism as 'rational ordering' within the social sciences and as 'anarchistic disordering' in the humanities and, more specifically, studies of the avant-garde. She avoids the formation or dismantling of hegemonies and argues instead that meaning is produced 'liminally in between'.[96] Borrowing Friedman's seminal pluralism, and acknowledging Stephen Ross's point that modernism has a 'persistently uncanny endurance', I offer another fibre for the fabric of modernist studies, a double thread that brings together mainstream British modernism and an alternative Russian-inflected aesthetics of the unseen.[97]

Notes

1. Leonard Woolf, *Beginning Again*, p. 48.
2. Hynes, *The Edwardian Turn of Mind*, p. 336.
3. Quoted in Garafola, *Diaghilev's Ballets Russes*, p. 316.
4. *Letters of Virginia Woolf*, II (1975), p. 5 (Woolf to Lytton Strachey, 1 September 1912).
5. Michael Sadleir, 'After Gauguin', *Rhythm*, 1.4 (1912), 23–9. *Über das Geistige in der Kunst* was first published in Britain as *The Art of Spiritual Harmony*, trans. M. T. H. Sadler (London: Constable, 1914). Michael T. H. Sadler changed his name to the older spelling of Sadleir in 1914 to differentiate himself from his father, Michael E. Sadler. I refer to Michael T. H. Sadler as Sadleir in the text to avoid confusion.
6. Not all of the Russian paintings arrived on time for the opening in October, but they were included in the rehanging in January 1913.
7. Hynes, *The Edwardian Turn of Mind*, p. 345.
8. For a full account see Henderson, 'The Free Russian Library in Whitechapel', in Beasley and Bullock, eds, *Russia in Britain*, pp. 71–86.
9. Anthony Cross, ed., *A People Passing Rude: British Responses to Russian Culture* (Cambridge: OpenBook, 2012); Rebecca Beasley and Philip Ross Bullock, eds, *Russia in Britain, 1880–1940: From Melodrama to Modernism* (Oxford: Oxford University Press, 2013).
10. Beasley and Bullock, 'Introduction Against Influence: On Writing about Russian Culture in Britain', in *Russia in Britain*, pp. 1–18.
11. Kaye, *Dostoevsky and English Modernism 1900–1930*; Kaznina, *Russkie v Anglii*; Marcus, *Tenth Muse*; Donald, Friedberg and Marcus (eds), *Close Up 1927–1933: Cinema and Modernism*; Clarke (ed.), *Translations from the Russian by Virginia Woolf and S. S. Koteliansky*; Garafola and Baer (eds), *The Ballets Russes and its World*; MacDonald, *Diaghilev Observed*; Senelick, *The Chekhov Theatre*; Blakesley and Reid (eds), *Russian Art and the West: A Century of Dialogue in Painting, Architecture, and the Decorative Arts*.
12. Oppenheim, *The Other World*, p. 396.
13. Hutchings, *Russian Modernism*, p. 8.
14. Sarabianov, 'The Many Faces of the Russian Avant-Garde', p. 272.
15. Kandinsky, 'Whither the "New" Art?', p. 101.
16. 'Das Staatliche Bauhaus in Weimar', *Beilage zur Thüringer Tageszeitung*, 3 January 1920, Bauhaus Archiv, Berlin, quoted in Washton-Long, 'Expressionism, Abstraction, and the Search for Utopia in Germany', p. 208.
17. Marks, *How Russia Shaped the Modern World*, p. 239.
18. Shields, *Reality Hunger*, p. 3.
19. Wilson, *Modernism and Magic*, p. 1.
20. Hutchings, *Russian Modernism*, pp. 7, 3, 221, 226.

21. Arnold, *The Works of Matthew Arnold*, IV (1903), p. 187.

22. Senelick, 'For God, for Czar, for Fatherland', p. 20.

23. Senelick notes that between 1854 and 1855 ten London theatres had twenty-five plays licensed for production that dealt with the conflict: 'For God, for Czar, for Fatherland', p. 21.

24. Bullock, *Rosa Newmarch and Russian Music*, p. 25.

25. Beasley, 'Russia and the Invention of the Modernist Intelligentsia', p. 28.

26. Richard Garnett, *Constance Garnett: A Heroic Life*, p. 75.

27. See Beasley and Bullock, eds, *Translating Russia, 1890–1935*, special issue of *Translation and Literature* (2011), for a discussion of the illusion of transparency in translation and of individual translators, including Jane Harrison, S. S. Kotelyansky and Koreny Chukovsky.

28. See Beasley, 'Reading Russian: Russian Studies and the Literary Canon', pp. 162–87.

29. A. T. Quiller-Couch, *Pall Mall Magazine*, February 1901. Quoted in Brewster, *East–West Passage*, p. 154.

30. Woolf, 'Character in Fiction', p. 426.

31. Mirksy, *The Intelligentsia of Great Britain*, p. 107.

32. Murry, *Between Two Worlds*, p. 369. Gordon Campbell described the intellectual debates that took place with the Lawrences at Murry and Mansfield's Rose Tree Cottage, The Lee, as 'the great Dostoevky nights, when Mansfield was always at her worst'; quoted in Alpers, *The Life of Katherine Mansfield*, p. 169.

33. Baring, *Landmarks in Russian Literature*, p. 261.

34. Pesmen, *Russia and Soul*, pp. 5, 6. See also Williams, *Russia Imagined: Art, Culture, and National Identity, 1840–1955* for a discussion of the origins of the 'Russian soul'; and Hellberg-Hirn, *Soil and Soul: The Symbolic World of Russianness* for a cultural studies approach to ideas of Russianness and the Russian soul.

35. Lethbridge and Lethbridge, *The Soul of the Russian*, pp. 1–2.

36. Stephens, ed., *The Soul of Russia*, pp. v–vi.

37. Kareev, 'How Far Russia Knows England', p. 101.

38. *The Times*, 23 December 1914, p. 10.

39. Harrison, *Russia and the Russian Verb*, p. 11. For a full discussion of Harrison's translations, see Schwinn Smith, '"Bergsonian Poetics" and the Beast: Jane Harrison's Translations from the Russian', in Beasley and Bullock, eds, *Translating Russia*, pp. 314–33.

40. May, *The Translator in the Text*, p. 31.

41. See Michael Hughes's *Beyond Holy Russia: The Life and Times of Stephen Graham* (Cambridge: OpenBook, 2014).

42. Garnett, 'Maxim Gorky', *The Speaker*, 11 March 1905, p. 570.

43. Smith, 'Edward Garnett: Interpreting the Russians', p. 302.

44. Garnett, 'Tolstoi's New Novel', *The Speaker*, 11 November 1899, p. 146.

45. Smith, *D. S. Mirsky*, p. 102. 'Introduction', in *Letters of Roger Fry*, I, p. 79.
46. The first performances at the Royal Opera House in Covent Garden in 1911 consisted of *Le Pavillon d'Armide, Le Carnaval, Polovtsian Dances from Prince Igor* (21 June), *Le Spectre de la rose* (24 June), *Les Sylphides* (27 June), *Cléopâtre* (7 July) and *Scheherazade* (20 July). See Macdonald, *Diaghilev Observed*, p. 26.
47. Leonard Woolf, *Beginning Again*, p. 49.
48. Garafola, *Diaghilev's Ballets Russes*, pp. 300, 322, 323.
49. Review of *Le Pavillon d'Armide, Daily Mail*, 22 June 1911. Quoted in MacDonald, *Diaghilev Observed*, p. 32.
50. Stravinsky's *L'Oiseau de feu* (The Fire Bird) premiered at the Royal Opera House in Covent Garden on 18 June 1912 and was the first ballet to capture the sense of the 'new'.
51. 'The Russian Ballet', *The Times*, 24 June 1911, p. 13; Swinnerton, *The Georgian Literary Scene*, p. 296.
52. Quoted in Chadd, 'The Rite of Spring', in *The Diaghilev Ballet in England* (exhibition catalogue), ed. Chadd and Gage, p. 22.
53. Liven, *The Birth of the Ballets Russes*, pp. 75–6.
54. Protopopova, 'Dostoevsky, Chekhov, and the Ballets Russes', p. 40.
55. For an overview and definitions of terms associated with occultism from the period, see Lewis Spence, *An Encyclopaedia of Occultism: A Compendium of Information on The Occult Sciences, Occult Personalities, Psychic Science, Magic, Demonology, Spiritism and Mysticism* (London: George Routledge, 1920). For more recent accounts, see *Dictionary of Gnosis and Western Esotericism*, ed. Wouter J. Hanegraaff et al. (Leiden: Brill, 2007); Nicholas Goodrick-Clarke, *The Western Esoteric Traditions: A Historical Introduction* (Oxford: Oxford University Press, 2008). For a full account of the history of theosophy in Russia and an account of Blavatsky's struggle to regain and retain her international reputation in her homeland, see Maria Carlson, *'No Religion Higher Than Truth': A History of the Theosophical Movement in Russia, 1875–1922* (Princeton: Princeton University Press, 1993).
56. Owen, *The Place of Enchantment*, p. 261 n11, n8.
57. Woolf, *Roger Fry*, p. 56. For a history of psychical research, see Alan Gauld, *The Founders of Psychical Research*.
58. See Owen, *The Darkened Room*, and Dixon, *Divine Feminine*.
59. Blavatsky, *Isis Unveiled*, 1, p. xxxvii.
60. Hanegraaff, 'Occult/Occultism', in *Dictionary of Gnosis and Western Esotericism*, pp. 884–9 (p. 885).
61. For a history of the Hermetic Order of the Golden Dawn, see R. A. Gilbert, *Revelations of the Golden Dawn* (London: Quantum, 1997).
62. Webb, *The Occult Underground*, p. 192; Wilson, *The Occult* (London: Hodder & Stoughton, 1971).

63. Banta, *Henry James and the Occult*; Harper (ed.), *Yeats and the Occult*; Ringbom, *The Sounding Cosmos: A Study in the Spiritualism of Kandinsky and the Genesis of Abstract Painting*.

64. Tryphonopoulos, *The Celestial Tradition*; Surette, *The Birth of Modernism*; Materer, *Modernist Alchemy*.

65. Clarke, *Energy Forms*; Luckhurst, *The Invention of Telepathy*, p. 5; Morrisson, *Modern Alchemy*, p. 11.

66. Henderson, *The Fourth Dimension and Non-Euclidean Geometry in Modern Art*; Hickman, *The Geometry of Modernism*.

67. Armstrong, *Modernism, Technology, and the Body*, p. 4.

68. Maddox, *George's Ghosts*, p. xv.

69. Owen, *The Place of Enchantment*, p. 6.

70. Owen, *The Place of Enchantment*, pp. 4, 12.

71. Vladimir Pavlovich Bykov, leader of the Moscow Circle of Dogmatic Spiritualists, estimated that 53 per cent of the subscribers to his spiritualist publications (*Spiritualist, Golos Vseobshchei Liubvi* and *Ottuda*) were civil servants and the military. See Carlson, *'No Religion Higher Than Truth'*, p. 27.

72. Carlson and Davis, 'Russian Occult Journals and Newspapers', in *The Occult in Russian and Soviet Culture*, ed. Rosenthal, pp. 423–43.

73. Carlson, *'No Religion Higher Than Truth'*, pp. 4–5, 26.

74. Carlson, *'No Religion Higher Than Truth'*, p. 9.

75. Carlson, *'No Religion Higher Than Truth'*, p. 15.

76. Rosenthal, 'Introduction', in *The Occult in Russian and Soviet Culture*, ed. Rosenthal, pp. 10, 28.

77. Jackson, *The Eighteen Nineties*, p. 160; Carlson, *'No Religion Higher Than Truth'*, pp. 7–8, 13.

78. Rosenthal, *The Occult in Russian and Soviet Culture*, p. 9.

79. Santucci, 'Theosophical Society', in *Dictionary of Gnosis and Western Esotericism*, pp. 1114–23 (p. 1114).

80. Carlson, *'No Religion Higher Than Truth'*, p. 41; Meade, *Madame Blavatsky*, p. 289.

81. Mr Hodgson's Report, 'Account of Personal Investigations in Ida, and Discussion of the Authorship of the "Koot Hoomi" Letters', in *Proceedings of the Society for Psychical Research, 1885*, III, p. 210.

82. 'Report of the Committee appointed to Investigate Phenomena connected with the Theosophical Society', p. 207.

83. Carlson, *'No Religion Higher Than Truth'*, pp. 205, 206.

84. Santucci, 'Theosophical Society', p. 1118.

85. Goodrick-Clarke, *The Western Esoteric Traditions*, p. 226.

86. Carlson, *'No Religion Higher Than Truth'*, pp. 7, 44.

87. Carlson, *'No Religion Higher Than Truth'*, pp. 61, 73.

88. Quoted in Carlson, *'No Religion Higher Than Truth'*, p. 74.

89. Ouspensky, *Letters from Russia 1919*, p. 28.

90. Hirschkop, 'Afterword', p. 265.
91. Woolf, *Diary*, I, p. 309 (4 November 1919); Woolf, 'A View of the Russian Revolution' (1918), pp. 338–40.
92. For accounts of the political bilateral relations between Britain and Russia, see Hughes, *Diplomacy before the Russian Revolution: Britain, Russia and the Old Diplomacy, 1894–1917* and Wilson, *The Policy of the Entente*.
93. Banfield, *The Phantom Table*, pp. 359–60; Goldman, *Modernism, 1910–1940*, p. 46.
94. Cover wrapper, *Close Up*, 1.4 (1927).
95. Eisenstein, 'The Fourth Dimension in the Kino', parts I and II, *Close Up* (1930). The essay was written in Russian in two parts in Moscow and then in London in 1929. The complete piece was published in Russian for the first time as 'Chetvertoe izmerenie v kino' ['The Fourth Dimension in Cinema'] in *Izbrannye Proizvedeniya* ['Selected Works'], vol. 2 (Moscow: Iskusstov, 1964), pp. 45–59; this is the title given in Richard Taylor's *Selected Works*, 4 vols (London: BFI Publishing, 1988), I, 181–94. Further references will be made to the version in Taylor's *Selected Works*.
96. Friedman, 'Definitional Excursions': *Modernism/Modernity* (2001), pp. 502, 505.
97. Ross, 'Uncanny Modernism', p. 41.

CHAPTER 1

'Splinters and Mosaics': Bloomsbury Aesthetics Reconsidered

In 1924 Virginia Woolf noted in her diary that we are 'splinters & mosaics; not, as they used to hold, immaculate, monolithic, consistent wholes'.[1] Mosaics, stone fragments cemented on to a hard surface, became an increasingly important visual metaphor for the writing process for Woolf in the late 1920s. Having visited the Byzantine mosaics at Monreale in 1927, the same year she began to contemplate writing *The Waves*, she wrote to her nephew Julian Bell advising him that 'trying to conglomerate words, like mosaic chips, together' had 'many advantages over fluent melody'. The method, she continued, is 'vivid and stark' but it 'asks extreme exactness and more attention'.[2] Piecing words together as a mosaic fits well with readings of modernist texts as montage or collage, fragments shored against collective ruin. Small stones are scattered throughout Woolf's work from the 'little green stone' on Mr Hilbery's watch chain to Phyllis Jones's words that 'peppered' the audience like a 'shower of hard little stones'.[3] But the connections between mosaics and Bloomsbury run deeper than a shared taste for scattered stones.

The Bloomsbury fascination for Byzantine mosaics was anticipated by Roger Fry's trips to Italy in 1891 and 1894, and the connections that he began to make between Byzantium and modern art, explored fully in J. B. Bullen's *Byzantine Rediscovered*. Fry's meetings with Matthew Prichard, former deputy director at the Isabella Stewart Gardner Museum in Boston, also encouraged Fry's developing interest in Byzantium. They met in 1905 in Boston and again in Paris in 1906. Bullen points to a formative moment in August 1907 in Venice, where Prichard wrote of the Pala d'Oro at the Basilica di San Marco that 'I shall not ever see a more glorious page in my life-time.' Fry was in Venice in the same month and 'may have been stimulated by Prichard's enthusiasm to look once again at Byzantine work'.[4] There followed more visits to Italy by Fry and various trips to Constantinople

by members of Bloomsbury (Woolf in 1906, Duncan Grant and
Maynard Keynes in 1910, and Fry and Vanessa and Clive Bell in 1911),
and Bullen notes that 'around 1912 Byzantinomania was at its height.
Duncan Grant designed "Byzantine" costumes for Granville Barker's
Macbeth, and Roger Fry visited Ravenna again'. And Clive Bell offered
Hagia Sophia as the 'supreme architectural expression' of his theory of
'significant form' in *Art* (1914).[5]

Central to the revival of Byzantium and its connection to Russophilia
in Britain was the arrival of the Russian mosaicist, Boris Anrep.
Ottoline Morrell described Anrep as 'clever, fat, good-hearted, sensual,
but full of youthful vitality and Russian gaiety'.[6] Fry was less enthu-
siastic, describing Anrep several years later as 'rather a bore with his
infinitely theoretical way of approaching everything'.[7] And in 1933
Woolf revealed an exasperated intimacy between herself and Anrep
in a postcard to the Russian ballet dancer Lydia Lopokova, who had
married Maynard Keynes in 1925: 'No, no, no – I cannot face another
conversation with B.A. – nor he with me – at the moment we're sick to
death of talking to each other – but united in love of L----a [Lydia].'[8]

Anrep is now known for his mosaics in the foyers of the National
Gallery, Westminster Abbey, the chapel at the Royal Military Academy
at Sandhurst, the Greek cathedral in London, the Bank of England
and Tate Britain. But years before these commissions, he curated
the Russian section of Fry's 'Second Post-Impressionist Exhibition'
in 1912. When he first arrived in Britain, to study at the Edinburgh
New College of Art in 1910, Bullen notes that the 'Byzanting impulse'
of Vanessa Bell and Duncan Grant was given a 'more serious tone'.
According to Augustus John, an early supporter of Anrep, he was
affected 'by the early Byzantine traditions still surviving in Russia'
and had succeeded in 'expressing modern conditions in terms which
have too long been considered obsolete'.[9] Building on Bullen's work
on Byzantium and Bloomsbury's visual arts, this chapter moves
the discussion into the verbal mosaics of Woolf's work. The focus is
the Russian mystical version of Byzantium that filtered through to
the aesthetics of Fry and Woolf. Anrep's theories of modern art, published in the preface to Fry's exhibition catalogue and his articles for
the Russian journal *Apollon* (1909–17), contribute to the splintering
of Bloomsbury's formalist aesthetics.[10] In one of his late lectures as
Slade Professor at Cambridge, Fry described the 'ideal work of art'
as the 'outcome of a free spiritual activity and its reception implies
a correspondingly free spiritual activity on the part of the apprecia-
tor'.[11] Fry's Byzantine-inflected post-impressionism injected a strand

of spirituality into Bloomsbury that can be read through into Woolf's work.

Russian arts in Britain

In January 2008, Adrian Searle, art critic for *The Guardian*, wrote that the Russian artworks hanging in the 'From Russia' exhibition at the Royal Academy were 'stirring and soulful and funny and, well, weird'.[12] Almost a century earlier, reviewing works by some of the same Russian artists exhibited in Roger Fry's 'Second Post-Impressionist Exhibition' of 1912, Rupert Brooke described them as 'heavy with soul, packed with a religious romanticism', and another critic referred to them as 'strange and unaccustomed'.[13] The idea of Russian artwork as the impenetrable expression of a deep Slavic soul, clothed in mysticism, romanticism and religion, is a resilient stereotype.

The Great Exhibition of 1851 included four galleries devoted to Russian art and objects. Although the exhibition opened on 1 May, the Russian display was not fully installed until 7 June. Queen Victoria recorded her visit on 11 June: 'We went first to look at the Russian exhibits, which have just arrived and are very fine: doors, chairs, a chimney piece, a piano as well as vases in malachite, specimens of plate and some beautifully tasteful and very lightly set jewelry.' *The Illustrated London News* declared that 'only a fairy palace could be furnished with such incredible malachite'. Scott Ruby notes that the exhibition was in many ways an attempt to 'combat Russophobia and the Russian stereotypes commonly held in the Western mind'.[14]

At the 1862 International Exhibition, seventy-eight canvases by Russian artists were exhibited, including paintings by Levitsky, Borovikovsky, Venetsianov, Fedotov, Briullov and Aivazovsky.[15] In 1872 twenty-five Russian paintings were loaned by the Russian Grand Duke Vladimir to the second British 'International Exhibition' in South Kensington. English art critic Joseph Beavington Atkinson published *An Art Tour to Northern Capitals of Europe* in 1873, in which he introduced the British public to a range of Russian artists and yet nine years later, reporting on an exhibition in Moscow, *The Times* correspondent claimed that Ivan Aivazovsky and Vasily Vereshchagin were the only two Russian artists known in England.[16] Reporting on the Coronation of the Tsar in Moscow in 1896, *The Times* correspondent denigrated the ecclesiastical art of the Assumption Cathedral for having preserved with 'pious conservatism' the 'stereotyped Byzantine forms' of the ninth century that lacked 'the humanizing and beautifying influences of the Renaissance'.[17] In 1884 Alfred Maskell published *Russian Art and Art Objects in Russia,* as part of his work selecting objects for phototype reproduction for the South Kensington Museum (which became the Victoria and Albert Museum in 1899). In 1901 the International Exhibition in Kelvingrove Park, Glasgow, included four Russian 'mediaeval' wooden pavilions designed by Fedor Shekhtel to house a selection of Russian artworks.

Diagilev's 'Exhibition of Russian Art' at the Salon d'Automne in 1906 raised the profile of contemporary Russian art in Paris. The ambitious aim of the exhibition was to present the development of Russian art from the fifteenth century to the present day. Artists associated with Diagilev's pro-Western magazine *Mir Iskusstva* ('The World of Art', 1898–1904) were represented, including Aleksandr Benua, Leon Bakst, Mstislav Dobuzhinsky, Evgeny Lansere, Sergei Maliutin, Nikolai Rerikh and Konstantin Somov. Works by Aleksandr Golovin and Mikhail Vrubel and ceramics from art patron Princess Mariya Tenisheva's Talashkino estate represented the arts and crafts movement. Natal'ia Goncharova and Mikhail Larionov were two of the youngest and more controversial exhibitors and, along with Rerikh, were chosen six years later by Anrep for Fry's exhibition. *The Times* noted on 9 October that 'The Russian sale, which was to be one of the great features of the exhibition, will not be ready before the 15th.'[18] Diagilev was keen to show the development of a distinctively Russian tradition of art and Goncharova and Larionov were key players in the movement to separate Russian art from Western influences. Towards the end of 1911 they distanced themselves from the 'Bubnovyi valet' ('Knave' or 'Jack' of Diamonds), a group that included Kandinsky and Aleksei Iavlensky (Alexej von Jawlensky), who were working in Germany.

Goncharova and Larionov announced their formation of the Donkey's Tail at the 1911–12 All-Russian Artists' Congress in St Petersburg, where the poet Sergei Bobrov defined it as a neo-primitive movement that aimed to return to 'Russian roots, to Russian archaism'. After Goncharova made her speech, Larionov, unable to attract the attention of the audience, apparently broke the lectern by slamming it with his fist, and threw himself into the crowd in a rage. The Donkey's Tail drew on a pre-classical heritage of Russian folk art, hand-coloured popular cartoons, children's art and Russian icons. Russian icons offered a model, notes Sarah Warren, for ways 'to break away from conventional modes of visual representation'.[19] Artwork by the Donkey's Tail appeared in the collection the *Worldbackwards*

(1912), edited with poetry and prose by Velimir Khlebnikov and Aleksei Kruchenykh. The same year saw the publication of the famous Hylaen's (later renamed Cubo-Futurism) manifesto called 'A Slap in the Face of Public Taste', which claimed the 'past is too tight' and offered to throw 'Pushkin, Dostoevsky, Tolstoy, etc., etc. overboard from the Ship of Modernity'.[20] By 1913 Goncharova claimed to have shaken the 'dust from my feet' and to have moved away from the West because she had 'passed through all that the West can offer'.[21]

In July 1908 Frank Rutter held a special exhibition of 'Modern Russian Arts and Crafts' at the Royal Albert Hall as part of his first Allied Artists' Association (AAA) Salon, which was opened by Mariya Tenisheva. The AAA was set up as an equivalent to the Salon des Indépendants and the Salon d'Automne in Paris, so that artists could 'submit their work freely to the judgment of the public without the intervention of any middleman, be he dealer or artist', and Rutter was clear that it should have an 'international aim'.[22] Rutter asked Tenisheva to curate the exhibition, continuing to promote the work of her colony, but she had asked Jan de Holewinski, a Polish artist living in Paris, to organise an exhibition in London, and so Holewinski and Rutter joined forces. Rutter was persuaded to hire the Royal Albert Hall and 175 exhibits were selected for the two South Galleries of 'a clan of Russian artists wishing to advance national art in alliance with the traditions of the past'. Holewinksi included embroideries by the 'skilful hands of the little peasant women of Smolensk' from Talashkino.[23]

Unlike Diagilev, Holewinski did not include many professional artists, although Rerikh and Ivan Bilibin were represented.[24] Sculptures by Konstantin Raush fon Traubenberg and designs by the architects Vladimir Pokrovsky and Aleksei Shchusev were displayed. As in Diagilev's catalogue of 1906, the traditional Russian qualities of the artworks were emphasised; Rerikh was described as creating an 'evocation of the ancient world and of prehistoric pagan Russia'.[25] The Times reviewer ignored the Russian section, simply noting that a 'sprinkling of foreign work is good, if only for comparison; but the association will probably find it desirable that this element should not become predominant'.[26] However, The Observer described the Russian section as 'an engrossingly interesting display' and Tenisheva's enamels as 'clearly derived from medieval Byzantine models'.[27] Although in subsequent years there was no dedicated foreign section, other Russian artists may have been encouraged to send in their work, including Vasily Kandinsky in 1909 (the first time he was exhibited in the UK) and the modernist Russian artists Il'ia Mashkov and Petr Konchalovsky in

1911. Although the response of the British press to the Russian works was generally positive, *The Observer* described Mashkov's 'Portrait' in 1911 as a 'Byzantine vision of a monstrously deformed human being'.[28]

In October 1910, a month before Fry's first 'Post-Impressionist Exhibition', an exhibition of about 430 Russian artworks by over ninety Russian artists was held at the Doré Gallery in Bond Street. In anticipation of the event, *The Times* described it as an exhibition of 'a novel and promising' character, which would include artists who had 'arrived' and those who had 'recently passed through the studios'.[29] In a review of the exhibition, *The Times* critic pointed out that the artists were keen to be known in the West where no Russian painter, save perhaps Vereshchagin, had a 'popular reputation'. Artworks singled out for comment included Vladimir Makovsky's paintings, Evgeny Lansere's bronze sculptures of Cossacks and horses, and a bust of Sof'ia Tolstoy by her son. However, the review concluded that if the artworks on display at the Doré Gallery were representative of contemporary Russian art, the genre had a 'long way to travel before she can meet Paris, London and Berlin on equal terms'.[30] Following Tolstoy's death in November 1910, an exhibition of portraits of the much-admired Russian author was held at the Doré Gallery; King George V and Queen Mary were among the visitors to the exhibition. The impact of Tolstoy's death was widespread in Britain and included a memorial service held at the Ethical Church in Bayswater and the Gramophone Company, which advertised its recording of 'Tolstoy's Last Message'.[31]

As well as those involving Russian artworks, a broad spectrum of contemporary exhibitions included 'Old Masters' at the Royal Academy of Arts (1910) and 'Eighteenth-Century Venetian Paintings' at the Burlington Fine Arts Club (1911); prior to 'Manet and the Post-Impressionists', the Grafton Galleries held an exhibition called 'Fair Women' in May 1910. The Whitechapel Art Gallery (founded in 1901) held a contemporary exhibition of 'Twenty Years of British Art 1890–1910' in the summer of 1910, which included three works by Roger Fry. Cézanne had exhibited at the Durand-Ruel exhibition at the Grafton Galleries as early as 1905 along with Monet, Degas, Manet, Renoir and Boudin. And in 1908 the International Society held an exhibition including works by Cézanne, Van Gogh, Gauguin and Matisse, inspiring Fry to write a letter to the Burlington Magazine, in which he called Cézanne and Gauguin 'proto-Byzantines'.[32]

Anna Gruetzner Robins notes that the Friday Club's exhibition in February 1911 at the Alpine Club Gallery showed Bell, Grant and Fry together for the first time. An exhibition of Picasso's drawings took place at the Stafford Gallery in April 1911 and an exhibition of Cézanne and Gauguin in November of the same year. The first exhibition of the Camden Town Group took place in June 1911 and the Sackville Gallery held an Italian futurist exhibition in March 1912. The Rhythm Group held an exhibition at the Stafford Gallery, which opened two days before Fry's exhibition on 3 October 1912.[33] Gruetzner Robins argues that it is 'highly probable' that Sadleir persuaded the gallery director John Neville to coincide with Fry's exhibition because, as Faith Binckes writes, this would raise the profile of both shows.[34]

Smaller galleries like Agnew's in Bond Street held an exhibition of watercolours by British artists in 1911, including William Turner, John Crome and Neville Lytton, but large international exhibitions were also popular. The Palace of Fine Arts in White City was erected in 1908 for the 'Franco-British Exhibition'. Measuring 350 by 200 feet, the space was divided equally between French and British artworks. In 1910 the same exhibition space was devoted to the Japanese–British Exhibition following the renewal of the Anglo-Japanese Alliance in 1905, which was affirmed again in 1911.

Despite the range of international art on display in Britain, Fry's first 'Post-Impressionist Exhibition' of 1910, 'Manet and the Post-Impressionists', caused, in Desmond MacCarthy's well-known phrase, 'The Art-Quake of 1910'.[35] *The Times* described the art as throwing 'away all that the long-developed skill of past artists had acquired', *The Morning Post* declared that the aim of the exhibition was 'intentionally made to look like the output of a lunatic asylum' and the *Daily Express* called it 'paint run mad'.[36] Even though they had been exhibited in London in previous years, Cézanne, Gauguin, Matisse and Van Gogh attracted the most press attention. The *Daily Express* referred to Gauguin's canvases as 'bizarre, morbid, and horrible', and one of Matisse's landscapes as 'epileptic' and 'only bearable from the next room'. Robert Ross referred to Cézanne as 'neither coherent nor architectural' and declared that if 'Van Gogh belongs to the School of Bedlam, M. Matisse follows the Broadmoor tradition'. By the end of the exhibition, the public response had mellowed and critics began to praise the vitality and colour of the French paintings. The *Daily Graphic* noted on the final Saturday of the exhibition that 'the general attitude was one of admiration and of regret that an exhibition which has furnished so much food for discussion must close'.[37] If the attitude towards French art in the British press became increasingly positive, the reception to Russian art in Britain during the period was less consistent.

'A spiritual revolution':
Fry's 'Second Post-Impressionist Exhibition'

Roger Fry's decision to include a British and a Russian section alongside the critically accepted French works for his 'Second Post-Impressionist Exhibition' of October 1912 was not unusual, but the range of contemporary Russian art he chose was wider than had been seen in Britain before. More of the key figures of the contemporary Russian art world were exhibited than had been displayed at Rutter's exhibition of 1908, including Rerikh, Goncharova, Larionov, Dimitry Stelletsky, Mikalojus Ciurlionis, Konstantin Bogaevsky, Kuzma Petrov-Vodkin, Vera Ivanovna Zhukova, Count Komarovsky, Sofiia Levitskaia, Evgeny Zak and Anrep himself. Fry was keen to make an impact, as he had with the first exhibition. He wrote to his mother that the 'British public has dozed off again since the last show and needs another electric shock'.[38] Of a total of about 250 artworks on view, less than a fifth were by Russian artists, a fifth were by British artists and the rest were French.[39] In his introduction to the catalogue, Fry wrote that it 'would of course have been possible to extend the geographical area immensely. Post-Impressionist schools are flourishing, one might almost say raging, in Switzerland, Austro-Hungary and most of all in Germany.' Despite giving no real rationale for his choice, he concluded: 'England, France and Russia were therefore chosen to give a general summary of the results up to date.'[40] A letter from Fry to Albert Rothenstein on 13 April 1911 offers a prosaic reason for the inclusion of the Russian artworks:

> I then thought it might still be possible to make up an exhibition from the works of younger artists together with yourself, John, Epstein, W. Sickert. Only I saw that with this we could not fill the Grafton, so I conceived the idea of having the exhibition divided, two rooms to this English group and two rooms to the works of the younger Russian artists which I thought ought to be better known in England. I thought that this would be an additional attraction and would be of great interest to English artists.[41]

Fry needed to fill the space in the Grafton galleries and, as Frances Spalding puts it in her biography of Fry, 'the younger artists had so far produced only a limited amount of work. The idea to include a Russian section provided the solution.'[42] But he also felt that the Russian art would appeal to the public as an 'additional attraction'. He wrote to Duncan Grant in 1912, 'A few of the Russian pictures have arrived; they're rather pretty and romantic – well, I daresay it's as well that the British Public should have something it'll like.'[43]

Fry's selection of countries and artists did not go unnoticed. Rupert Brooke wrote in the *Cambridge Magazine* in November 1912:

> It is a pity that the committee could not have included works by, at any rate, Erbslöh, Jawlensky, and Kandinsky of Munich, Pechstein of Berlin, and Kokoschka of Vienna, who paint pictures at least as good and as interesting as most of those here.[44]

Kandinsky, in particular, is a surprising omission, given that he had exhibited at the AAA in London since 1909, and his theories had been brought to the British public in the journal *Rhythm* earlier in 1912. The connection with *Rhythm* may have been one of the reasons why he was excluded. Anrep, who made the selection of the Russian paintings, visited Larionov's studio in Moscow in the summer of 1912. The previous year Larionov broke with the Jack of Diamonds group, with which Kandinsky had exhibited, and this meeting may have reinforced Anrep's position. Kandinsky and Aleksei Iavlensky were working in Germany and were more connected with the European avant-garde than with the Donkey's Tail neo-primitive movement, which drew on Russian folk art, children's art, and icons.

On 12 September 1912 Boris Anrep wrote to Ottoline Morrell, apologising for not having replied to her previous letter in good time because he was 'so busy in writing a short preface to the catalogue of the [sic] Fry's exhibition, which I could not succeed to manage very easily bekause [sic] the lack of common english expressions in my head'.[45] Frances Partridge described the effect of Anrep's idiosyncratic use of language: 'one was for ever trying to fix some wonderful phrase in memory, only to have it ousted by another'.[46] Anrep's preface begins with the claim that 'Russian spiritual culture has formed itself on the basis of a mixture of its original Slavonic character with Byzantine culture and with the cultures of various Asiatic nations.' European influences may be discerned in 'later times' but, Anrep argues, these influences do not 'take hold of the Russian heart, that continues to stream the Eastern blood through the flesh of the Slavonic people'. And the 'innermost recesses' of 'the Russian heart', he writes, are 'filled with mystical passions'. Although the thrust of his argument is that Russians have different blood to those in the West, he borrows Fry's language to define contemporary Russian art. Eastern art, he argues, is disposed towards 'decorative translations of life' and 'imaginative design'. Western influences, he continues, are considered by the Russian nationalists as 'foreign and noxious to the growth of the Eastern elements of the Russian art'.[47]

Anrep's praise for the Russian artists who preserve the 'beauty and expressivity' of ancient Russian art and avoid the 'noxious' influences of the West echoes Diagilev's claim in 1899 that the 'true Russian nature is too pliant to be broken under the influence of the West'.[48] The West cannot taint the 'tender Russian quality', according to Diagilev, but its threat is more potent for Anrep. Their rhetoric may differ but both Anrep and Diagilev reinforce the stereotype of a strong, sensitive Russian soul.

Anrep praised Stelletsky, who approached 'ancient forms', and Rerikh, who belonged to a 'new Byzantine group'.[49] Although there is no record as to why Anrep replaced Rerikh's *Battle in the Heavens* in the rehang in January 1913, the painting is a good example of Anrep's 'new Byzantine group' with its strong dark contours (Fig. 1). The layers of horizontal sky are similar to the layers of water in Duncan Grant's *Bathing*, bringing together British and Russian post-impressionism via Byzantium (Fig. 2). Rerikh was interested in ancient Slavic history and its connections with Eastern cultures and religion. He and his wife, Elena Ivanovna Shaposhnikova-Rerikh, became members of the Russian Theosophical Society, and Elena worked on a Russian translation of Helena Blavatsky's *Secret Doctrine*. In the 1920s and 1930s the Rerikhs formed their own version of Theosophy, Agni Yoga,

Fig. 1 *Battle in the Heavens*, 1912 (tempera, graphite pencil and gouache on board), Nikolai Rerikh, 1874–1947, Russkii muzei (Russian Museum), St Petersburg.

Fig. 2 *Bathing*, 1911 (oil on canvas), Duncan Grant, 1885–1978. © Tate, London 2013. © ADAGP, Paris, and DACS, London 2013.

a synthesis of Eastern and Western philosophies. Rerikh went on to found the Corona Mundi in 1922, an international art centre that gave support to a wide range of international cultural and social activities.[50]

Goncharova, according to Anrep, aimed for a true representation of the 'ancient Russian God' in her depiction of 'stern, severe and austere, hard and bitter' saints (Fig. 3). 'Sweetness, joy, tenderness and voluptuousness' are as far from Goncharova's art, wrote Anrep, 'as they are far from the Russian conception of the Divinity'.[51] Whilst certainly a severe and austere-looking quartet, the saints display some dancelike features, unnaturally elongated hands and fingers, and their feet are turned outwards in identical poses, and reflect the colours of their robes: violet, grey, blue and green. Their gestures mirror each other, like the figures in Matisse's *La Danse* (1909), also displayed at Fry's exhibition, adding a flicker of movement and fluidity to the saints' contemplation. Although Goncharova claimed to have distanced herself from the West, she had not completely shaken all post-impressionist dust from her shoes.

Anrep concluded his preface to the Russian section of Fry's exhibition with reference to three artists whom he described as 'more explicit to a modern European artist's mind' because they keep 'their art in close

Fig. 3 *Four Panels Depicting the Four Evangelists*, c. 1910–11 (oil on canvas), Natal'ia Goncharova, 1881–1962, private collection, Calmann & King Ltd, The Bridgeman Art Library. © ADAGP, Paris, and DACS, London 2013.

connection with their philosophical substance'. He included Petrov-Vodkin because he gives 'great spiritual meaning to the gestures of his figures', and the desert landscape in *The Dream* certainly evokes the Last Temptation of Christ. Bogaevsky is also included here because his landscapes 'terrify the Russian soul as if they were terrible omens'.[52] The flood in Bogaevsky's *Apocalyptic Star* appears to emanate from the star itself and the picture was singled out as 'powerful' in the *Athenaeum*.[53]

The third artist in Anrep's philosophy category was Lithuanian artist and composer Ciurlionis, who was included because of his devotion to 'the mysteries of the Cosmos and to the music of the empyrean aether'. The fire in the centre of his painting *Rex* (Fig. 4) is 'surrounded by the horizon of an occult world, by the mounting spheres and by the shadow of angels'.[54] Echoing Anrep's preface, four years later, Rosa Newmarch described how *Rex* 'perplexed visitors to the Salon in 1909 as much as those who saw it at the Grafton Galleries in 1913' because

in this kind of cosmic symphony, the fire which glows at the heart of it forms the centre of an occult world; it is encircled by mysterious shadows, the mounting spires of the heavenly spheres, and peopled by winged messengers. It is a subject such as Scriabin treated musically in his 'Prometheus,' and we realize that in this painter's soul sounds and visions are practically interchangeable.[55]

Ciurlionis, like Kandinsky, considered himself a synaesthete with the ability to perceive music and colours simultaneously. In *Rex* the emerging globe, tower, shooting stars, sun and moon appear to hover over each other in translucent layers, creating the illusion that things are happening simultaneously. Ciurlionis's *Mountain* (1906) depicts an unearthly mound rising above a cityscape, with a foreground of trees. The mountain is flooded with light, casting the landscape below into shadow. George Kennaway has argued that Ciurlionis may have seen reproductions of Cézanne's *Mont-Saint Victoire* paintings in Warsaw or during his tour of European art galleries in 1906, although there is no evidence for this, and he links the two artworks in terms of composition, the profile of the mountains and parts of their palette. There does seem to be a parallel in the sculptural quality on the right-hand side of both mountains, and the link would certainly support

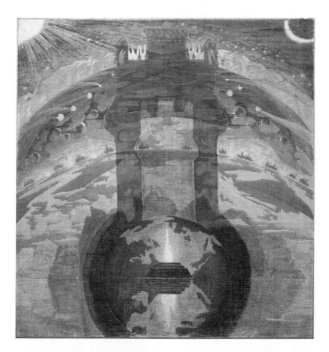

Fig. 4 *Rex*, 1909 (tempera on canvas), Mikalojus Konstantinas Ciurlionis, 1875–1911, The M. K. Ciurlionis National Museum of Art (Kaunas, Lithuania).

Anrep's claim that Ciurlionis was one of the Russian artists exhibited who were closest to the 'modern European artist's mind'.[56]

Jacqueline Falkenheim and Jane Goldman have tracked the shift from romantic to classic in Fry's rhetoric from the First to the Second Post-Impressionist Exhibition catalogues, highlighting the idea of the romantic genius that was superseded by significant form.[57] Clearly a dominant principle of the second catalogue, significant form should not, however, be read as synonymous with pure form. The connections between modern art and spirituality recur throughout the preface to Fry's second exhibition. Bell concludes his section with the claim that the French paintings are 'manifestations of a spiritual revolution', Fry claims that post-impressionism sets free a 'disembodied spirit' and Anrep begins with a discussion of 'Russian spiritual culture' and later reminds us of the 'mystical passions' running through the Russian blood.[58] The emphasis on the paintings as external expressions of inner spirituality cuts across national boundaries but also had its roots in the first exhibition.

Writing about the first 'Post-Impressionist Exhibition', art critic C. Lewis Hind noted that although he had been 'charged with hypnosis' for calling it a 'spiritual movement [. . .] when one is in harmony with the spirit that informs the movement, one has a clearer vision of the vital things in life'. For Cézanne, wrote Hind, 'the spiritual meaning was everything' and the exhibition provoked a strong response, he claimed, because behind 'the movement there is a purpose, an idea partaking more of the spiritual than the material'.[59] Having been the victim of much critical abuse during the first 'Post-Impressionist Exhibition', Cézanne was exempt from negative reviews by 1912, and was set up as the 'spiritual father of these moderns'.[60] This position was reinforced by the addition of more than thirty works by Cézanne in the exhibition in January 1913 to fill the spaces left by the Matisse and Picasso works that had been sent to the Armory Show in New York. *The Times* critic wrote that Cézanne, 'like another Giotto, found a new music in masses, and he has, perhaps, given a new start to European painting'.[61]

The response to the 'Second Post-Impressionist Exhibition'

Most of the press coverage of the 'Second Post-Impressionist Exhibition' was devoted to Matisse and Picasso. Before the transfer to the Armory Show, Matisse was represented by forty-two works, which included oil paintings, drawings, sculptures and lithographs, and Picasso was represented by thirteen analytical cubist paintings and three drawings.

Matisse's use of design, rhythm and colour were praised but his treatment of the human figure was denigrated. *The Times* critic wrote that the figures in *La Danse* were 'merely hideous' and evidence of Matisse's 'peculiar unhumanity [sic]'.[62] The juxtaposition of cubist works by Picasso and Braque marked the first occasion on which Picasso's position as the dominant artist was established.[63] Although Picasso was defined as the leader of cubism, he came under fire for painting non-representational figures. Hind wrote that Picasso's portraits were 'as unsympathetic as they are unintelligible'. And just as Van Gogh had been referred to as an 'adult maniac' in the first exhibition by Robert Ross, P. G. Konody called Picasso's portraits 'the incoherent ravings of a lunatic' in the second.[64]

The British artworks received relatively little coverage in the press. Amongst the British artworks on display there were five works by Roger Fry and six by Duncan Grant, as well as work by Frederick Etchells, Bernard Adeney, Henry Lamb, Wyndham Lewis, Eric Gill, Charles Ginner, Spencer Gore and Vanessa Bell. *The Times* reported that the British pictures 'are inferior to the French just where we should expect them to be, in their rendering of mass and form' and Konody described them in *The Observer* as 'dull and almost colourless compared with the surrounding orgies in primaries'.[65]

Despite the general passion for all things Russian in Britain the response to the Russian section, as it had been with the British, was surprisingly limited. The lack of press attention was partly due to the small number of Russian paintings in comparison to the French, but also because some of the Russian paintings, including three by Natal'ia Goncharova, one by Mikhail Larionov, one by Bogaevsky and one by Armenian artist Martiros Sari'an, did not arrive on time. Rupert Brooke wrote in the *Cambridge Monthly*: 'When I last visited it, for instance, on November 5th, it had been open just a month. And still some of the best Russian pictures, referred to in the preface, were not hung.'[66]

The critical response to the Russian artwork that was already on show was mixed. Konody credited the Russian paintings with 'decorative effectiveness' in *The Observer*, but he claimed that 'these Russian paintings are too far removed from the Western European conception of art to arouse a deeper interest than that of passing curiosity'. And in his article after the rehang, he called the new Russian pictures 'curiosities' full of 'intolerable affectations'.[67] *The Times* stated that the Russian artworks 'do not seem to us to promise much' and doubted 'whether any of the artists really feel Byzantine'.[68] Writing for the *Cambridge Magazine*, Rupert Brooke analysed the cultural divide:

The Russians in this exhibition have hitherto been unknown to England; almost, I should think, to Western Europe. They have almost no connection with the French, German and English 'Post-Impressionists.' In his preface, indeed, M. von Anrep especially disclaims Western influence. Their work is difficult to appreciate at first. It is heavy with soul, packed with a religious romanticism. The first attitude an ignorant Western mind takes up towards it is one of suspicious awe. The pictures seem to vary between pomposity and real mysticism.[69]

Brooke's claim that the Russian artists were unknown to Western Europe was not true, as Rerikh, Larionov and Goncharova had all been exhibited in Paris six years earlier. Rerikh had also been exhibited at the AAA in London and was also known for his designs for Aleksandr Borodin's 'Polovtsian Dances' (Act 2 of *Prince Igor*), which premiered in Paris in 1909 and was performed in London in 1911. Brooke directly lifted phrases from Anrep's preface – for example, 'heavy with soul' and 'religious romanticism' – and yet he was one of the few critics to devote a good portion of column space to the Russian artists, and praised Stelletsky to some extent for the 'desperate and gloomy heat of unquiet' that 'tinges all these Russian pictures'.[70]

The Standard referred to the 'Russian group' as 'particularly interesting' because the 'general characteristics are imaginative power, good colour, intricate design, and a strong racial flavour, expressed in the use of Byzantine conventions'. Putting the Russian artworks into a British context, Ciurlionis's *Rex*, according to the *Standard*, was a 'Blake-like composition of angels and comets about a white-flamed altar'. And *The Connoisseur* argued that the Russian artworks were some of the 'most original pictures' in the exhibition and that in their 'deep mystical feeling and intense though enigmatical utterance' they recall the works of William Blake. The Russian paintings, the reviewer continued, were 'conceived in beautiful form, and with sufficient coherence to arrest the imagination of the spectator and allow him to weave their mystical utterance into harmony with his own thoughts'. Borrowing from Anrep's preface, the critic for *The Morning Post* separated 'from the general debauchery the work of the Russian Group' because their pictures make an effort to 'regain their freedom from Western ideals, whose bondage was as bad for their art as the bondage of Siberia is or was to the life of Russia'.[71]

Anrep chose to present a very positive version of the British response to the Russian artworks in the Russian journal *Apollon* in February 1913. Similar to *Mir Iskusstva* in its editorial approach,

Apollon has been described as the 'last of the great journals to be set up during Russia's Silver Age'. Its founder and editor, Sergei Makovsky, believed in a renewal of Russian culture, and yet the title, Apollo, the Greek god of light and art, demonstrated its pro-Western approach. The journal published a range of material, but Christina Lodder and Peter Hellyer have tracked how it began to move away from the mysticism associated with symbolism in 1910 and towards Nikolai Gumilev and Sergei Gorodetsky's 'new direction' of acmeism ('from the word acme, the highest degree of something'), which stressed clarity, rigour, craftsmanship and concrete imagery.[72] Anrep wrote in his article for *Apollon* in 1912:

> In general, these [Russian] artists appealed to the general public incomparably more than the French and the English; it's a fact that enthusiastic exclamations could be heard. The success of the Russian artists with the crowd of visitors was such that the organisers even started to give lectures, right there at the exhibition, about symbolism, the occult, spiritualism and other inner strengths of the Russian artists.[73]

Although the response in *The Standard* and *The Connoisseur* had been positive, Anrep's claim about impromptu lectures is not recorded elsewhere and reveals his embellishment for the audience in Russia.

In the same article Anrep narrates the shift in the British response to Fry's first and second exhibitions. He explains that modern art was initially explained as giving 'rise to certain spiritual emotions' and that the aim of it was 'to create a visual music'. Viewers, he asserts, were not expected to 'find reflections of nature in the pictures but should strive to understand the underlying spiritual motives'.[74] Anrep complains that this guidance was vague. He does not, however, reveal that the emphasis on spiritual emotions, visual music and underlying spiritual motives is a reference to Fry's preface to the second exhibition.[75] Compare, for example, Anrep's phrase, 'the aim of modern art is to create a visual music', and Fry's 'purely abstract language of form – a visual music'. The narrative of Anrep's article (that the first exhibition failed and the second was a success) required him to describe a shift in the critical reception and yet, perhaps due to the lack of English phrases in his head, he borrowed Fry's language from the second catalogue to illustrate the inadequacy of the first.

Anrep admired the 'freshness' of colour, originality and charm of Matisse's paintings, but, he argued, 'this charm will not retain its power for long, just as one cannot nourish one's soul on a charming exterior'. Matisse will not provide 'sustenance for the soul', wrote Anrep; he 'wanted only to seduce it'. Whereas British critics praised the rhythm they observed in Matisse's work, Anrep rejected the 'shallowness' of Matisse because, he argued, Russians respect images 'of the divine, created with piety by our icon painters, for whom spiritual symbols have unique meaning'. The art of Matisse would work better, according to Anrep, if it were condensed into square-inch enamels to sell 'in the magnificent antique shops of Old Bond Street'. By imagining Matisse's paintings as 'beautiful enamel behind a clear glaze and no bigger than the palm of one's hand', Anrep converted them into a traditional form of enamelled Russian icon.[76] But as Lodder and Hellyer note, *Apollon* was committed to openness and sought to foster debate, and Anrep's article can be read alongside that of Iakov Tugenkhol'd, the Paris correspondent, who praised Matisse's *Dance* and *Music* for the 'naïve monumentality of the primordial age' in the December 1910 issue.[77]

Picasso's early drawings and etchings were, according to Anrep, inspired by 'the spirit of El Greco' because both artists express 'the same endless torment and gentle pity' in their figures. However, Picasso's downfall came with a 'shocking change' in his 'artistic personality', attributed by many to 'mental illness' when he became 'the father of Cubism'. The cubists, according to Anrep (adopting the psychiatric vocabulary of the British art critics), were 'maniacs, fascinated by one idea, by some irresistible glimpse of reason', whose art is simply a 'boring reshuffling of grey geometric shapes'. Anrep concluded that artists involved in cubism are 'weak in body' and must have 'strained nerves', and spend their 'last penny on stimulating and intoxicating drugs'. Anrep asks whether 'this is just a passing phase and Picasso will recover?'[78]

If the cubists were physically sick or intoxicated, the British artworks were 'impersonal and pale', wrote Anrep. They were a 'provincial echo' of French modern art and 'lag significantly behind the French and the Russians at this exhibition'. Although he singled out one or two paintings for praise – 'Grant – "The Seated Woman"; "Dancers"; Lewis – "Creation" a good graphic; Fry – "Angles sur Langlin landscape"', he summarised their efforts as including 'a little romanticism, a little realism, a little Post-Impressionism'. Unlike the British and French painters, the Russian artists 'occupied a special position in the exhibition' because of the 'impression they made on the public at large with their "exoticism"'. As well as the Russians being exotic, Anrep claimed that the English critics admired the 'purity of nature' in the work. The British public, he continued, were able to appreciate how Russian artists, more than others, were able to evolve their work into 'fantastic compositions' in order to create the 'visual musicality' that he had disparaged only a few paragraphs before. Anrep admitted that some critics detected a certain coldness in some of the Russian pictures, and a 'measured anecdotalism and illustration', which 'damaged the purity of the painting'. And, more importantly, he noted a 'spiritual indifference' to the 'expressiveness of contours', which 'detracts from the structure of the painting'. But Anrep concluded with a rousing finish, celebrating the diversity of the Russian artworks exhibited at the Grafton: 'Russian art has met with great success: in it people have found the beauty of completely opposing styles.'[79]

Whilst Anrep presented the reception of the Russian artists in a favourable light in *Apollon*, he was simultaneously concerned about the lack of press attention in England, and particularly the response to his own six works that were exhibited at the Grafton. In a letter to Ottoline Morrell on 4 November 1912, he described the rejection he would feel if he was not mentioned in the newspapers. Although he claimed to be 'much more above the critics', he admitted to 'eagerly look[ing] through what they say'. Anrep began to promote the paintings himself. On 13 November he wrote to Morrell to enlist her support. He wrote: 'It would be so kind of you if you would mention to your friends the Russian pictures by Stelletzsky who needs selling, Komarovsky too.' He points out that the prices are flexible: 'they all I am certain are willing to reduce there [sic] prices if any offers should be made'.[80]

Reconsidering Fry's aesthetics

Only Jacob, carrying in his hand Finlay's Byzantine Empire, which he had bought in Ludgate Hill, looked a little different; for in his hand he carried a book, which book he would at nine-thirty precisely, by his own fireside, open and study, as no one else of all these multitudes would do.[81]

Byzantium 'operated as a facilitating myth', argues Bullen, because it came from 'a culture which would seem alternately authoritarian, romantic and decadent'. It offered a space for those who felt themselves to be on the margins of the establishment, a space occupied intermittently by Roger Fry as he challenged conventional views on modern art.[82] Accompanied by Vanessa and Clive Bell, Fry went to Constantinople in 1911 and on their return Vanessa Bell wrote to Fry:

I'm trying to paint as if I were mosaicing, not by painting in spots but by considering the picture as patches, each of which has to be filled in by the definite space of colour as one has to do with mosaic or woolwork, not allowing myself to brush the patches into each other.

She felt that this ought to give her 'something of the life one seems to get with mosaics', evident in her *Byzantine Lady* of 1912. Duncan Grant apparently agreed that 'mosaic is the one thing to be done'.[83] This was by no means exclusive to Bloomsbury. In 1911 Rutter described van Gogh as building up 'a mosaic of bright colour with small touches of pure pigment uncompromisingly juxtaposed'.[84] In the spring of 1911 Roger Fry asked Duncan Grant to design murals for Borough Polytechnic, the results of which were *Bathing* and *Football*. These, along with murals from Fry, Frederick Etchells, MacDonald Gill, Bernard Adeney and Albert Rutherston, were placed along two long walls. A Tate Gallery catalogue from the 1960s notes that as the panels progressed they 'decided to employ the technique of gradating the colour tones to a dark contour to increase the rhythm of the design, as in Byzantine mosaics'.[85] And Bullen notes that the Byzantine effect was picked up by Robert Ross in *The Morning Post*, who described the water in *Bathing* as similar to the 'strata and streaks such as you see in Christian Fifth Century mosaics at Rome or Ravenna'.[86]

In 1914 Clive Bell strengthened Fry's connections between post-impressionism and Byzantium in his influential book, *Art*. Post-impressionism, argues Bell, is one of those 'huge slopes' into which we can divide 'the history of art and the spiritual history of mankind'. We shall 'compare Post-Impressionism', continues Bell, with that 'vital spirit which, towards the end of the fifth century, flickered into life amidst the ruins of Graeco-Roman realism'. For Bell, Hagia Sophia was one of the best examples of significant form, and Cézanne was the only artist who could be compared favourably with Byzantium: 'since the Byzantine primitives set their mosaics at Ravenna no artist in Europe has created forms of greater significance unless it be Cézanne'.[87] Fry had connected Cézanne and Byzantium via El Greco in the *Burlington Magazine* a few years earlier:

Was it not rather El Greco's earliest training in the lingering Byzantine tradition that suggested to him his mode of escape into an art of direct decorative expression? and is not Cézanne after all these centuries the first to take up the hint El Greco threw out?[88]

El Greco was also chosen by Anrep as a symbol of all that was good in Picasso because both artists expressed 'the same endless torment and gentle pity' in their figures.[89] Fry and Bell were not alone in their veneration of Cézanne as a modern Byzantine. T. E. Hulme described Cézanne's *Large Bathers* (1906) as 'more akin to the composition you find in the Byzantine mosaic (of the empress Theodora) in Ravenna, than it is to anything which can be found in the art of the Renaissance'.[90] Hulme, Fry and Bell were shifting, in their individual ways, away from the traditional emphasis on the Renaissance towards a modern Byzantium.

And yet Cézanne represented more than Byzantium for Fry and Bell; his work moved them to expressions of mysticism.[91] Bell wrote that everything in Cézanne's work 'can be seen as pure form, and behind pure form lurks the mysterious significance that thrills to ecstasy', and Fry wrote of Cézanne's *Les Maisons jaunes*, that its 'magic art distils for us this strange and haunting vision'.[92] In his book on Cézanne published nearly twenty years later, Fry wrote that in describing Cézanne's works he is 'like a mediaeval mystic before the divine reality, reduced to negative terms. I have to say first what it is not.'[93] The connections between Cézanne, Byzantium and spirituality offered a model for their engagement with contemporary Russian art. Cézanne and Byzantium stood for the experimentation with form, abstraction, spirituality and texture in the world of modern art.

The texture of the surface of the mosaic was important to Anrep's indirect method, in which the tesserae were glued to strong paper with the design in reverse. Frances Partridge described watching Anrep work:

> After cementing the fireplace surround, the whole thing was rapidly pressed against it by Boris and his Italian henchman, working like fiends in Hell; they then rubbed away the paper exposing the reverse side of the complete mosaic to our delighted eyes. The final operation, which had to be carried out before the cement had completely hardened, consisted in deftly hammering individual pieces of mosaic so that they caught the light and produced that slight unevenness of surface that gave it life.[94]

Fry referred to the 'material beauty' of Anrep's work, and noted that the new interest in the 'picture surface' amongst post-impressionists, combined with the 'new sympathy for Byzantine art', led to mosaics becoming a 'peculiarly satisfactory method' of expression.[95] Charles Aitken, former Director of the Tate Gallery, remarked on Anrep's mosaic at the Tate as having 'the quality of old tapestry' with 'varying joints showing between, which gives a beautifully varied effect over the whole floor', unlike the 'commercial mosaics' of Italian skilled workmen which lack 'this rough quality'.⁹⁶ The spaces between the stones were as important as the stones themselves for Anrep. He described how the workshop at the Vatican 'prides itself on possessing 22,000 shades of enamel. Cut to microscopic dimensions' and that 'these tesserae can perform at will any acrobatic feat of pseudo-painting'.⁹⁷ Anrep's mosaics were not paintings in stone; the cement was part of the composition, a breathing space, similar to the visibility of brushstrokes and canvas in a post-impressionist painting. Anrep mocked his own profession and the acrobatic pseudo-painting of Italian mosaics in a good-humoured postcard to Mary Hutchinson in 1924, extolling the virtues of Venice but exclaiming 'I hate mosaics!'⁹⁸

Anrep himself was quick to point to the spiritual qualities of his work. He noted in the catalogue for a solo exhibition at the Chenil Gallery in 1913 that his stones would reveal their 'beauty and Soul' in order to 'bring forth their Spirit', and twenty years later, giving a speech at the National Gallery, he referred to the 'magic power of my material'.⁹⁹ Jane Williams has noted that Anrep's mosaics captured not only the 'monumental qualities' of Byzantine mosaics but also the 'inner spirituality' evident in Russian icons, which he 'injected' with modernity to produce new visual expression.¹⁰⁰

Fry's decision to include a selection of Russian paintings in his 1912 exhibition may have been influenced by his ongoing, fluctuating, intellectual engagement with spirituality and mysticism. Mysticism is a vague term and it was used interchangeably with occultism around the turn of the century, as both were concerned with animism, unity of spirit and matter, and correspondences between earthly and spiritual things.¹⁰¹ The extent of Fry's mysticism, like his interest in the idea of the spiritual, is difficult to ascertain and certainly shifted throughout his career. Initially influenced by Giovanni Morelli and Bernard Berenson's spiritual approach to art history, towards the end of his life Fry declared, 'I wish I hadn't got so hot about mysticism. But I must go on because I've found a perfect description of mysticism – it's the attempt to get rid of mystery.'¹⁰² The attempt to get rid of mystery is a useful way to approach Fry's aesthetics; his theories are characterised by their attempt to define the indefinable or to eliminate the unknown. Fry's interest in the unseen has received little analysis because it does not, at first, appear to correlate with his formalist aesthetics.

However, recent scholarship on Fry has begun to move his aesthetics away from narrow definitions of formalism. Christopher Green questioned the image of Fry as 'the rigid formalist, whose separation of art from life not only conserved art as the privilege of the few, but opened the way to the Anglo-American formalism of Clement Greenberg from the 1940s onwards'. And Christopher Reed has redefined Fry's formalism as an open 'methodology of doubt'.[103] Elizabeth Prettejohn noted that the 'familiar word "formalist" is certainly relevant, but too crude to capture the complexity of Fry's evaluative criteria or of his descriptive language'. And Richard Shone cautions against creating a 'Holy Trinity of formalism' of Roger Fry, Vanessa Bell and Duncan Grant.[104] Continuing this move to open out his aesthetics, I want to consider Fry's theories in relation to Byzantium, mysticism and Russian aesthetics.

Fry's unpublished early writings show a marked interest in the mystical and spiritual during his time at Cambridge. Fry won a science scholarship to King's College in 1884, but during the course of his university career, and with the eventual support of his parents, he decided to pursue a career in the arts. While at Cambridge, Fry attended meetings of the Society of Psychical Research (SPR), which had been set up in 1882 with Henry Sidgwick, Professor of Moral Philosophy at Cambridge, as President. One of the committees of the SPR was charged with the investigation of apparitions and haunted houses (other committees investigated areas such as clairvoyance, telepathy and mesmerism). According to Woolf's biography, Fry 'visited haunted houses in a vain pursuit of ghosts' when he was at Cambridge.[105]

Woolf's comment appears to be validated by a satirical account from 1885 found amongst Fry's papers at King's College. The narrator tells us that the President of the SPR is 'at his wits end' because of a lack of evidence of 'Haunted Houses' and subscribers are tired with the 'monotonous negative results of that accurately scientific society'. The narrator and his friend are sent to investigate a 'depressingly commonplace', 'black stuccoed' lodging house 'of the most barbarous description' in the West Country. The garden is 'laid out regularly with black asphalt paths' and the friends are disappointed because they have been led to believe that apparitions occur in 'chambers of medieval castles'. And yet, odd things begin to happen: the window blind blinks like 'the malign wink of an evil face' and the ceiling moves with a 'strange rhythmic contortion'. The friend notes the contortions as 'apparent peristaltic contraction of the rays'. This obscure short piece, attributed to Fry, reveals both his engagement with the unseen and his early commitment to aesthetics. The aesthetics of the house are more dangerous than the apparitions: the 'infectious hideousness' of the 'foul gimcracks' may damage good taste. In a final moment of bathos Fry's narrator states the 'following important & interesting conclusions:– '.[106] The ellipsis mocks the concluding remarks of many SPR reports. For example, 'Notes on the Evidence, Collected by the Society, for Phantasms of the Dead' written by Eleanor Sidgwick, concluded: 'As regards present conclusions, the result of the investigation will, I fear, appear to many very unsatisfactory. But I do not myself think that we ought to expect so quickly to come to a conclusion.'[107]

Fry's election to the Cambridge Conversazione Society, known as the Apostles, which involved 'nearly everyone of distinction who was at Cambridge during the last fifty years', was central to his intellectual development and his willingness to challenge the establishment.[108] Ann Banfield credits Fry with bringing aesthetics to Cambridge philosophy, quoting Quentin Bell, who described 'Cambridge at the turn of the century' as 'aesthetically blind'.[109] In a paper for the Apostles dated 1888, Fry described an individual who wakes up as a mystic and cannot see 'anything clearly', only the 'broad effects of light and shade'. The 'great abstract outlines of the scene' are then 'filled in' with colour, light and shade, anticipating the post-impressionists' slabs of colour, and suddenly 'everything is significant' and 'worth while'. He moves from an Emersonian mystical state to 'the kingdom of Epicurus' and concentrates on the 'minutest detail not for its own sake but for its relation with the whole'. A seedling here, then, of Fry's aesthetics: the relationship of the detail to the whole, and slabs of colour that make everything significant.[110]

Fry's interest in the unseen was not unusual amongst his contemporaries at Cambridge. John McTaggart (who went on to become a Hegelian philosopher) believed in the 'Saul-feeling' or a mystical experience of being at one with the world. Goldsworthy Lowes Dickinson, another important figure in Fry's early career, believed in the immortality of the soul and in an unseen pattern behind the appearance of things.[111] The cult of friendship circulating in Cambridge during the period was encouraged by a visit from the socialist, mystic, poet and campaigner for homosexual equality, Edward Carpenter, in July 1886. There is scope for further study into the intellectual relationship between Fry and Carpenter but a letter from Carpenter to Fry in 1894 reveals their shared interest in 'the timeless relation of each "spirit" to all the others' as 'infinitely various'.[112]

Fry lamented that 'nothing similar to the octave has been discovered in the vibrations of ether which give colour' in a talk to the Apostles in 1888.[113] In 1905 theosophists Annie Besant and Charles Leadbeater produced a detailed account of colours produced by vibrations so that when 'a musical note is sounded, a flash of colour corresponding to it may be seen by those whose finer senses are already to some extent developed'.[114] For Besant and Leadbeater music and thoughts produced forms, whereas for Fry form produced emotions. Certain 'proportions of lines in space' or certain 'proportions of rapidity of vibration in air', explained Fry, 'arouse in us intense emotional activity'.[115] And we find this theory developed over twenty years later in the *Fortnightly Review*, where Fry wrote that particular 'rhythms of line and particular harmonies of colour have their spiritual correspondences, and tend to arouse now one set of feelings, now another'.[116] Bertrand Russell defined mysticism as an 'attitude towards life' rather than a 'creed about the world', and Russell's insistence that 'the greatest men who have been philosophers have felt the need both of science and mysticism' applies well to Fry. A former scientist, Fry wrote in later life that science can only begin when you accept mystery and then seek to 'clear it up'. The effect of science, for Fry, 'is none the less always to increase mystery for with every new avenue that's cleared up you get a fresh vista into the world beyond'.[117]

So how do Fry's early experimental aesthetics affect our reading of his later formalism? As already mentioned, the traditional trajectory is to track his idea of the romantic genius through to the high formalism expressed in the catalogue to the 'Second Post-Impressionist Exhibition'. Falkenheim argues that the shift occurred with his idea of the 'Classic spirit' that was 'synonymous with pure form' and a 'necessary characteristic of any art he considered successful in establishing a harmonious relationship among structural elements'.[118] Although Fry was clearly concerned with formal qualities of art by 1912, his notion of the 'Classic spirit' was more than 'pure form'. It was not 'dull, pedantic, traditional, reserved', wrote Fry; it was the 'setting free a pure and as it were disembodied functioning of the spirit' that 'communicates a new and otherwise unattainable experience'. As science was the attempt to clear up mystery, the juxtaposition of 'classic' and 'spirit' captures the duality of Fry's aesthetics.[119]

Despite Fry's emphasis on the spiritual in art, he was not ready to abandon figurative form in 1912. He wrote that the

> logical extreme of such a method would undoubtedly be the attempt to give up all resemblance to natural form, and to create a purely abstract language of form – a visual music; and the later works of Picasso show this clearly enough. They may or may not be successful in their attempt. It is

too early to be dogmatic on the point, which can only be decided when our sensibilities to such abstract form have been more practised than they are at present.[120]

And yet, only a year later, in a review of an exhibition at the AAA in 1913, he referred to the three abstract works by Kandinsky as 'by far the best pictures there'. Fry continued to struggle with the tension between abstract and figurative art throughout his career.[121]

In Fry's first comprehensive outline of his aesthetics in 1909, he argued that an artist might, if he chooses, 'take a mystical attitude' and 'the fullness and completeness of the imaginative life he leads may correspond to an existence more real and important than any that we know of in mortal life'. The imaginative life of the artist offered a new way of seeing, a heightened 'clearness of perception' in which the whole, rather than the 'labels', of everyday life are visible, rather like his hypothetical Emersonian who emerges into Epicureanism. The 'cinematograph' and the mirror serve as analogies for this clarity because the screen or reflection creates a 'visionary quality' where we see 'everything equally' as opposed to its constituent parts.[122]

Between the years 1909 and 1920 Fry's use of the term 'spiritual' increased. The 'imaginative life', outlined in 'An Essay in Aesthetics', became the 'spiritual life' in 'Art and Socialism', published as 'The Artist in the Great State' in H. G. Wells's collection *The Great State* (1912): art 'is one of the chief organs of what, for want of a better word, I must call the spiritual life'.[123] By 1917 Fry claimed that scientists were ready to admit 'not only the necessity but the great importance of aesthetic feeling for the spiritual existence of man'.[124] But by 1920 Fry pulled back in his conclusion to *Vision and Design*. Interrupting himself, he wrote that aesthetic emotion created the 'peculiar quality of "reality" which makes it a matter of infinite importance' for those who experience it, but 'any attempt I might make to explain this would probably land me in the depths of mysticism. On the edge of that gulf I stop.' Preferring to leave his theory of aesthetic emotion unexplained, Fry characteristically opens up a fresh vista.[125]

By 1919 Fry's theory of the 'clearness of perception' had evolved into the idea of a 'creative vision' or a 'fourth kind of vision'. The idea of a fourth dimension of space (as opposed to time) was popular in the 1910s, and it involved pushing the boundaries of human perception in order to visualise a new space existing in parallel to three-dimensional space (which is explored in Chapter 3). Fry wrote in *The Athenaeum* that the 'artist's main business in life' is 'carried on by means of yet a fourth kind of vision, which I call the creative vision', in which 'objects as such tend to disappear, to lose their separate unities, and to take their places as so many bits in the whole mosaic of vision'. For Fry the best analogy for this new, creative, 'fourth kind of vision' was a mosaic.[126]

A 'resting point for the mind': revisiting Woolf's aesthetics

In December 1912 Woolf wrote to Violet Dickinson: 'The Grafton, thank God, is over; artists are an abominable race.'[127] Although Woolf clearly felt frustrated with the furore around the exhibition (which was not over until January 2013), her work is often associated with the aesthetics of post-impressionism. In 1934 Woolf wrote: 'not in our time will anyone write a life as Sickert paints it. Words are an impure medium; better far to have been born into the silent kingdom of paint.'[128] Scholars, including Jane Goldman and Diane Gillespie, have successfully liberated Woolf from the patriarchal straitjacket of 'significant form' but there is scope here to think about Fry's and Woolf's aesthetics together again in relation to mysticism and mosaics.

Recent Woolf scholarship has focused on Woolf's engagement with science, mathematics and astronomy. Patricia Waugh argues that science was 'misread as "mysticism" by those contemporaries and later critics for whom science necessarily and exclusively constitutes a reductive materialism associated with the "anti-modernism" of Wells and Bennett'. Woolf's 'insubstantiality', Waugh argues, was in fact an artistic engagement with new philosophical and scientific ideas of her day, including the idea that science could not offer final conclusions.[129] For Ann Banfield, the analytic philosophy of Bertrand Russell was more important for Woolf's aesthetics than the process philosophy of Bergson, but her book also opens up the potential for mysticism within Bloomsbury aesthetics. Russell's essay, 'Mysticism and Logic' (1914), writes Banfield, offers 'evidence of a contemporary debate which took in the aesthetic question' and 'concentrates the ideas about mysticism circulating between Cambridge and Bloomsbury'.[130] Taking into account these studies, which show how scientific and philosophical discourses required a revision of the available theories of knowledge, I want to create a parallel space for the contribution of the 'unseen' in spiritual and mystical terms, as well as the scientific and philosophical. One of Woolf's audience members in *Between the Acts* is overheard saying 'odd that science, so they tell me, is making things (so to speak) more spiritual . . . The very latest notion, so I'm told is, nothing's solid . . .' Waugh notes the indication here of the 'multiple ways of being "spiritual"'.[131] Michael Whitworth unpicks the satirical next sentence between the ellipses: '. . . There, you can get a glimpse of the church through the trees . . .', signalling the thinning out of matter, the thinness of the argument and, more importantly, the tendency of popular science writers to interpret scientific theories in religious terms: for example, Bertrand Russell's reference to 'the Creator'.[132] Science, religion and spirituality are all fodder for Woolf's satire.

Woolf was clear about her lack of interest in spiritualism and mocked those who 'dabbled in mysticism' and 'made tables walz [sic]', including Mrs Shaw who 'rolled herself up in Indian mysticism, like a caterpillar in a cocoon'. However, we know that she listened to the physicist and spiritualist Oliver Lodge on the radio, went to hear the theosophist Annie Besant in 1917, and was impressed by Yeats's theories of the 'unconscious soul' when she met him in 1930. She called her own theories 'crude and jaunty' next to his.[133] We also know that she read books on Eastern religion, as well as popular science, that dealt with 'new ideas about evolution, the development of civilisation, the universe as waves, time as a fourth dimension'.[134] In 1930 Woolf referred to her illness as ' – how shall I express it? – partly mystical', and defined periods when she felt that words took on a 'mystic quality'. Her illness induced synaesthesia during which words became colours: 'We grasp what is beyond their surface meaning, gather instinctively this, that, and the other – a sound, a colour, here a stress, there a pause – '[135] However, I am less concerned here with moments of mysticism experienced in her daily life, and more concerned with whether we can trace a spiritual post-impressionism in Woolf's fiction.

Woolf's ongoing engagement with Russian literature throughout her career is well known. During the late 1910s and early 1920s, as she was writing her early experimental fiction, she was engaged in writing dozens of essays and reviews of Russian literature. She collaborated with the Ukrainian émigré Samuel Kotelyansky on the translation of three Russian texts for publication with the Hogarth Press. Eight out of twenty-seven of the Hogarth Press publications in its first years, up to 1923, were Russian translations.[136] Writing in *The Times Literary Supplement* in 1918, Woolf claimed that the Russians had produced 'the most spiritual of modern books'. She was referring to the stories of Elena Militsina, which showed 'little sense of form' and yet produced 'an effect of spirituality'.[137] In 'The Russian Point of View' (1925), Woolf described the Russian soul as 'not restrained by barriers. It overflows, it floods, it mingles with the souls of others.'

As for many of her contemporaries, Dostoevsky was the epitome of the Russian soul. Without defining 'it', Woolf evoked the experience of drowning in this 'perplexed liquid', how 'it tumbles upon us, hot, scalding, mixed, marvellous, terrible, oppressive – the human soul'.[138] Earlier, in 1917, she wrote that Dostoevsky was 'alone among writers' in being able to reconstruct 'swift and complicated states of mind, of rethinking the whole train of thought in all its speed, now as it flashes into light, now as it lapses into darkness'. For Woolf, Dostoevsky suggested the 'dim and populous underworld of the mind's consciousness where desires and impulses are moving blindly beneath the sod'.[139]

Marcus has adeptly highlighted Woolf's response to and her construction of the strangeness, fragmentation, speed, depth, freedom and inconclusiveness of Russian texts.[140] If Dostoevsky triggered metaphors of speed, depth and fragmentation, Chekhov triggered ideas about freedom and inconclusion. Woolf described reading Chekhov and feeling that 'the solid ground upon which we expected to make a safe landing has been twitched from under us', a feeling that is 'giddy, uncomfortable, inconclusive'; but through this, she added, 'we have gained a sense of astonishing freedom'.[141] This freedom was also, of course, a result of the freedom she felt at publishing through the Hogarth Press rather than Duckworth. A year later, in 1919, in another review of Chekhov (*The Bishop and Other Stories*), Woolf argued that 'we are by this time alive to the fact that inconclusive stories are legitimate'.[142] When she was beginning to think about writing *Jacob's Room*, Woolf wrote in her new notebook: 'I think the main point is that it should be free.'[143] And on finishing the novel she wrote: 'I think Jacob was a necessary step, for me, in working free.'[144] Chekhov's lack of conclusions, combined with the new Press, offered Woolf a sense of freedom, but it was balanced by repose: 'somehow or other' the stories 'provide a resting point for the mind – a solid object casting its shade of reflection and speculation'.[145]

Woolf explored the tension between freedom and repose in her short story, 'Solid Objects', written in 1918–19 and published in 1920. The story opens with John, a politician, walking on the beach with an old friend. They sit and John absent-mindedly buries his hand in the sand. His fingers touch a lump of green glass and he brings to the surface a 'full drop of solid matter'. In this moment he loses his 'background of thought and experience' and begins to lead a life devoted to stones, glass, china and metal. Surface and depth are conflated in the act of pulling out the glass drop and John is drawn into the present. As his collection grows, the small round pieces of 'anything – china, glass, amber, rock, marble' begin to take on their own existence, defined by their relationship with each other. Alone they remain discarded objects but together they form something else. For John, the

> contrast between the china so vivid and alert, and the glass so mute and contemplative, fascinated him, and wondering and amazed he asked himself how the two came to exist in the same world, let alone to stand upon the same narrow strip of marble in the same room. The question remained unanswered.[146]

By leaving the question unanswered, Bill Brown argues that Woolf grants the materials 'their sovereignty' not from 'a state of abjection, but in a state of wonder'. Brown's theory is that the use value, sign value or cultural capital of things produces *objects*. He writes that things are *things* through their 'misuse value', their dislocation, their 'fetishistic overvaluation or misappropriation' and subsequent reanimation. Fetishised objects have agency in Brown's theory: by 'engaging the shard', he argues, things become 'all but magical'.[147] A piece of broken china for Woolf's politician 'looked like a creature from another world – freakish and fantastic as a harlequin. It seemed to be pirouetting through space, winking like a fitful star'.[148] Adopting Brown's thing theory, we can see how, taken out of context and fetishised, John's fragments become magical.

Jacob's Room is a novel of fragments and 'nobody sees any one as he is'.[149] Characters make brief appearances. For example, Mrs Norman, an early incarnation of Mrs Brown, sits opposite Jacob on the train to Cambridge and offers us her view of him as 'nice, handsome, interesting, distinguished, well built' and we must 'do the best one can with her report' (37), or there is Miss Marchmont, who is seeking sometimes 'one thing, sometimes another'. She sits next to Jacob in the British Library and like her shifting interests, her books overbalance and fall into 'Jacob's compartment' (143). The narrative playfulness exposes the apparently inefficient workings within the novel so that when the narrator moves from the 'salt gale' that blew in at Betty Flanders's bedroom window back to 'Jacob and Sandra' climbing the Acropolis at night, they 'had vanished. There was the Acropolis; but had they reached it?' (224). We are reminded that the attempt to represent any moment in its entirety is futile, as in the famous moment when Jacob runs, sobbing, on the beach, towards his nanny and the 'waves came round her. She was a rock' (7). The gap between perception and reality is a prelude to the horror of the 'blocks of tin soldiers' that reel 'slightly this way and that' and fall flat, 'save that, through field-glasses, it can be seen that one or two pieces still agitate up and down like fragments of broken match-stick' (216). Structure and chaos are held in tension in the novel, represented by the silent solid Parthenon and the 'European mysticism' scorned by Jacob. Before she began writing *Jacob's Room*, Woolf decided that there would be 'no scaffolding; scarcely a brick to be seen; all crepuscular, but the heart, the passion, humour, everything as bright as fire in the mist'.[150] Kate Flint connects this to Woolf's view of *Jacob's Room* as a 'structure, as an architectural space', but the crepuscular diary entry could equally be read through the prism of Fry's pure and free disembodied spirit, or the fire burning at the heart of Ciurlionis's *Rex*.[151]

Fragments are built up to create temporary structures and then are broken down again in the novel. The light comes through the stained glass window in King's College Chapel and the 'stone is softly chalked red, yellow, and purple' (38). Earlier, Mrs Flanders's tears 'spangled the kitchen with bright knives' (4); lights 'falling on the cobbles' in Cambridge pick out 'dark patches of grass and single daisies' (54); the lamps 'made large greasy spots of light upon the pavement' in Soho (109) and Great Russell street was 'glazed and shining – here yellow, here, outside the chemist's, red and pale blue' (148). Jacob's friends arrange themselves into a fractured work of art as they sit in his rooms at Cambridge, their 'gestures of arms, movements of bodies, could be seen shaping something in the room'. Jacob stands up and our perspective reverses 180 degrees so that we see him framed from the other side of the window, and behind him the 'shape they had made, whether by argument or not, *the spiritual shape*, hard yet ephemeral, as of glass compared with the dark stone of the Chapel, was dashed to splinters, young men rising from chairs and sofa corners, buzzing and barging about the room' (69, 71, emphasis added). The formation and disintegration of the shape is a verbal account of Fry's pure and free disembodied spirit that communicates a new experience. The students embody post-impressionism; they do not imitate form, they create a spiritual shape with their bodies. The image, like glass, is 'dashed to splinters' as the young men stand up and move about, like the pieces of a stained glass window, the discarded fragments in 'Solid Objects', or the stones of a mosaic.

The Waves is arguably Woolf's most experimental, mosaic-like book. The gestation period for the book was one of Woolf's longest: she began to refer to the novel as *The Moths* in her diary from 1927, but she wrote the book between 1930 and 1931. After the 'continuity and narrative' of *Orlando*, Woolf was ready to turn once more to experimental prose.[152] She wrote early on in her notes that she wanted to tell the 'story of the world from the beginning'.[153] In 1930 she decided that the book was to be 'Childhood; but it must not be <u>my</u> childhood' and in the same year she referred to it as a 'litter of fragments'. Yet, by the end of the year, she decided that she did not want the 'waste' that the break of chapters creates, but rather she sought a 'saturated, unchopped, completeness'.[154] The book is a collection of monologues from six characters circling around the death of the seventh, Percival, the character based on her brother Thoby. Like the 'fragments' in Chekhov that have the 'air of coming together by chance', *The Waves* is a series of scattered notes drawn together through the narrative interludes that describe the rising and setting of the sun over the sea.[155]

Identity is splintered in *The Waves*, like the image in a mosaic is splintered, yet whole, and the characters seek solidity through their connections. Louis has 'roots' that 'go down to the depths of the world, through earth dry with brick', and he wants to 'exist here and now and not in streaks and patches'.[156] Like the streaks and patches of a Byzantine mosaic, Louis wants to escape fragmentation and to nail impressions to a board, in the same way that Rhoda stretches her toes to touch the rail at the end of the bed to assure herself 'of something hard' (19). Louis's 'shattered mind is pieced together by some sudden perception' and Neville's completeness comes suddenly: 'descended upon me the obscure, the mystic sense of adoration, of completeness that triumphed over chaos' (28, 37). Bernard feels that he is not 'one and simple, but complex and many' and later is 'turned to small stones', and Rhoda is 'broken into separate pieces; I am no longer one' (56, 66, 79). Bernard and Rhoda are fragile structures composed of small stones and it is Jinny who holds the pieces together. Like Mrs Ramsay, Jinny appears to create solidity, she 'seems to centre everything', as in Larionov's rayonnism, so that 'tables, lines of doors, windows, ceilings, ray themselves, like rays round the star in the middle of a smashed window-pane'. Jinny 'seems' to centre everything, but the centre is 'smashed'. Percival, however, creates true solidity: 'without Percival there is no solidity. We are silhouettes, hollow phantoms moving mistily without a background' (91).

As she was coming to the end of the novel, Woolf asked: 'How to end, save by a tremendous discussion, in which every life shall have its voice – a mosaic – a –. I do not know.'[157] Here the mosaic represents simultaneity of perception, where every voice is apparent but only together creates the whole. Like Anrep's mosaics, the novel does not smooth over its artifice or conceal its means of construction; it lays bare the cement between the stones. Neville reflects that, for Rhoda and Louis, it 'is not enough to wait for the thing to be said as if it were written; to see the sentence lay its dab of clay precisely on the right place, making character; to perceive, suddenly, some group in outline against the sky' (151). But in *The Waves*, the dab of clay is exactly enough. Like the street market, where 'every sort of iron rod, bolt and screw is laid out' (124), the voices and interludes in *The Waves* are laid out like stones on cement.

Woolf described writing the novel to a 'rhythm and not to a plot' because the 'rhythmical is more natural to me than the narrative' and because the novel was 'completely opposed to the tradition of fiction'.[158] The novel plays with the notion of subjective language and how to answer Bernard's famous question about how to 'describe the world seen without a self' (314). Flint argues that the novel demands 'that we consider the subjectivity inherent in all expression' and yet that we 'simultaneously acknowledge that language cannot control, cannot stabilize our sense of selfhood'.[159] Circularity and rhythm are privileged over linearity, embodied by Bernard, who creates narrative obsessively and yet is aware of its limitations. His phrases come 'so easily' and he loves 'what comes next' but he realises he is 'weakly making phrases to my circumstances' (169). He has difficulty finishing stories and letters, and as a young man decides that if he had been born without knowing that 'one word follows another', he might have been 'who knows, perhaps anything' (143). As he gets older, Bernard abandons stock phrases in favour of 'words of one syllable' (314). He longs for 'broken words, inarticulate words, like the shuffling of feet on the pavement' (183). Like tesserae, words of one syllable are privileged over phrases in the novel, although, of course, Bernard's concluding monologue, an attempt to 'sum up' the meaning of his life, contradicts the novel's own aesthetic ambition (260). Bernard's monologue brings the narratorial interludes into the main body of the text. He repeats the passage from the second intervention (indicating that he has narrated the others?) that reads: '*Sharp stripes of shadow lay on the grass, and the dew dancing on the tips of the flowers and leaves made the garden like a mosaic of single sparks not yet formed into one whole*' (29). Bringing the novel full circle, Bernard says 'all the drops are sparkling, trembling, as if the garden were a splintered mosaic, vanishing, twinkling; not yet formed into one whole' (270). The incompleteness of the image of the mosaic is central to the novel's unity and shape.

Woolf wrote about her interest in mysticism during the period she was planning to write *The Waves*. A diary entry from 1928 reads, 'now, if I write The Moths I must come to terms with these mystical feelings' and that it would be an 'abstract mystical eyeless book: a playpoem'. She described the entire process two years earlier as an 'endeavour at something mystic, spiritual; the thing that exists when we aren't there', and yet by 1928 she is concerned that there 'may be affectation in being too mystical, too abstract'. According to her diary, Roger Fry, Duncan Grant, Vanessa Bell and Ethel Sands all admired this tendency.[160] Woolf was reading James Jeans as she wrote *The Waves*, and recorded a discussion with Clive Bell, Lytton Strachey and Lord David, during which they talked about 'the riddle of the universe (Jeans' book) whether it will be known; not by us'.[161] She was referring either to Jeans's 1930 book *The Mysterious Universe* or *The Universe Around Us* (1929). In the former, Jeans wrote that 'we are beginning to suspect that we live in a universe of waves, and nothing but waves' and in the latter that the information we have is 'fragmentary' and that if we are to compare it to anything it would be the 'pieces of a jig-saw puzzle'. If we had all the pieces, argued Jeans, we might be able to form a 'single complete consistent picture' but many of the pieces are still missing.[162]

Mosaics were one of many important influences on Bloomsbury aesthetics in the 1910s and 1920s. Grant and Bell described their attempts to paint as though they were daubing colours in a mosaic, while Woolf described the writing process as placing mosaic chips next to one another. Anrep's connections with Bloomsbury and his mosaics in the Tate Gallery and the National Gallery drew mosaics into the contemporary art world and formed a concrete manifestation of the fragmentation of post-impressionism and its concern with artifice, texture and surface. Mosaics create unity from fragments, and their Byzantine heritage added a spiritual flavour contributing to Fry's existing spiritual, scientific formalism. Woolf's post-impressionist aesthetics, often illustrated by her description of 'colour burning on a framework of steel; the light of a butterfly's wing lying upon the arches of a cathedral', can be reimagined as the splintered stones of a mosaic that catch the light, or as Fry's objects that 'lose their separate unities', and yet 'take their places as so many bits in the whole mosaic of vision'.[163]

Notes

1. Woolf, *Diary*, II (1978), p. 314 (15 September 1924).
2. Woolf, *Letters*, III (1977), p. 549 (25 October 1928).

3. Woolf, *Night and Day*, p. 4; Woolf, *Between the Acts*, p. 48.

4. Bullen, 'Byzantinism and Modernism, 1900–1914', *Burlington Magazine*, p. 669.

5. Bullen, *Byzantium Rediscovered*, p. 183.

6. *Ottoline: The Early Memoirs*, ed. Gathorne-Hardy, p. 204. Wendy Rosslyn notes that Anrep ceased using the German form of his name 'Boris von Anrep' some time after 1912, presumably at the outbreak of the Great War; see Rosslyn, 'Boris Anrep and the Poems of Anna Akhmatova', *Modern Language Review* (1979), p. 885.

7. *Letters of Roger Fry*, ed. Sutton, II, p. 448 (to Vanessa Bell, 11 March 1919). Fry's relationship with Anrep's wife, Helen, began in the winter of 1924–5.

8. Woolf, *Letters*, V, (1979), p. 197 (16 June 1933).

9. John, 'Five Modern Artists', *Vogue*, 3 October 1928, p. 104, quoted in Bullen, *Byzantium Rediscovered*, p. 183.

10. For a formalist account of Fry's aesthetics, see Falkenheim, *Roger Fry and the Beginnings of Formalist Art Criticism* (1980).

11. Fry, 'Vitality', in *Last Lectures*, ed. Clark, p. 38.

12. Searle, 'One Damn Masterpiece after Another', *The Guardian*, 23 January 2008, p. 23.

13. Brooke, *Cambridge Magazine*, in Bullen, ed., *Post-Impressionists in England*, p. 407; *Westminster Gazette*, 7 October 1912, quoted in Gruetzner Robins, *Modern Art in Britain*, p. 105.

14. C. H. Gibbs-Smith, *The Great Exhibition of 1851* (London, 1964), p. 21, quoted in Ruby, 'The Crystal Palace Exhibition and Britain's Encounter with Russia', in Cross, ed., *A People Passing Rude*, pp. 92, 93. For an account of Russophobia, see John Howes Gleason, *The Genesis of Russophobia in Great Britain: A Study of the Interaction of Policy and Opinion* (Cambridge, MA, and London, 1950).

15. Cross, 'By Way of Introduction', in *A People Passing Rude*, pp. 1–36 (p. 27).

16. 'Art at Moscow', *The Times*, 3 October 1882, p. 4.

17. 'Latest Intelligence: Coronation of the Tsar from Palace to Cathedral', *The Times*, 27 May 1896, p. 5.

18. 'The Salon D'Automne', *The Times*, 9 October 1906, p. 10.

19. Warren, *Mikhail Larionov and the Cultural Politics of Late Imperial Russia*, pp. 140, 98.

20. The manifesto is reprinted in *Words in Revolution*, ed. Lawton, pp. 51–2.

21. In Sharp, *Russian Modernism between East and West*, p. 1.

22. 'Foreword', in *Allied Artists' Association Catalogue* (1912), p. xiii; Rutter, *Since I was Twenty-Five*, p. 183.

23. *Allied Artists' Association Catalogue* (1908), p. 147.

24. See Hardiman, 'Infantine Smudges of Paint . . . ', in Cross, ed., *A People Passing Rude*, p. 136.

25. *Allied Artists' Association Catalogue* (1908), p. 147.

26. 'The London Salon', *The Times*, 13 July 1908, p. 10.

27. Konody, 'Art Notes: Allied Artists', *The Observer*, 12 July 1908, p. 12.

28. 'Art and Artists: The London Salon', *The Observer*, 9 July 1911, p. 4, quoted in Hardiman, 'Infantine Smudges of Paint . . .', p. 144.

29. 'Russian Art in London', *The Times*, 26 October 1910, p. 6.

30. 'Exhibition of Russian Art', *The Times*, 1 November 1910, p. 11.

31. 'The King and Queen', *The Times*, 12 December 1910, p. 13; see Beasley, 'Russia and the Invention of the Modernist Intelligentsia', pp. 19–20.

32. Quoted in Bullen, ed., *Post-Impressionists in England*, p. 5.

33. See Gruetzner Robins, *Modern Art in Britain*, pp. 181–5.

34. Gruetzner Robins, *Modern Art in Britain*, p. 108; Binckes, *Modernism, Magazines, and the British Avant-Garde*, p. 139.

35. MacCarthy, 'The Art-Quake of 1910', *The Listener*, 1 February 1945.

36. '"Post-Impressionist" Painting', *The Times*, 7 November 1910, p. 12.

37. Cook, 'The Post-Impressionists', *Morning Post*, 19 November 1910, p. 4; 'Paint Run Mad: Post-Impressionists at Grafton Galleries', *Daily Express*, 9 November 1910, p. 8; Ross, 'The Post-Impressionists at the Grafton: The Twilight of the Idols', *Morning Post*, 7 November 1910, p. 3; 'An Art Victory: Triumphant Exit of the Post-Impressionists', *Daily Graphic*, 16 January 1911, p. 15. All in Bullen, ed., *Post-Impressionists in England*, pp. 118, 119; 105, 106; 102, 104; 184.

38. *Letters of Roger Fry*, I, p. 359 (28 June 1912).

39. Gruetzner Robins has a count of 157 French, 35 Russian and 49 British artworks in *Modern Art in Britain*, p. 183. Some of the Russian paintings did not arrive in time for the opening of the exhibition but they are all listed in the Re-arrangement Catalogue, 4–31 January 1913 (Grafton Galleries, 1913). Anrep also took the opportunity to replace three works by Rerikh and two by Komarovsky with three of his own and one by Bogaevsky during the rehang.

40. Roger Fry, 'Introduction', in *Catalogue of the Second Post-Impressionist Exhibition*, in Bullen, ed., *Post-Impressionists in England*, p. 348.

41. *Letters of Roger Fry*, I, pp. 345–6 (13 April 1911).

42. Spalding, *Roger Fry*, p. 148.

43. *Letters of Roger Fry*, I, p. 360 (autumn 1912).

44. Brooke, *Cambridge Magazine*, in Bullen, ed., *Post-Impressionists in England*, p. 404.

45. HRHRC, Ottoline Morrell Collection, Series II, Correspondence 1894–1938, box 33, folder 5 (Anrep to Morrell, 12 September 1912).

46. NAL, Manuscript, MSL/1974/16160, 'Unpublished Memoir of Boris Anrep by Frances Partridge', p. 3.

47. Anrep, 'The Russian Group', in Bullen, ed., *Post-Impressionists in England*, pp. 356, 358.

48. Diaghilev, 'Principles of Art Criticism' [second issue of *World of Art* (1899)], trans. Olive Stevens, in *The Ballets Russes and its World*, ed. Garafola and Baer, p. 91.

49. Anrep, 'The Russian Group', in Bullen, ed., *Post-Impressionists in England*, p. 357.

50. See Carlson, '*No Religion Higher Than Truth*', pp. 194–5.

51. Anrep, 'The Russian Group', in Bullen, ed., *Post-Impressionists in England*, p. 357.

52. Anrep, 'The Russian Group', in Bullen, ed., *Post-Impressionists in England*, pp. 357, 358.

53. 'The Grafton Galleries', *Athenaeum*, 4446, 11 January 1913, p. 50.

54. Anrep, 'The Russian Group', in Bullen, ed., *Post-Impressionists in England*, p. 358.

55. Newmarch, *The Russian Arts*, p. 272.

56. See Kennaway, 'Lithuanian Art and Music Abroad', p. 243.

57. See Falkenheim, *Roger Fry*, and Goldman, *The Feminist Aesthetics of Virginia Woolf*.

58. Bell, 'The English Group'; Fry, 'The French Group'; Anrep, 'The Russian Group'. All in Bullen, ed., *Post-Impressionists in England*, pp. 351; 355; 356, 358.

59. Hind, 'The Post Impressionists', in Bullen, ed., *Post-Impressionists in England*, pp. 187, 188, 189.

60. Hind, 'Ideals of Post Impressionism', *Daily Chronicle*, 5 October 1912, p. 6, in Bullen, ed., *Post-Impressionists in England*, p. 366.

61. [Ross?], 'Cézanne and the Post-Impressionists', *The Times*, 8 January 1913, p. 10, in Bullen, ed., *Post-Impressionists in England*, p. 411.

62. [Ross?], 'A Post-Impressionist Exhibition: Matisse and Picasso', *The Times*, 4 October 1912, p. 9, in Bullen, ed., *Post-Impressionists in England*, p. 363.

63. Gruetzner Robins, *Modern Art in Britain*, p. 73.

64. Ross, 'The Post-Impressionists at the Grafton'; P. G. Konody, 'Art and Artists – More Post-Impressionism at the Grafton', *The Observer*, 6 October 1912, p. 6. All in Bullen, ed., *Post-Impressionists in England*, pp. 103; 369.

65. [Ross?], 'The Post-Impressionists: Some French and English work', *The Times*, 21 October 1912, p. 10; P. G. Konody, 'Art and Artists: English Post-Impressionists', *The Observer*, 27 October 1912, p. 10. All in Bullen, ed., *Post-Impressionists in England*, pp. 381; 386.

66. Brooke, *Cambridge Magazine*, in Bullen, ed., *Post-Impressionists in England*, p. 404.

67. Konody, 'Art and Artists: English Post-Impressionists'; Konody, 'Art and Artists – More Post-Impressionists', in Bullen, ed., *Post-Impressionists in England*, pp. 389; 415.

68. [Ross?], 'The Post-Impressionists: Some French and English Work', in Bullen, ed., *Post-Impressionists in England*, p. 380.

69. Brooke, *Cambridge Magazine*, in Bullen, ed., *Post-Impressionists in England*, p. 407.

70. Brooke, *Cambridge Magazine*, in Bullen, ed., *Post-Impressionists in England*, p. 407.

71. Quoted in Kennaway, 'Lithuanian Art and Music Abroad', p. 241.

72. Lodder and Hellyer, 'St Petersburg/Petrograd/Leningrad. From Aesthetics to Revolutionaries', in *The Oxford Critical and Cultural History of Modernist Magazines*, ed. Brooker et al., II, pp. 1254, 1259.

73. Anrep, 'Po Povodu Londonskoi Vystavki s "Uchastiem" Russkikh" Khudozhnikov Salon' ('Report of an Exhibition in London in which Russian Artists Participated'), *Apollon*, 2 (1913), p. 47. I am grateful to Elizabeth Hibbert for this translation. Future references to the article will be in English, while page references refer to the Russian version in *Apollon*. Some sections from the article have been translated and published as 'Apropos of an Exhibition in London with Participating Russian Artists' in *Russian and Soviet Views of Modern Western Art 1890s to Mid-1930s*, ed. Ilia Dorontchenkov, trans. Charles Rougle (Berkeley: University of California Press, 2009), pp. 106–8.

74. Anrep, 'Report of an Exhibition in London', pp. 40, 41.

75. Fry refers to 'certain spiritual experiences' in 'A Postscript on Post-Impressionism', in Bullen, ed., *Post-Impressionists in England*, p. 148. Fry compares painting to music in 'Post Impressionism', *Fortnightly Review*, 95 (May 1911), in Bullen, ed., *Post-Impressionists in England*, p. 168.

76. Anrep, 'Report of an Exhibition in London', p. 43.

77. Ya. Tugendkhol'd, 'Osennyi salon', *Apollon*, 12 (December 1910), 26–36, quoted in Lodder and Hellyer, 'St Petersburg/Petrograd/Leningrad', p. 1257.

78. Anrep, 'Report of an Exhibition in London', p. 44.

79. Anrep, 'Report of an Exhibition in London', pp. 45, 46, 47, 48.

80. HRHRC, Ottoline Morrell Collection, Series II, Correspondence 1894–1938, box 33, folder 5 (Anrep to Morrell, 4 November 1912); (Anrep to Morrell, 13 November 1912).

81. Woolf, *Jacob's Room*, p. 87.

82. Bullen, *Byzantium Rediscovered*, p. 13.

83. MS. in King's College Library, Cambridge, quoted in *Letters of Roger Fry*, I, p. 40.

84. Rutter, *Revolution in Art*, p. 41.

85. Chamot, Farr and Butlin, *Tate Gallery Catalogue: The Modern British, Paintings, Drawings and Sculpture*, I, p. 6.

86. Quoted in Bullen, *Byzantium Rediscovered*, p. 182. Bullen notes: 'I have been unable to identify the precise reference for Robert Ross's words, in the cuttings collection of the Tate Gallery': p. 235, n239.

87. Bell, *Art*, pp. 47, 130.

88. Fry, 'Introduction to Cézanne I, by Maurice Denis', in *Burlington Magazine*, (1910), p. 207.

89. Anrep, 'Report of an Exhibition in London', p. 44.

90. T. E. Hulme, 'Modern Art and its Philosophy' (1914), in Csengeri, ed., *Collected Writings*, p. 281.

91. Maud Lavin notes that Fry's formalism is 'clothed in mysticism' when he writes about Cézanne; see Lavin, 'Roger Fry, Cézanne, and Mysticism', *Arts Magazine* (1983), p. 100. S. K. Tillyard argues that Fry thought that Cézanne 'was possessed of a kind of efflorescent naturalness', almost putting him forward as 'proof of spiritualism'; see S. K. Tillyard, *The Impact of Modernism*, p. 91.

92. Bell, *Art*, p. 209; Fry, 'Acquisition by the National Gallery at Helsingfors', *Burlington Magazine* (1911), p. 293.

93. Fry, *Cézanne: A Study of his Development*, p. 2.

94. NAL, Manuscript, MSL/1974/16160 'Unpublished Memoir of Boris Anrep by Frances Partridge', p. 9.

95. Fry, Preface, in 'Works by Boris von Anrep', *Chenil Gallery Catalogue*, np; Fry, 'Modern Mosaic and Mr. Boris Anrep', *Burlington Magazine* (1923), p. 277.

96. Charles Aitken, discussion following Anrep's paper 'Mosaics', *Journal of the Royal Institute of British Architects* (1927), p. 211.

97. Anrep, 'Mosaics', *Journal of the Royal Institute of British Architects* (1927), p. 204.

98. HRHRC, Mary Hutchinson Papers, Series II, Correspondence 1910–77, box 2, folder 1 (Anrep to Hutchinson, 29 November 1924).

99. Anrep, 'Works by Boris von Anrep', *Chenil Gallery Catalogue*, np; NAL, Manuscript, MSL/1974/16160 'Anrep's Speech at Opening of East Vestibule of National Gallery', 13 November 1933.

100. Williams, 'A Russian Interpretation of British Society in Mosaic', paper given at 'Russia in Britain 1880–1940' conference (2009).

101. Owen, *The Place of Enchantment*, p. 21.

102. See Hinojosa, *The Renaissance, English Cultural Nationalism, and Modernism*, Chapter 6; quoted in Woolf, *Fry*, p. 271.

103. Green, ed., *Art Made Modern: Roger Fry's Vision of Art*, p. 14; Reed, 'Revision and Design: The Later Essays', in Reed, ed., *A Roger Fry Reader*, p. 309.

104. Prettejohn, 'Out of the Nineteenth Century', in Green, ed., *Art Made Modern: Roger Fry's Vision of Art*, p. 34; Shone, *The Art of Bloomsbury*, p. 11.

105. Woolf, *Fry*, p. 56.

106. Fry, 'Satirical Piece on Psychical Phenomena, untitled authored manuscript', 1885–9, KCAC, The Papers of Roger Eliot Fry, REF 1/7.
107. Mrs H. Sidgwick, 'Note on the Evidence, Collected by the Society, for Phantasms of the Dead', in *Proceedings of the Society for Psychical Research*, III, p. 150.
108. *Letters of Roger Fry*, I, 114 (Fry to his mother, 26 May 1887).
109. Banfield, *The Phantom Table*, p. 11.
110. Fry, 'Epicurus or Emerson', autograph manuscript papers to the Cambridge Conversazione Society, 11 February 1888, pp. 7, 8; KCAC, The Papers of Roger Eliot Fry, REF 1/10.
111. See *The Autobiography of G. Lowes Dickinson*, ed. Proctor, p. 68.
112. For a longer account of Carpenter and modernism, see Henderson, 'Mysticism as the "Tie that Binds"', *Art Journal*, 46.1 (1987), 29–37. Edward Carpenter to Fry, 27 February 1894, KCAC, The Papers of Roger Eliot Fry, REF 3/28. For Carpenter and Woolf, see Gerrard, 'Brownness, Trees, Rose Petals, and Chrysalises', in Burrells et al., *Woolfian Boundaries*, pp. 15–21.
113. Fry, 'Must Mahomet go to the Mountain?', autograph manuscript papers to the Cambridge Conversazione Society, June 1888, p. 2; KCAC, The Papers of Roger Eliot Fry, REF 1/10.
114. Besant and Leadbeater, *Thought-Forms*, p. 75.
115. Fry, 'Are we Compelled by the True & Apostolic Faith to Regard the Standard of Beauty as Relative?', autograph manuscript papers to the Cambridge Conversazione Society, October 1889, p. 5; KCAC, The Papers of Roger Eliot Fry, REF 1/10.
116. Fry, 'Post-Impressionism', in Bullen, ed., *Post-Impressionists in England*, p. 173.
117. Russell, 'Mysticism and Logic' (1914), in *Mysticism and Logic and Other Essays*, pp. 11, 1; Woolf, *Fry*, p. 271.
118. Falkenheim, *Roger Fry*, pp. 24, 25.
119. Fry, 'The French Group', in Bullen, ed., *Post-Impressionists in England*, p. 355.
120. Fry, 'The French Group', in Bullen, ed., *Post-Impressionists in England*, p. 353.
121. Fry, 'The Allied Artists', in Bullen, ed., *Post-Impressionists in England*, p. 459.
122. Fry, 'An Essay in Aesthetics', in *Vision and Design*, pp. 14, 16, 12, 13.
123. Fry, 'Art and Socialism', in *Vision and Design*, p. 36.
124. Fry, 'Art and Life', in *Vision and Design*, p. 9.
125. Fry, 'Retrospect', in *Vision and Design*, p. 199.
126. Fry, 'The Artist's Vision', in *Vision and Design*, p. 33.
127. Woolf, *Letters*, II (1976), p. 15 (Woolf to Violet Dickinson, 24 December 1912).
128. Woolf, *Walter Sickert*, p. 13.

129. Waugh, 'Science and the Aesthetics of English Modernism', *New Formations* (2003), pp. 43, 42.
130. Banfield, *The Phantom Table*, pp. 359, 360.
131. Waugh, 'Science and the Aesthetics of English Modernism', p. 43.
132. Woolf, *Between the Acts*, p. 123; Whitworth, *Einstein's Wake*, pp. 168–9.
133. Woolf, *Diary*, I (1975), p. 114 (25 January 1918); Woolf, *Letters*, II (1976), p. 103 (Woolf to Katherine Cox, 25 June 1916); *Diary*, III (1980), p. 330 (8 November 1930).
134. Lee, *Virginia Woolf*, p. 621.
135. Woolf, *Diary*, III (1980), p. 287 (16 February 1930); 'On Being Ill' (1926), in *Essays*, IV (1994), p. 324.
136. See *Translations from the Russian*, ed. Clarke. See also the recent biography of Kotelyansky by Diment, *A Russian Jew of Bloomsbury*, and Rubenstein, *Virginia Woolf and the Russian Point of View*. Marcus, 'Introduction', in *Translations from the Russian*, p. x.
137. Woolf, 'The Russian View', *Times Literary Supplement*, 19 December 1918, p. 641.
138. Woolf, 'The Russian Point of View' (1925), *Essays*, IV (1994), p. 187.
139. Woolf, 'More Dostoevsky', *Times Literary Supplement*, 22 February 1917, p. 91.
140. Marcus, 'The European Dimensions of the Hogarth Press', in Caws and Luckhurst, eds, *The Reception of Virginia Woolf in Europe*, and Marcus, 'Introduction', in *Translations from the Russian*, ed. Clarke.
141. Woolf, 'Tchehov's Questions' (1918), *Essays*, II (1987), p. 245.
142. Woolf, 'The Russian Background', *Times Literary Supplement*, 14 August 1919, p. 435.
143. Quoted in Lee, *Virginia Woolf*, p. 436.
144. Woolf, *Diary*, II (1978), p. 208 (8 October 1922).
145. Woolf, 'The Russian Background', p. 435.
146. Woolf, 'Solid Objects', in *The Complete Shorter Fiction*, pp. 103, 102, 104, 105.
147. Brown, 'The Secret Life of Things', pp. 7, 2, 8, 7.
148. Woolf, 'Solid Objects', p. 105.
149. Woolf, *Jacob's Room*, p. 36. Subsequent references appear as page numbers in the text.
150. Woolf, *Diary*, II (1978), pp. 13–14 (26 January 1920).
151. Flint, 'Introduction', in Woolf, *Jacob's Room*, p. xii.
152. Woolf, *Diary*, III (1980), p. 203 (7 November 1928).
153. Quoted in Lee, *Virginia Woolf*, p. 24.
154. Woolf, *Diary*, III (1980), p. 236 (23 June 1929); p. 287 (16 February 1930); p. 343 (30 December 1930).
155. Woolf, 'The Russian Background', p. 435.

156. Woolf, *The Waves* (1931) (London: Penguin, 1992), pp. 7, 129. Subsequent references appear as page numbers in the text.
157. Woolf, *Diary*, III (1980), p. 298 (28 March 1930).
158. Woolf, *Letters*, III (1977), p. 204 (Woolf to Ethel Smyth, 28 August 1930).
159. Flint, 'Introduction', in *The Waves*, p. xxxviii.
160. Woolf, *Diary*, III (1980), p. 203 (7 November 1928); p. 114 (30 October 1926); p. 203 (7 November 1928).
161. Woolf, *Diary*, III (1980), p. 337 (18 December 1930).
162. Jeans, *The Mysterious Universe*, p. 44; Jeans, *The Universe Around Us*, p. 15.
163. Woolf, *To the Lighthouse*, p. 78; Fry, 'The Artist's Vision', in *Vision and Design*, p. 34.

CHAPTER 2

Russian Aesthetics and British Periodicals: Kandinsky, Sadleir and *Rhythm*

In the fourth issue of the modernist magazine *Rhythm*, published in the spring of 1912, its editor, the aspiring art critic Michael Sadleir, declared that Vasily Kandinsky had 'voiced the inarticulate ideals of a multitude'.[1] The article in which this remark appeared, 'After Gauguin', claimed to describe Gauguin's legacy, but was in fact primarily a critique of Kandinsky's new book, *Über das Geistige in der Kunst*, published in Germany earlier that year. Sadleir's article was the first to introduce the British public to the Russian artist's aesthetics. Sadleir went on to translate *Über das Geistige in der Kunst*, which was published as *The Art of Spiritual Harmony* in 1914.[2]

Rhythm, published between 1911 and 1913, was one of the more aesthetically radical of the pre-war magazines that have shaped our understanding of the modernist period. The term 'modernist magazine' is in line with Peter Brooker and Andrew Thacker's recent critical and cultural history of modernist magazines, in which they argue for a heterogeneous field that includes avant-garde 'little magazines' (such as *Rhythm*, *Blast* and *The Egoist*), as well as the 'more neutral sounding' periodicals, journals, papers and reviews (such as *The New Age*, *The Athenaeum* and *Criterion*).[3] Like other modernist magazines of the pre-war period, *Rhythm* was keen to assert itself as avant-garde. In the first issue, the editor, John Middleton Murry, declared that 'Rhythm is a magazine with a purpose.' That purpose was to 'provide art, be it drawing, literature or criticism, which shall be vigorous, determined, which shall have its roots below the surface, and be the rhythmical echo of the life with which it is in touch'.[4] And in a very early usage of the term, he declared that 'modernism' 'penetrates beneath the outward surface of the world' and 'disengages the rhythms that lie at the heart of things'.[5] However, *Rhythm*'s manifesto appears modest alongside Wyndham Lewis's manifesto in *Blast*, which described itself as 'an avenue for all those vivid and violent ideas that could reach the Public in no other way' or Dora Marsden's declaration in the *New Freewoman* that 'in the clash of opinion we shall expect to find our values'.[6] *Rhythm*'s purpose was milder; rather than spar with the European avant-garde, it sought to appropriate it to its own purposes.

Rhythm was first published in the summer of 1911, edited by Murry and Sadleir, with the Scottish painter John Duncan Fergusson as art editor. Murry's partner, Katherine Mansfield, became assistant editor on the fifth issue in July 1912. Breaking her connections with A. R. Orage's weekly, *The New Age*, Mansfield replaced Sadleir at the request of Charles Granville, of Stephen Swift and Co., who had published her first collection of short stories, *In a German Pension* (1911), and had now taken over the publication of *Rhythm*. Mansfield co-edited the February and March 1913 issues, before the journal folded due to severe financial difficulties after a total of fourteen issues.

Rhythm tends to be referred to as Bergsonian in philosophy and Scottish fauvist in aesthetics, with a strong emphasis on French literature and art.[7] Its fauvism was that of the Scottish colourists Fergusson and S. J. Peploe. Fergusson's close friend, Georges (Dorothy) Banks, and his partner of the time, Anne Estelle Rice, were also regular contributors. Fergusson's access to the Parisian art world resulted in the reproduction of works by artists associated with fauvism, including André Dunoyer de Segonzac, André Derain, Auguste Herbin and Auguste Chabaud, as well as drawings by Picasso and Henri Gaudier-Brzeska. *Rhythm* published literary works by the Parisian-based writers Tristan Derème and Francis Carco in French. As Marysa Demoor has remarked, 'one is struck by the sheer number of French contributions to *Rhythm*'.[8] Less frequently discussed, though often noted, is the wider international focus of the magazine. In addition to the work coming out of Paris, *Rhythm* published Yone Noguchi's articles on Japanese aesthetics and showed a particular interest in Russian art and literature: it printed prose by Leonid Andreev, drawings by Natal'ia Goncharova, reviews of productions by Sergei Diagilev's Ballets Russes, and stories written in the style of Tolstoy and Dostoevsky. Two of the international-sounding authors, Boris Petrovsky and Lili Heron, were in fact Mansfield's pseudonyms, reminding us, as Faith Binckes notes, that 'cosmopolitanism, or internationalism, was also about image and performance'.[9]

Rhythm embraced its cosmopolitan status, listing both 'Agents for *Rhythm* Abroad' on the back cover and 'foreign correspondents' on the contents page. Agents in Paris, New York, Munich and Berlin, and an

American correspondent were listed by the fifth issue. The critic and translator Floryan Sobieniowski, who famously introduced Mansfield to the works of Chekhov, was added as the Polish correspondent in the sixth issue, and by August 1912 agents in Warsaw, Krakow and Helsinki were included. Mikhail Likiardopulo, secretary to the directors of the Moscow Art Theatre, was added as the Russian correspondent, and Francis Carco, Tristan Derème, Georges Banks and Anne Estelle Rice were all listed as French correspondents from August 1912.

The significance of Sadleir's article on Kandinsky is understood when read in conjunction with a cross-section of articles in magazines from the same period. Kandinsky's book is not mentioned in other British magazines in early 1912 because it had only just been published in Germany. Sadleir was given advance notice because Kandinsky himself had mentioned it in a letter to him in October 1911.[10] By comparison, Huntly Carter's art column in *The New Age* on 7 March 1912 focused on the first futurist exhibition held at the Galerie Bernheim-Jeune in Paris. The 'Notes from Russia' column in *The Athenaeum* on 9 March included information about the number of public libraries in Russia (633) and the publication of the first volume of *The Fauna of Russia*, detailing every species of fish in the 'Russian Empire'.[11] The March 1912 issue of the *English Review* published the first translation by Stephen Graham of an essay by Viacheslav Ivanov on the 'Theatre of the Future', in which he wrote that the 'presence of rhythm is indispensable' in art.[12] *Rhythm*, we can see, was not unusual in its focus on Russian aesthetics, or on rhythm, but Sadleir's personal connection with Kandinsky positioned the magazine at the heart of a new, spiritually inflected Russian aesthetics.

Brooker's and Thacker's history of modernist magazines and the digitisation of many of the publications themselves has opened up scholarship into this 'dialogic matrix of modernism'. Modernist magazines should not be read in isolation; they function in (often competitive) dialogue with each other as a 'network of cultural formations'.[13] In light of this argument, borrowed from Brooker and Thacker, this chapter argues that the appearance of Kandinsky's aesthetics in *Rhythm* was not anomalous, but part of a wider network of aesthetic concerns in British periodicals during the pre-war period. Russian culture and modernism were connected to a growing interest in spiritual aesthetics, an interest that grew from a mixture of sources, including the Victorian fashion for spiritualism, the turn-of-the-century theosophical movement, and a reaction – in some quarters – against empiricism.

Rhythm's Russian aesthetics

The December 1912 issue of *Rhythm* included two lithographs by
Natal'ia Goncharova that were titled *La Vendange,* and are now
known as *Women with Basket of Grapes* and *Men with Basket of
Grapes* (Fig. 5). Goncharova's rhythmic representation of the harvest-
ing of grapes shows the arms of the harvesters in identical dancelike poses. The designs were based on the *Picking Grapes* polyptych
(1911). As Anthony Parton suggests, the polyptych brought together
Goncharova's neo-primitive research and practice within a Christian
framework.[14] The 'drawing' that appears a few pages later, attributed
to Mikhail Larionov, depicts a typically Russian-looking scene. In
fact, this was a lithograph based on Goncharova's 1910 painting,
The Storm, created as a postcard for the Donkey's Tail exhibition in
Moscow in 1912.[15] It shows a man on horseback and another man following through a pine forest, in which the rain is so heavy it bends the
trees. The angle and thickness of the strokes of the lithograph, like the
brushwork in the painting, indicate rain and also fragment the composition into triangular sections (Fig. 6), working against the angle of
the figures.

The December 1912 issue of *Rhythm* went to press after the opening
of Roger Fry's 'Second Post-Impressionist Exhibition' on 5 October
1912, in which Goncharova and Larionov were to exhibit, although
their works, along with those of some others, did not arrive in time for
the opening and were added to the exhibition in January 1913. It may
have been coincidence that the editors of *Rhythm* wanted to include
Fry's exhibitors (although in fact they included only one of them), but
it is likely that there was also a competitive element. As mentioned
in Chapter 1, earlier in 1912 the opening of the exhibition of the
'Rhythmists' at the Stafford Gallery, which included Jessica Dismorr,
Fergusson, Peploe, Rice and Ethel Wright, had been postponed from
June to October in order to coincide with Fry's exhibition.

As well as reproducing Russian visual art, *Rhythm* printed poems
and stories purporting to be by Russian writers. In the same issue
in which Sadleir wrote about Kandinsky, Mansfield used her alias
'Boris Petrovsky' for the first time, claiming to be 'his' translator. Yet
the poems by Petrovsky/Mansfield – 'Very Early Spring' and 'The
Awakening River' – draw on a range of national styles. They appear,
first, to parody contemporary Georgian pastoral poetry, a volume
of which was published the same year.[16] Mansfield's reference to the
river running away with the birds to the sea in 'Very Early Spring'

NATALIE GONTCHAROVA

THE OPAL DREAM CAVE

In an opal dream cave I found a fairy :
Her wings were frailer than flower petals—
Frailer far than snowflakes.
She was not frightened, but poised on my finger,
Then delicately walked into my hand.
I shut the two palms of my hands together
And held her prisoner.
I carried her out of the opal cave,
Then opened my hands.
First she became thistledown,
Then a mote in a sunbeam,
Then—nothing at all.
Empty now is my opal dream cave.

KATHERINE MANSFIELD

NATALIE GONTCHAROVA

SEA

The Sea called—I lay on the rocks and said :
"I am come."
She mocked and showed her teeth,
Stretching out her long green arms.
"Go away," she thundered.
"Then tell me what I am to do," I begged.
"If I leave you, you will not be silent,
But cry my name in the cities
And wistfully entreat me in the plains and forests ;
All else I forsake to come to you—what must I do ?"
"Never have I uttered your name," snarled the Sea.
"There is no more of me in your body
Than the little salt tears you are frightened of shedding.
What can you know of my love on your brown rock pillow . . . .
Come closer."

KATHERINE MANSFIELD

Fig. 5 *Women with Basket of Grapes* and *Men with Basket of Grapes*, after the motifs of the *Picking Grapes* polyptych, 1911, Natal'ia Goncharova (1881–1962), Russkii muzei (Russian Museum), St Petersburg. Reproduced as *La Vendange* in *Rhythm*, 2, no. 11 (December 1912), pp. 306–7. © ADAGP, Paris, and DACS, London 2013.

MICHAEL LARIONOFF

Fig. 6 Natal'ia Goncharova, *Autumn*, after the motifs of *Autumn Study (Direct Perception)* (1911), Russkii muzei (Russian Museum), St Petersburg. Reproduced as Mikhail Larionov, *Drawing*, in *Rhythm*, 2, no. 11 (December 1912), p. 317. © ADAGP, Paris, and DACS, London 2013.

gently mocks the tendency of pastoral poets to be seduced by nature. But they also bear a striking resemblance in theme and tone to Paul Selver's translation of the Polish poet, Kazimierz Przerwa-Tetmajer, whose lyrical 'Song of the Night Mists' was published in *The New Age* in January 1912. This was noted by *The New Age* contributor Beatrice Hastings (Emily Alice Haigh), who referred to the 'flapping and wappering' of the stanzas, and to the entire issue of *Rhythm* as 'dutifully imitative' of the latest issue of *The New Age*.[17] Selver's translation of Przerwa-Tetmajer's poem reads, 'Softly, softly, let us wake not streams that in the valley sleep, / Let us with the wind dance gently o'er the spaces wide and deep.' Three months later, in 'Very Early Spring', Mansfield wrote, 'A wind dances over the fields. / Shrill and clear the sound of her waking laughter, / Yet the little blue lakes tremble.'[18] Given the contentious relationship between Mansfield and Hastings, and Mansfield's fondness for satire, it seems likely that these poems were intended to amuse readers of *The New Age* and *Rhythm*. Hastings asks, 'Aware that Miss Mansfield has, on occasions, a sense of humour, we wonder if it is all a joke; especially as the verse is solemnly asserted to be a translation from the Russian!'[19]

Frank Harris published 'The Holy Man (After Tolstoi)', a version of Tolstoy's 'The Three Hermits', in the June 1912 issue of *Rhythm*. Tolstoy's story was based on a legend he had heard from a wandering storyteller in 1879, and had first been published in Britain in 1906 in *Twenty-Three Tales*, a collection of his stories translated by Louise and Aylmer Maude. Harris adapts the story for a British readership: he explains that 'Men are commonly called "souls" in Russia as they are called "hands" in England', and in case we might find the holy man who is the subject of the story too sincere for authenticity the Bishop protagonist tells us he was not trying to 'show off' but that his 'sincerity was manifest and his goodness too'.[20] Whereas Tolstoy's Bishop asks that we pray for 'us sinners', Harris's Bishop is abandoned in mid-sentence at the end of the story to effect the transfer of the story from a nineteenth-century Russian context to a British modernist one: 'I only wish – '[21] More important than the changes made by Harris to Tolstoy's tale, however, is the editorial decision to include a nineteenth-century spiritual Russian folk legend in the first place. Its publication was also likely to have been financially motivated. Binckes notes that, given Harris's financial contribution to the magazine, Murry owed Harris 'plenty of positive publicity'.[22] This argument is reinforced by the advertisement in the same issue for a talk at Claridges by the 'greatest English master of the short story', none other than Frank Harris himself.[23]

Mansfield's 'Tales of a Courtyard' in the August 1912 issue have more in common with the moral ambiguity found in a Dostoevsky novel than the Tolstoyan spirituality of 'The Three Hermits'. The tales were published a month after her parody in *The New Age*, 'Green Goggles', in which 'Olga Petrovska' (related to Boris Petrovsky?) arrives in disguise, wearing, of course, green goggles, and her words fall upon the soul of 'Dimitri Tchernikofskoi' like snow flakes, leaving him wondering 'how large his soul was' and 'how many flakes it would take to cover it completely'.[24] The first story in 'Tales of a Courtyard' involves a group of neighbours admiring a budding chestnut tree and jeering at the 'swollen distorted body' of a Russian girl walking out of the courtyard. The final story tells the story of Feodor, an aspiring poet who works as a doorman for a drapery establishment. He steals a book of poetry from an old man sitting on the stone bench in the courtyard. He is tortured by his theft but unable to return the book, only to discover the old man has died in the courtyard overnight.[25] Moral degradation and spiritual inspiration are combined in Leonid Andreev's 'The Present', published in *Rhythm* two months later. A worker, Sazonka, visits his apprentice, Senista, in hospital and promises to return but instead spends his Easter holiday drinking. When he eventually returns to the hospital Senista is dead. Sazonka walks away from the city, lies down on a hill and falls 'upon his split lip, rigid, in a fit of silent despair'. But, unlike 'Tales of a Courtyard', Andreev's story ends with the comfort of 'Eternal mother earth' who took 'her guilty son to her bosom and comforted his sad heart with the warmth of her love and hope. Far away in the city the Easter chimes were ringing gaily . . .'[26]

The Ballets Russes featured strongly in *Rhythm*, as they did in many publications of the period: for example, *The New Age, The Egoist* and *Little Review*. Huntly Carter in *The New Age*, for example, described the first performance of the Ballets Russes as the 'finest thing of the kind that has been seen in this country'.[27] Georges Banks illustrated and wrote *Rhythm*'s first review of the Ballets Russes for the July 1912 issue. *Petrushka*, wrote Banks, 'has the eternal something, the "incommunicable thrill of things," which belongs to all great art'. The reason for this, according to Banks, is the unity of sound and visual art; the music becomes '*visual* in form', and the feeling of 'world tragedy' is created by the 'designs in colour, line and music'.[28] In August 1912, Anne Estelle Rice described the visual impact of Leon Bakst's set for *Sheherazade* as though it were a post-impressionist painting:

> full of the visions of Asia, a tropical heat, not of stillness, but of new life born every instant, where realism and fantasy combine and multiply into a fluidity of moving reds, blues, oranges, greens, purples, triangles, squares, circles, serpentine and zigzag shapes.

For Rice, Bakst's use of line and colour broke new ground:

> Bakst takes all colours, every nuance of each colour from its extreme brilliancy downwards, and all directions of line and compositions of line, harmonizes everything; and by his simple but fully expressive effect, convinces the spectator of the artist's belief in his power to create, as opposed to the apologetic grovelling of the aesthetic before nature.[29]

Unlike the impressionists' grovelling, the Ballets Russes offered a powerful new aesthetic experience in which the boundaries between sound and image were no longer fixed.

Russian art and literature, therefore, served two very different functions in *Rhythm*. The inclusion of Russian visual art, including that of the Ballets Russes, established the magazine's position at the cutting edge of modernism, and contributed to the magazine's promotion of a distinctive interpretation of post-impressionism, made up of Anglo-American fauvists, Scottish colourists and the Russian artists, Goncharova and Kandinsky. *Rhythm* claimed in the third issue, not without cause, that it had 'given the world better drawing than has been seen in one magazine before'.[30] The fourth issue advertised a case costing half a crown, designed 'in colours by J. D. Fergusson' for binding issues of *Rhythm*, indicating that it aspired to be an art work in itself rather than a disposable journal. By contrast, the Russian literary works, apart from the story by Andreev, were simulated versions of Russian literature, mediated through Frank Harris and Katherine Mansfield. The creation of quasi-Russian literature in *Rhythm* points to both the editorial ambition for internationalism and a desire to experiment, sometimes playfully, across perceived national styles.

Kandinsky and *Rhythm*

Michael Sadleir's first opportunity to view Kandinsky's work in Britain would have been at the second exhibition of the AAA in 1909, in the form of two paintings, *Jaune et rose* and *Paysage*, and twelve engravings.[31] Louise Hardiman notes the difficulty in identifying the paintings, as the titles do not correspond with the *catalogue raisonné* entries for the relevant dates.[32] Kandinsky's work continued to be included in the AAA exhibitions (with the exception of 1912, although he was listed as a contributor in the catalogue) until 1914, when the onset of war brought the larger AAA shows to an end, although smaller exhibitions were held at the Grafton Galleries until 1920. Sadleir bought six of Kandinsky's woodcuts from the 1911 AAA exhibition. They were part of the proofs for *Klänge*, a book of Kandinsky's poems and woodcuts that was published in Germany in 1913. Sadleir wrote in his memoir of his father that the woodcuts 'were strange productions, semi-representational, and with an element of hieratic rigidity which presumably appealed at that time to some Schwärmerei of my own'.[33] Gruetzner Robins notes that Rutter must have written to Kandinsky about the sale because Kandinsky wrote back in August 1911, sending '16 small texts' and an account of *Klänge*. He described these as his 'compositions for the stage', which consist of 'gesture (movement of "dance"), colour (movement of painting) and of sound (musical movement – this will be done by the famous composer Hartmann) on the principle of pure theatre'. Rutter replied to say that he had passed on the texts to Sadleir, who had bought the prints.[34]

On 2 October 1911, Sadleir wrote to Kandinsky to say how pleased he was to have the woodcuts and that he believed 'this artistic revolution' to be so important that he would like to 'reproduce one of them in my quarterly journal *Rhythm*'.[35] Kandinsky wrote back on 6 October:

> Thank you for sending me your periodical. I am very glad to give permission for the reproduction of my wood-cuts. I am very pleased that the so-called modern art movement is mirrored in your journal and meets with interest in England. Mr Brooke from Cambridge also told me about this last winter. I enclose for you the prospectus of the art periodical that I have founded, the first issue is due to appear in January. Also this month my book 'Über das Geistige in der Kunst' will be published. I will send you a copy. Please write back with your impression.[36]

Although he did not publish Kandinsky's woodcuts in *Rhythm*, Sadleir was made aware in October 1911 of two of Kandinsky's major theoretical works: *Über das Geistige in der Kunst* and the *Blaue Reiter* almanac, both of which were published in Germany in 1912. In December 1911 Kandinsky wrote to Sadleir that the 'great inner relationship of all arts is coming gradually ever more clearly to light'. And in the same letter he advised Sadleir to read the texts of *Klänge* without 'looking for an explicit narration' but to let them 'work on your feeling, on your soul' and then they will 'become clear'.[37]

Sadleir apparently let the *Klänge* texts work on his soul because in the spring 1912 issue of *Rhythm* he positioned Kandinsky and Derain as 'neo-primitive' successors to Gauguin. Binckes argues that the article was primarily intended as a way to establish connections between *Rhythm* and 'related, high-caste, publishing ventures', including Kandinsky's *Der blaue Reiter* and Apollinaire's *L'Enchanteur pourrissant* (1909).[38] Although this was no doubt part of his purpose, Sadleir's genuine enthusiasm for Kandinsky's theories of abstraction is clear. Sadleir summarised Kandinsky's aesthetics as 'virtually a statement of Pantheism', or a belief in 'a "something" behind externals, common to nature and humanity alike'. New art for Kandinsky, wrote Sadleir, will 'act as intermediary for others, to harmonize the *inneres klang* of external nature with that of humanity'.[39]

Sadleir's interpretation relies on a knowledge of Kandinsky's theories in *Über das Geistige in der Kunst*. One of the first theoretical discussions of abstract art, the book sets out to define what Kandinsky saw as the contemporary status of spiritualism in art. According to

Kandinsky, the spirit of the age in the early twentieth century was connected to that of 'the Primitives' because artists from both periods were seeking to express 'internal truths' without concern for 'external form'. The souls of artists in the early twentieth century, argued Kandinsky, were emerging from the 'nightmare of materialism' towards 'subtler emotions'. Kandinsky argued that literature, music and art were all approaching each other in terms of their 'spiritual development' because they were 'striving towards the abstract, the non-material'. Music, for Kandinsky, was the 'best teacher' because it revealed 'that modern desire for rhythm in painting, for mathematical, abstract construction, for repeated notes of colour, for setting colour in motion'. The second half of the book is devoted to the 'psychological working of colour', influenced by Besant and Leadbeater's *Thought-Forms* (1901), which Kandinsky owned in a German translation from 1908. Different colours create different psychic effects, or 'spiritual vibration', argues Kandinsky, and different forms each have their individual 'spiritual value'.[40] In *Thought-Forms*, 'definite thought produces a double effect – a radiating vibration and a floating form'.[41] The power of thought to create form clearly appealed to Kandinsky as a model for aesthetic process.

In his early account of Kandinsky's engagement with theosophy, Sixten Ringbom noted that the influence of *Thought-Forms* on Kandinsky 'worked on a more general and fundamental level than in isolated details such as the meaning of single colours'.[42] There *are* some overlaps in the colour theories – for example, blue is connected to the spiritual and vermillion to passion – but it quickly diverges; yellow, for Kandinsky, is 'earthly' whilst for Besant and Leadbeater it is pure intelligence. Ringbom points out that in his autobiography (*Rüblicke 1901–13*), Kandinsky described a synaesthetic experience during a production of Wagner's *Lohengrin* at the Moscow Court Theatre in the 1890s. In *Thought-Forms*, Besant and Leadbeater describe how music leaves behind an 'impression' of form and colour, and in the case of Wagner, 'successively retreating ramparts of a mountain' and 'billowy masses of cloud' and rocks, which represent 'in size, shape and color' the 'general effect of one of the sections of the piece of music as seen from a distance'.[43] The abstract shapes and forms that illustrate *Thought-Forms* bear striking resemblance to Kandinsky's early abstract work.

Kandinsky was influenced by theosophy from a number of sources, including Aleksandra Unkovskaia's 'The Method of Color-Sound Numbers'.[44] He also read works by Blavatsky and Steiner, and attended

Steiner's lectures at the *Architektenhaus* in Berlin in 1907 and 1908, in which he discussed the disintegration of the atom. One of Kandinsky's notebooks from 1908 refers to Blavatsky's *The Key to Theosophy*, Katherine Tingley's *International Theosophical Chronicle* and Édouard Schuré's *The Great Initiates*. In 1961 Peter Fingesten emphasised that what 'some choose to see today in terms of pure aesthetics, was to Mondrian (and Kandinsky as well) an expression of pure spirit'.[45] Or, to put it another way, artists find new ways to express the unseen. The recent Hayward Gallery exhibition, 'Invisible: Art About the Unseen 1957–2012', took this to its logical extreme: total invisibility.[46] Eichner claims that Kandinsky was interested in the concept of thought transference and the idea that artists' creations would, eventually, 'radiate in space without any material media'.[47] Whether or not this was true, we can conclude here that Kandinsky's move to abstraction emerged from a struggle to describe the unseen, rather than as a rejection of realism as style.

Six months before writing his review of *Über das Geistige in der Kunst*, and around the time of his initial correspondence with Kandinsky, Sadleir argued that Van Gogh never used colour to 'create illusion' but rather to 'suggest deeper meaning'. Sadleir was not in favour of the 'purposely divided' colour of the impressionists, which would 'fuse in the eye from the proper distance'. He attacked the way the 'actual value' of 'each pure red or blue or yellow went to create another composite value, and there was no attempt beyond the creation of a suffused brilliance'.[48] By contrast, fauvists, argued Sadleir, kept the integrity of each colour by using definite slabs rather than creating an artificial surface.

However, Kandinsky's theory of synaesthesia or, in Sadleir's words, 'the possibility of hearing colour, seeing sound, touching rhythms, and so forth', was too systematic for Sadleir, who preferred the simpler idea that 'colour can convey a more immediate and subtle appeal to the inner soul than words'.[49] Sadleir argued that the 'deeper meaning' of colour should be apparent but not articulated. Synaesthesia had become an increasingly popular phenomenon at the beginning of the twentieth century, as epitomised by Aleksandr Skryabin's *Prometheus* (1910) for piano, orchestra, optional choir and *clavier à lumières* (keyboard with lights). *Prometheus* premiered in Britain on 1 February 1913 at the Queen's Hall and, as Bullock notes, it was deemed so important that it was performed twice on the same evening. Rosa Newmarch wrote to Skryabin after the concert to tell him that the 'impression was quite shaking, strange' and that the audience responded with 'sincere and spontaneous applause'.[50] And later, Duncan Grant's *Abstract Kinetic Collage Painting with Sound* or *The Scroll* (1914) involved an abstract pattern of painted rectangles on a scroll of paper to be viewed through an opening in a lit box to the sound of the Adagio from Bach's *First Brandenburg Concerto*. The availability of theories of synaesthesia is apparent in Yone Noguchi's throw-away comment *in Rhythm*: 'Oh how I wish to write my poetry to be smelled!'[51]

Before writing on Kandinsky in *Rhythm*, Sadleir reviewed *Über das Geistige in der Kunst* in *Art News* in March 1912. Again, Sadleir was critical of Kandinsky's system:

> I think Kandinsky inclines over-much to the scientific in some of his theories. Sane art need not mean scientific art, and the chief danger of this new idea is the growth of formulae, by which the impressions to be given by a picture will be manufactured from recipes. Such a line will excite, such a colour soothe.[52]

Having criticised Kandinsky for being too scientific in this review of 1912, in the introduction to his 1914 translation he attacked Kandinsky's 'vague and grandiloquent language'.[53] Sadleir's criticisms perhaps fostered a sense of empathy with readers who might find the language off-putting, but he also engendered a sense of exclusivity. In his review in *Art News* in 1912, Sadleir adopted a belligerent tone, and accused those who objected to new forms of art as 'uneducated enemies' of the new movement. He challenges these 'enemies' to produce work themselves that creates the 'psychological effect given by the best work of the new school'. If they can, he writes that he will 'salute them as artists. If not, I would suggest that they mind their own business.'[54]

Kandinsky's theory of 'innerer Klang' and the 'inner need' of artists bolstered the Bergsonian aesthetics of *Rhythm*. Murry, we remember, stated that modernism 'penetrates beneath the outward surface of the world' and in the same article he indicated that *Rhythm*'s primary ambition was to spread the theories of Bergson to England.[55] Sadleir emphasised Kandinsky's idea that the artist realises 'what lies underneath the life which inspires him'.[56] The aesthetic faculties of humanity, according to Bergson, prove that we can access our intuition or inner life, in the same way an artist is able to understand life by 'placing himself back within the object' and by breaking down 'the barrier that space puts up between him and his model'. The idea of a common soul running through generations is also an important connection between Kandinsky's aesthetics and the Bergsonian philosophy so fundamental to *Rhythm*. Bergson's theory of evolution 'implies a real persistence of the past in the present, a duration which is, as it were, a hyphen, a connecting link'. Bergson builds on the notion of a connecting link to formulate his theory of transformism, which he defines broadly as 'a visible current' passing from generation to generation that 'has become divided amongst species and distributed amongst individuals without losing anything of its force'.[57] It was this concept of a 'visible current' that Murry used to represent art in his opening article for *Rhythm*, where he used an alchemical metaphor to define it as a 'golden thread that runs through a varied texture, showing firm, brilliant, and unbroken when the fabric has fallen away'.[58] Kandinsky argued for a 'vital impulse of life' and, like Murry's aesthetic golden thread, this impulse runs through the ages so that the relationship between art of different times 'is not a relationship in outward form but in inner meaning'. The artist, according to Kandinsky, must 'watch only the trend of the inner need', as opposed to the 'conventions of form' and 'demands' of 'his particular age'.[59] Sadleir's version of Kandinsky's theories reinforced the idea of a spiritual life connecting art of all ages that had begun with the interpretation of Bergson's philosophy in the pages of *Rhythm*.

Rhythm and the spiritual

Kandinsky's reference to 'that modern desire for rhythm in painting' draws attention to the widespread use of the term 'rhythm' that spanned art movements and time periods.[60] Just weeks before the first issue of *Rhythm* was published, Roger Fry wrote in a discussion of post-impressionism that 'Rhythm is the fundamental and vital quality of painting, as of all the arts – representation is secondary to that, and must never encroach on the more ultimate and fundamental demands of rhythm.'[61] Although Fry would later move towards the idea of 'significant form' to define (with equal ambiguity) post-impressionism, at this stage rhythm was the fundamental principle of his aesthetics, a principle that defined the 'vital quality' of painting.

The idea and terminology of rhythm was such common currency amongst British art critics that D. S. MacColl, Keeper of the Tate Gallery, developed a theory of classic and romantic rhythms to categorise art of all ages. MacColl referred to the 'tyrannic imposition of rhythm' in Romantic drawing, 'a rhythm of the artist's excitement' rather than 'the rhythms of the objects' in classic art.[62] Laurence

Binyon's *Flight of the Dragon* (1911), a formal analysis of Chinese and Japanese art, brought together rhythm and spirituality in its translation of the first principle of ancient Chinese art: 'Rhythmic Vitality, or Spiritual Rhythm expressed in the movement of life'.[63] Reviews of Fry's Post-Impressionist exhibitions routinely described the work of Matisse in terms of rhythm. Desmond MacCarthy, for example, referred to Matisse's search for 'an abstract harmony of line, for rhythm', and *The Times* reviewer observed that Matisse does not 'impose this rhythm' on his figures but 'has wrung it, as it were out of the figures themselves'. In fact, although the artists associated with *Rhythm* were keen to assert their independence from Fry's post-impressionism, to the wider public, post-impressionism and rhythm were considered synonymous. Art critic for *The Observer*, P. G. Konody, wrote in 1911 that 'Post-Impressionism has evidently come to stay. It now has its official organ in the shape of the new shilling quarterly "Rhythm".'[64] By 1912 Frank Rutter claimed that rhythm was 'the magic word of the moment'. Even if 'the numerous attempts made at defining it were not very convincing', he argued, 'one "knew what it meant"'.[65] The ambiguity of the term was clear when C. J. Holmes admitted in *Rhythm* itself that 'until it was suggested that I should write an article' on the subject 'it had never occurred to me to find out what the word "Rhythm" meant'.[66]

Ideas about spirituality, rhythm and art were evolving outside as well as inside the pages of *Rhythm*, then, and, as in *Rhythm*, Russian art was a particular focus for this complex of ideas. The art critic for *The New Age*, Huntly Carter, wrote in his book, *The New Spirit in Drama and Art* (1912), that 'the enormous importance of rhythm in life is already beginning to be felt'. Rhythm was one of Carter's four 'modern principles', alongside 'simplicity, unity, continuity', that distinguished the Moscow Art Theatre and the Ballets Russes from contemporary theatre in London and Paris. One of the reasons for this, according to Carter, was that the 'Russian decorators' have discovered, 'as the early Egyptians expressed it', that 'mysticism' is a 'definite thing, having strength and vitality, and enthroned in a blinding white light' rather than being 'necessarily vague and indefinite and buried in darkness'.[67]

Carter was an important figure for the *Rhythm* artists. His promotion of their work in his book is acknowledged by a sketch of Carter by Banks in the January 1913 issue of *Rhythm* called 'The New Spirit in Art and Drama' (Fig. 7). Adrian Glew calls this sketch a 'Kandinsky-like skit' but the title must be a reference to Carter's book.[68] Carter had written of 'the strong direction of line and colour' in one of Banks's works that

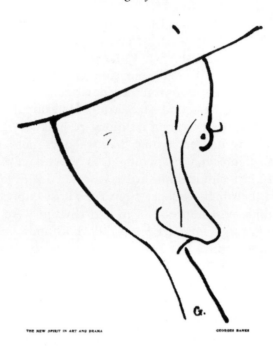

THE NEW SPIRIT IN ART AND DRAMA   GEORGES BANKS

Fig. 7 'The New Spirit in Art and Drama', 1913, George [Dorothy] Banks, in *Rhythm*, 2, no. 12 (1913), p. 13.

'seems to proclaim the fact that the study is about to walk out of the frame'.[69] As though in response to Carter's remark, Banks's drawing of Carter appears to push against the edges of the sketch. In a review for *The Egoist*, Carter compared Kandinsky's book with Clive Bell's *Art*, both published in the spring of 1914. Given Carter's admiration for spiritualism in art, and Russian art in particular, it is not surprising that he favoured Kandinsky – whom he called a 'spiritual harmonist' who (adding a touch of Bergson) believes that 'art passes through the world as a flux of spirit' – over Bell, who saw art as 'frame or form'.[70]

The importance of Sadleir's article 'After Gauguin' and his subsequent translation of *Über das Geistige in der Kunst* is evident in the contemporaneous reception of Kandinsky, and his current international status. The Japanese edition of his book, for example, appeared as early as 1924.[71] Reviews of *The Art of Spiritual Harmony* were mixed. Solomon Eagle, the reviewer for the *New Statesman*, praised Kandinsky's sincerity and yet referred to his pictures as 'puzzling' because they reminded him of 'enlarged photographs of bacteria'. Eagle called Kandinsky's book the work of a 'single minded – though conceivably misdirected – artist', and argued that Kandinsky had difficulty 'convincing us that his forms really are abstract'. *The Saturday Review* complained that 'intelligent review of this book is not easy; it is vague and confusing, sincere, occult and idealistic; philosophical, psycho- logical and dogmatic. In much it seems to us soundly critical, in much unsound in its philosophy.' The reviewer for *The Athenaeum* (probably Murry), praised Kandinsky's classification of colours, and yet inexpli- cably complained that 'he exaggerates the inertness of green', presum- ably referring to Kandinsky's theory that green is 'the "bourgeoisie" – self-satisfied, immovable, narrow'. For *The Athenaeum* the problem was 'one of planning' because Kandinsky 'has a mania for classifying in detail, but the main divisions are loosely related'. Frank Rutter was one of the only reviewers to praise Kandinsky's book unequivocally as 'the most lucid and best reasoned account of the aims of abstract painting that has yet been written'.[72]

The vorticist artist Edward Wadsworth reviewed Kandinsky's theo- ries of aesthetics positively in the first issue of *Blast* in June 1914: 'This book is a most important contribution to the psychology of modern art.'[73] However, Wyndham Lewis was disparaging in the second issue. He was dismissive of Kandinsky's desire to be 'passive and medium-like', and argued that his art avoided 'almost all powerful and definite forms', and that he was 'at the best, wandering and slack'.[74] Henri Gaudier-Brzeska remarked in 1914 in *The Egoist*, 'I have been told that he is a very great painter', but that his own [i.e. Gaudier's] 'temperament does not allow of formless, vague assertions'.[75]

Kandinsky's reputation in London was enhanced by an endorse- ment from Fry, even though Fry and Anrep did not choose to include Kandinsky in the Russian section of the 'Second Post-Impressionist Exhibition'. On 11 March 1913 Sadleir's father wrote to Kandinsky that

> Mr Roger Fry has been staying with us and was deeply interested in your drawings. He asked if I would lend them for an exhibition which he and some friends are organizing next week in London, and of course I gladly consented.

Kandinsky was thus exhibited at the Grafton Group show at the Alpine Club Gallery in March 1913. When Fry went to the AAA exhibi- tion later the same year, he wrote in his review for *The Nation* that 'by far the best pictures there seemed to me to be the three works by Kandinsky', because they had the most 'definite and coherent expres- sive power'. Fry described Kandinsky's paintings as 'pure visual music', and decided that he could not 'any longer doubt the possibility of emotional expression by such abstract visual signs'.[76]

Sadleir's interpretation of Kandinsky's spiritualist aesthetics in 1912 crystallised a set of aesthetic concerns that had been emerging and evolving in Britain since the late nineteenth century. Ideas about the spiritual vision of the artist and the vogue for Russian culture cut across literature, philosophy and the visual arts, bringing together Bergsonian philosophy, ideas about rhythm in art, the Ballets Russes, synaesthesia and colour theory. Sadleir's introduction of Kandinsky's aesthetics to the British public formed a significant contribution to *Rhythm*'s search for 'an art that strikes deeper, that touches a profounder reality, that passes outside the bounds of a narrow aestheticism, cramping and choking itself, drawing its inspiration from aversion, to a humaner and a broader field'.[77]

John Middleton Murry

John Middleton Murry is not usually awarded much space in modernist studies other than accounts of his excessive editing of Mansfield's works in order to create 'a composite image of literary perfection'.[78] Kotelyansky, for example, was so horrified by what Murry had done that he cut off ties with his old friend. As Rachel Polonsky rightly notes, Murry erased Mansfield's 'dialogue with Chekhov' from the last years of her life, including the astute critical insights that run through her letters and notebooks, which Murry often passed off as his own. This part of the chapter, whilst acknowledging the importance of Mansfield's engagement with Chekhov, and the translations she undertook with Kotelyanksy, is concerned with her engagement with the Russian-inflected spiritual aesthetics in *Rhythm* and aims to establish how it played out in the writings of both Mansfield and Murry. Although Murry's early fiction does not merit much critical analysis, it is worth tracking the shift in focus from an early spiritual rhythm, which morphed into an ultimately religious concept of harmony in his later work. There is also scope for work on the early aesthetics of art critic Michael Sadleir in relation to Kandinsky, but it is not addressed here.[79]

Murry's early aesthetics were closely aligned with a Bergsonian concept of rhythm in art that developed into a more overtly mystical, and ultimately religious, concept of harmony during the course of his career. Critics like Ernest Griffin and Sharron Greer Cassavant concentrate on Murry's mysticism after Mansfield's death in 1923 and link it to the development of his religious beliefs.[80] But my argument is that Murry's mystical aesthetics originated in *Rhythm*, and developed in his first novel, *Still Life* (1916), and his study of Dostoevsky of the same year. Murry's mystical aesthetics can also be tracked as they were played out in the romanticism versus classicism debate with T. S. Eliot in *The Adelphi* and *The Criterion*.

By contrast, despite the circumstances of her death, Mansfield argued that writing and mysticism should remain separate. In a review of Victor Neuburg's poems in 1912, Mansfield described 'mysticism' as

> perverted sensuality; it is 'passionate admiration' for that which has no reality at all. It leads to the annihilation of any true artistic effort. It is a paraphernalia of clichés. It is a mask through which the true expression of the poet can never be discerned.[81]

Despite these assertions, Mansfield was certainly interested in the Maori mysticism she encountered during her trip through the Urewera district in the north of New Zealand in 1907.[82] And so, although moments of what might be termed aesthetic mysticism are apparent in Mansfield's early work, they should not be read as a prelude to her decision to join Georgy Ivanovich Gurdzhiev's 'Institute for the Harmonious Development of Man' in Fontainebleau in 1922.

The 'revival of mysticism' in the 1890s, mentioned by Holbrook Jackson in 1913, was distinct from the popular spiritualism of the late nineteenth century.[83] According to Owen, the mystical revival was 'rampantly eclectic' and was used across the 'ideological board to identify a range of spiritual alternatives to religious orthodoxy that sprang up in the 1880s and 1890s'. More than a surrogate faith to replace religion, mysticism 'spoke to a new taste for philosophical idealism and European vitalism'. If occultism was the search for a hidden reality and the 'arcane secrets of existence', mysticism was the experience of 'oneness with a variously conceived divinity, an experience that could be received as a divine gift regardless of training or preparation'.[84]

Evelyn Underhill's *Mysticism* (1911) was a popular account of the recent eponymous trend. Her text had its roots in Anna Bonus Kingsford's esoteric Christianity and her theory of the power of mystical revelation. After leaving the Theosophical Society, Kingsford set up the 'Hermetic Society', which became the forerunner of the influential 'Hermetic Order of the Golden Dawn', established in the late 1880s. Underhill broke from the 'Hermetic Order of the Golden Dawn', and 'denounced practical occultism in favor of mystical Christianity'.[85] Her book was published in the same year as the first issue of *Rhythm* and she defined mysticism as 'the expression of the innate tendency of the human spirit towards complete harmony with the transcendental order', words that could have been lifted straight from Kandinsky's spiritual treatise on art, or one of Murry's early essays for *Rhythm*.[86]

Murry produced over fifty books, including three novels, two volumes of poetry, two verse dramas, numerous essays and reviews, as well as editing *Rhythm* (1911–13), *The Blue Review* (1913), *The Athenaeum* (1919–21) and *The Adelphi*, which he founded in 1923 and which continued in various formats until 1948. Murry's early definition of 'Modernism' as the penetration 'beneath the outward surface of the world' in order to disengage 'the rhythms that lie at the heart of things' aligned his aesthetics with those of Underhill. She argued that writers must rearrange words 'in accordance with the laws of rhythm' in order to reveal 'the life-movement of the universe'.[87]

If rhythm was the pivotal term of Murry's aesthetics during the lifespan of the magazine, harmony became its successor in his novel *Still Life*. The novel tells the story of Maurice, a young writer who falls in love and embarks on an affair with Anne Craddock, the wife of the editor of the journal for which he writes. During the period he was writing *Still Life*, Murry noted in his autobiography that harmony was a 'magic word' that remained 'mysterious' to his protagonist, who rarely had 'any glimmering of its meaning'. Occasionally, harmony is 'a symbol of something remotely seen, infinitesimally apprehended' for Maurice.[88]

Two years before Murry wrote *Still Life*, Sadleir translated Kandinsky's book as the 'The Art of Spiritual Harmony'. The inclusion of 'Harmony' in the title was inaccurate. Solomon Eagle wrote in the *New Statesman* that the

> title of the English book is not good. If I remember rightly, the literal translation of the German translation would be 'The Spiritual in Art'. This is a horse of another colour. The title Mr. Sadler has hit upon has a crankish air.[89]

Crankish or not, the idea of harmony certainly pervades Kandinsky's text. In the introduction he argued that 'harmony or even contrast of emotion' in art can 'preserve the soul from coarseness'. And abstract drawing, for Kandinsky, created a 'real harmony' through the 'non-material sense of the object' and this 'true harmony' exercised a 'direct impression on the soul'. Harmony, then, for Kandinsky had a direct link to the soul, and could act as the soul's protector.[90]

In *Still Life* Maurice argues that you 'can't carve a harmony in the soul', but 'you can believe in it and leave room for it, so that other people can feel it'. As in Kandinsky's text, harmony, or a space set aside for harmony, resides in the spectator, not the artwork. Maurice argues that 'the true artist' realises 'what the harmony in the soul may be' and this is more apparent in a 'Greek statue' than 'this modern stuff' (34). But even so, harmony is not *in* the 'Greek statue' but 'belongs to us', if 'we could only get to it'. Harmony, therefore, was aligned with classicism and was in conflict with the 'modern stuff' that was associated with a 'return to the savages' or 'the primitive, uncontrolled people. They're splendid, unconscious . . . ' (23). Primitivism, in relation to modernism, reflected a desire by writers and artists to appropriate the 'supposed simplicity and authenticity to the project of transforming Western art', exemplified by, for example, Conrad's *Heart of Darkness* (1899), Picasso's African masks in 'Les Demoiselles d'Avignon' (1907) and Vatslav Nizhinsky's 'L'Après-midi d'un faune' (1912).[91] Sadleir referred to Kandinsky and Gauguin's neo-primitivism, through their 'technique reminiscent of primitive and savage art', in his article of 1912.[92]

Harmony does not have an easy presence in Murry's novel. At the British Museum, Anne 'liked to ascribe her quieting to a mysterious potency belonging to [the Elgin Marbles] alone' and, like the statues around her, she reveals for Maurice the 'glimmering of [harmony's] meaning' (54, 220). Her ability to perceive the mysterious potency of the marbles exposes the 'calm of her eyes [. . .] complete repose, of balance, of harmony' (219–20). Contrary to Kandinsky's theory that the artist must 'harmonize the *inneres klang* of external nature with that of humanity', Anne's harmony does not translate into inner purity or external harmony; she appears unable to empathise with others.[93] The *Times Literary Supplement* reviewer noted in 1916 that the title, *Still Life*, implies a 'vision of something calm and exquisite' and yet all is 'turmoil, apprehension, and disgust'.[94]

Like rhythm, harmony was in wide circulation during the period. For example, in *Creative Evolution* Bergson argued that evolution is the result of an underlying harmony and Underhill argued that mysticism was the innate drive of the human spirit towards 'complete harmony'.[95] Although Murry's interest in harmony would have been fuelled by Bergson and Underhill, amongst others, his location of harmony within the soul during aesthetic contemplation and his discussion of harmony in relation to 'primitivism' create a compelling case for his engagement with Kandinsky's aesthetics in his first novel.[96] Harmony does not function effectively as a purification process in the novel, but it is an important component of aesthetic experience that shifts the emphasis from the formal qualities of art to the spiritual experience of the spectator.

Murry's critical analysis of Dostoevsky stimulated his increasing taste for mysticism. Dostoevsky the mystic was a widely held view, and Murry was no exception: Dostoevsky was not a 'novelist' for Murry but something 'more difficult to define', and a new creation requires a new form of criticism.[97] Although he may have felt that he was pioneering a new criticism, Murry's response to Dostoevsky was very much of its time. Peter Kaye, building on Helen Muchnic's earlier work on the reception of Dostoevsky in England, notes that the 'Russian author was acclaimed as mystic, prophet, psychologist, irrationalist, a chronicler of the perverse, and sometimes as a novelist'. The lack of English translations of Dostoevsky's fiction between 1889 and 1911, and the fact that few people in Britain spoke Russian meant that the reception of Dostoevsky in England at the turn of the twentieth century was dictated by the voices of a few Russian immigrants. Kaye cites novelist, poet and critic Dmitry Merezhovsky, who concentrated on Dostoevsky's 'hasty, sometimes clearly neglected language', and Petr Kropotkin, who referred to 'the atmosphere of a lunatic asylum' in his novels.[98] Evgeny Solov'ev's *Dostoievsky: His Life and Literary Activity*, also published in 1916, played out the stereotype of the passion and simplicity in the Russian writer, referring to Dostoevsky as a 'psychopath', and to the 'fire, the nervousness, the inequality of his talent' as well as to his 'clear and simple outlook' and 'guarded affection' for the masses.[99] Although Edward Garnett's 1906 article in *The Academy* and Maurice Baring's *Landmarks in Russian Literature* (1910) went some way to redress the balance, when Constance Garnett's translation of Dostoevsky's *The Brothers Karamazov* was published in 1912, the British literary world was not used to discussing Dostoevsky in terms of his literary merit.[100]

Like many of his contemporaries, Murry believed that English writers had much to learn from Russian literature because 'in Russia the things of the spirit are held in honour above all others'.[101] For Murry, the experience of writing the Dostoevsky book resembled automatic writing: 'Suddenly the whole thing had fallen into pattern; and I was, for the first time, the victim of the strange sensation of being hardly more than the amanuensis of a book that wrote itself.'[102] If writing the book was automatic, reading Dostoevsky was like witnessing an ancient cult or getting a glimpse of 'the tremendous rites of some secret Brotherhood to which we are not initiate'. Murry turned Dostoevsky's texts into mystical doctrines, in which his characters were 'spirits' and their voices called 'without sound', suns grew 'cold', and time stopped so that we see with 'the eye of eternity' and the universe is 'frozen'. The novels are 'fragments of dialogue', spoken in darkness. 'In truth', Murry argued, Dostoevsky 'was a God-tormented man', who 'dreamed that there might be a secret hidden from his conscious seeking', which would 'serve him as a key to the mystery'.[103]

In the 1920s, harmony, for Murry, became a religious rather than an aesthetic aspiration. If some artists are capable of 'knowing' harmony, Murry argued, those who make contact with the 'divine reality' can 'elucidate and reveal it'. The religious artist, Murry continued, reveals 'harmony immanent in the world' and 'thrills us and brings us peace'.[104] Harmony is no longer an abstract magical concept that cannot be attained; it is a palpable object that can be transferred to humanity and provides peace. Faith gave stability to Murry's account of harmony.

Katherine Mansfield

Although she never went, Mansfield was fascinated by Russia through-out her life. She smoked Russian cigarettes, signed her name as Katerina and Kissienka, and described her mind 'like a Russian novel'.[105] Joanna Woods's biography offers a detailed account of her engagement with Russian culture, ranging from her early introduction to the music of Tchaikovsky and the literature of Tolstoy, Dostoevsky and Turgenev at Queen's College, Harley Street, between 1903 and 1906, to her later introduction to the works of Chekhov by Floryan Sobieniowski in the spa town of Bad Wörishofen in 1909. In one of her daydreams she wanted to adopt a Russian baby, call him Anton and 'bring him up as mine with Kot [Kotelyansky] for a godfather and Mme Tchekhov for a godmother. Such is my dream.'[106] She acknowl-edged her debt to Chekhov in a little rhyme she wrote on the fly-leaf of her copy of Garnet's translation of *The Lady with the Dog* (1917): 'This book is bound to belong to me. Besides I am sure that you agree. I am the English Anton T.' And later, she wrote beneath it, 'God forgive me, Tchehov, for my impertinence.'[107] After reading *War and Peace*, Mansfield wrote to Garnett in 1921, to thank her for the 'whole other world' and to say that her translations 'have changed our lives, no less. What would it be like to be without them!'[108]

Accusations of plagiarism against Mansfield have been thoroughly documented and will not be reiterated here.[109] By 1911 Mansfield had published her first collection of short stories, *In A German Pension*, and it was at this point that she sent a short story to the editor of *Rhythm*, John Middleton Murry. In April 1912 Mansfield invited Murry to take a room in her flat in Clovelly Mansions on Gray's Inn Road, leaving him the now well-known note on his first morning which read: 'This is your egg. You must boil it. K. M.'[110] By June 1912 Mansfield was listed on the contents page of *Rhythm* as editorial assistant and Mansfield and Murry had become lovers. Mansfield's interest in Russian culture contributed to the Russian flavour of the magazine in the form of her Petrovsky poems and her 'Tales of a Courtyard' short stories, complementing the articles on the Ballets Russes, Frank Harris's story 'After Tolstoi' and Leonid Andreev's story 'The Present'. Shortly after the demise of the magazine, Murry began work on a series of translations of little-known works with Kotelyansky, with which Mansfield was closely involved. These included a collection of Chekhov stories called *The Bet and Other Stories* (1915), Dostoevsky's *Pages from the Journal of an Author* (1916), Aleksandr Kuprin's *The River of Life and Other Stories* (1916), and finally, the publication that interested Mansfield most, *Anton Tchekhov and Other Essays* (1916) by Lev Shestov.

Murry's work on Dostoevsky and the death of her younger brother in France in 1915 coincided with the period when Mansfield returned to one of her most important works, initially 'The Aloe', which later became 'Prelude'. Mansfield noted that when Dostoevsky turns 'a soft but penetrating full light' on the character of Ivan Shatov in *The Possessed*, 'we have managed to gather a great deal of knowledge of his character from the former vague sidelights and shadowy impressions'.[111] Vague sidelights and shadowy impressions are important in 'Prelude'. Published by the Hogarth Press in 1918, things have a 'habit of coming alive' for Linda Burrell, the mother of three children who has moved with her family to the country. The day after the move, she stays in bed with a headache and traces her finger over a poppy bud on the wallpaper. She feels it as though it is a real bud, 'the sticky, silky petals, the stem, hairy like a gooseberry skin, the rough leaf and the tight glazed bud'. She often 'had seen' the tassels on the fringe of her quilt changing into a 'funny procession of dancers with priests attending'; some of the tassels did not dance but 'walked stately, bent forward as if praying or chanting'. The medicine bottles above the washstand often turned into a 'row of little men with brown top-hats on' and the washstand jug sat 'in the basin like a fat bird in a round nest'.[112]

Linda's things 'swell out with some mysterious important content' and, as in thing theory, fetishised or misappropriated objects are given magical agency. When Linda's objects have swollen full, 'she felt that they smiled'. Their smiles, however, were

> not for her, only, their sly secret smile; they were members of a secret society and they smiled among themselves. Sometimes when she had fallen asleep in the daytime, she woke and could not lift a finger, could not even turn her eyes to left or right because THEY were there, sometimes when she went out of a room and left it empty, she knew as she clicked the door to that THEY were filling it. (27)

The objects, swollen with 'mysterious content', are like members of an occult sect, 'a secret society', impenetrable to human perception. The capitalised lack of definition gives the objects a vague, yet dominant presence. Like Betty Flanders in *Jacob's Room*, who felt that 'behind the door was the obscene thing, the alarming presence' (124), Linda cannot escape from the perceptive capabilities of things: 'THEY knew how frightened she was; THEY saw how she turned her head away as she passed the mirror' but 'if she gave herself up and was quiet, more than quiet, silent, motionless, something would really happen.' Only when Linda becomes inert do things come alive 'down to the minutest, tiniest particle', blurring the boundaries between the material and animate world (28).

Linda's daughter Kezia is similarly drawn to inanimate objects. Kezia and her sister are left behind at the old house for a few hours because there is no space for them in the 'buggy' to travel to the new one. Kezia moves through the empty house, finding small objects in each room: a 'pill box black and shiny outside and red in' in her parents' room; a 'stray button' and 'some beads and a long needle' in the servant girl's room. From her grandmother's room she watches the daylight disappear and is 'suddenly quite, quite still, with wide open eyes and knees pressed together'. Like her mother, who is silent and motionless as things come alive, Kezia is rendered still by the presence of something indefinable: 'IT was just behind her, waiting at the door, at the head of the stairs, at the bottom of the stairs, hiding in the passage, ready to dart out at the back door' (14, 15). Kezia's undefined fear is singular ('IT'), unlike her mother's ('THEY'), but inertia is the trigger for both. The moment when Kezia is unable to move parallels Mansfield's description of crossing someone on the stairs: 'IS someone there? The "fright" – the pause – the unknown in each other glaring through the dark & then passing (which is almost too terrifying to be borne).'[113] Linda and Kezia occupy a different space from the others in the story,

a space inhabited by animated objects, and yet their particular respon-
siveness to their surroundings impedes their connections with the true
source of animation around them – their family.

In her notes for her unpublished novel, *Maata*, Mansfield described
Rhoda in a moment of rapturous ecstasy as she waits for the arrival of
her beloved Maata: '"A-ah", she breathed in a surge of ecstasy.' The
narrator mocks Rhoda for her self-importance as she sees herself in
the garden clothed in clichés: 'in her white gown, with flowing hair – a
saint in a holy picture of a garden, glorying and triumphant'.[114] Saikat
Majumdar has argued that *Maata* is based on the notes Mansfield
made during her tour of the New Zealand countryside, and was influenced by the cultural ethnology of writers like Elsdon Best, who wrote
extensively on Maori culture, including *The Spiritual and Mental
Concepts of the Maori* (although this was not published until 1922, but
Best was running the Government Store in Te Whaiti in 1907 when
Mansfield travelled through it). Mansfield visited a site that saw most
Maori men slaughtered in 1866 and Majumdar notes the tension in her
work between 'routine-encased domestic space on one hand' and the
'powerful undercurrent of violence and trauma on the other', both of
them 'uneasy and unavoidable legacies of colonial history'.[115] Whilst
Maori mysticism and colonial narratives were clearly important, we
also find in her notebook an account of an evening spent with May
Gilmer just after her trip to the Urewera area, who later became known
for her political activism in welfare and women's organizations: 'She is
extremely graceful, dressed in white – she floats along', an image very
close to Rhoda's fantasy.[116]

Mansfield referred to her short story 'Bliss' as '*our* new story' to
Murry, in 1918.[117] The story has a romantic vernacular with a modernist tone. Bertha Young experiences moments of intensity or 'bliss'
inspired by the pear tree in her garden. However, she does not experience the tree directly but observes it through the window of her
drawing-room, and then through closed eyes, and she 'seemed to see
on her eyelids the lovely pear tree with its wide open blossoms as a
symbol of her own life' (*Bliss*, 96). After a dinner party during which
one of her guests, Pearl Fulton, a beautiful woman, seemed to have
'something strange' about her, Bertha and Pearl stand looking at the
tree, and it seemed 'like the flame of a candle, to stretch up, to point,
to quiver in the bright air'. The narrator asks 'how long did they stand
there?' and refers to them as 'creatures of another world' (95, 102).

Mansfield parodies different genres within the story. A member
of the party comments that 'the trouble with our young writing men

is that they are still too romantic' (103), satirising, perhaps, Bertha's moments of bliss. If the romantics are mocked, so is contemporary poetry: its banal evocation of the everyday is parodied in the conversation in which one of the dinner guests, Eddie, describes 'an *incredibly* beautiful line: "Why Must it Always be Tomato Soup?"' (105). Clearly not '*incredibly* beautiful', the phrase precedes the moment when Bertha sees her husband in the hallway turn Miss Fulton 'violently to him' and sees 'his lips' say 'I adore you' (105). We see, rather than hear, the words and it is not clear if the affair is imagined or real. The story ends with Bertha running over to the pear tree, which, in apparent disloyalty, is 'as lovely as ever and as full of flower and still' (105). Modern poetry about soup has little merit but romantic moments involving pear trees have value.

Although Mansfield had strong aversions to the clichés of mysticism, she displayed moments in her fiction, notebooks and letters in which the process of writing shares something with the traditions of mysticism. Mansfield explored the idea that the boundaries between the self and the world were fluid. In October 1917, she wrote to Dorothy Brett:

When you paint apples do you feel that your breasts and your knees become apples, too? Or do you think this the greatest nonsense. I don't. I am *sure* it is not. When I write about ducks I swear that I am a white duck with a round eye, floating in a pond fringed with yellow blobs and taking an occasional dart at the other duck with the round eye, which floats upside down beneath me. In fact this whole process of becoming the duck (what Lawrence would, perhaps, call this 'consummation with the duck or the apple') is so thrilling that I can hardly breathe, only to think about it. For although that is as far as most people can get, it is really only the 'prelude'. There follows the moment when you are *more* duck, *more* apple or *more* Natasha than any of these objects could ever possibly be, and so you *create* them anew. [. . .] I don't see how art is going to make that divine *spring* into the bounding outlines of things if it hasn't passed through the process of trying to *become* these things before recreating them.[118]

Mansfield's dissolution of the self is not a desire to unite with the universe, but with the objects of her fiction. Unlike Murry's dissolution of the self in order to achieve inner harmony, the dissolving boundaries between objects and self are artistic tools for Mansfield. Like Bergson's artist, who dissolves the boundaries around things, for Mansfield the 'divine spring into the bounding outlines of things' is the defining moment of artistic creation, and it occurs when the self dissolves into the objects before writing.

Mansfield's interest in Russian theosophy began when A. R. Orage, editor of *The New Age* (1907–14), introduced her to *Cosmic Anatomy: or the Structure of the Ego* (1921) by M. B. Oxon, a work with strong affinities to the theories of the Russian theosophist Petr Ouspensky.[119] Mansfield wrote, 'What saved me finally, [from a state of depression about her work] was reading a book called Cosmic Anatomy and reflecting on it.'[120] In 1921 Lady Rothermere paid for Ouspensky to come to London, and Mansfield attended one of his lectures about the teachings of his friend and mentor Georgy Gurdzhiev on 14 September 1922 at Rothermere's house. Woods notes that the 'house was dimly lit and a Russian woman checked the names at the door. Inside was a small room in which the audience waited in silence.'[121] Quoting Ouspensky's friend, Carl Bechhofer Roberts, James Webb describes the audience in *The Harmonious Circle*: 'one saw doctors, psychologists, psycho-analysts, editors, writers, civil servants, theosophists of both sexes, clergymen and a sprinkling of the men and women who are always attracted by the lure of the mysterious'.[122] Mansfield met Ouspensky alone on 30 September and later referred to him in a letter to Murry as 'an extraordinarily sympathetic person' and urged Murry to take him out to dinner.[123]

After unsuccessful X-ray treatment of her lungs by the Russian doctor Ivan Manukhin in Paris, Mansfield made the decision to enter Gurdzhiev's Institute for the Harmonious Development of Man near Fontainebleau in 1922. Members of the Institute were required to take part in a combination of dance, physical labour and exercises, designed to break 'habitual patterns of thought and life and bring the intellectual, emotional and instinctual aspects of the self into harmony'.[124] Her decision to join Gurdzhiev's Institute interrupted her writing. Unlike Murry, for Mansfield mysticism and writing were unconnected:

> If I write at present I 'falsify' my position [. . .]. If I am sincere I can only say we *live* here – every moment of the day seems full of life. And yet I feel I can't enter into it as I shall be able to; I am only on the fringe. But write about it I can't.[125]

Murry and Mansfield's modernism can be constructed in the context of the spiritual aesthetics of Kandinsky, the vitalism of Bergson and the growing trend for mysticism during the period. Rather than being triggered by Mansfield's death at Fontainebleau in 1923, Murry's engagement with mysticism can be traced back to his early articles and the development of his theories of rhythm, which were overtaken by a spiritual theory of harmony in his work on Dostoevsky and in his first novel, *Still Life*. Mansfield was less explicit about her interest in the unknown in relation to her work, as opposed to her life and her pursuit of recovery, but her early fiction is underpinned by a romantic yet mysterious belief in the potency of things.

Notes

1. Michael T. H. Sadler, 'After Gauguin', *Rhythm*, 1.4 (1912), p. 29. Michael T. H. Sadler changed his name to the older spelling of Sadleir in 1914 to differentiate himself from his father, Michael E. Sadler. Hereafter I will refer to Michael T. H. Sadler as Sadleir in the text to avoid confusion.
2. Kandinsky, *The Art of Spiritual Harmony*, trans. M. T. H. Sadler (London: Constable, 1914).
3. Brooker and Thacker, 'General Introduction', in *The Oxford Critical and Cultural History of Modernist Magazines*, p. 13.
4. [Murry], 'Aims and Ideals', *Rhythm*, 1.1 (1911), p. 36.
5. Murry, 'Art and Philosophy', *Rhythm*, 1.1 (1911), p. 12.
6. [Lewis], 'Long Live the Vortex', *Blast*, 1 (1914), p. 7; Dora Marsden, 'Views and Comments', *New Freewoman*, 1.2 (1913), p. 25.
7. See Binckes, *Modernism, Magazines, and the British Avant-Garde* (2010); Mark Antliff, *Inventing Bergson* (1993); and Gruetzner Robins, *Modern Art in Britain* (1997).
8. Demoor, 'John Middleton Murry's Editorial Apprenticeships', *English Literature in Transition, 1880–1920*, 52 (2009), p. 130.
9. Binckes, *Modernism, Magazines, and the British Avant-Garde*, p. 81.
10. Kandinsky to Sadleir, 6 October 1911, in Kandinsky, *Concerning the Spiritual in Art*, trans. Michael T. H. Sadler (London: Tate, 2006), appendix B, letter 2, p. 115.
11. Carter, 'Art and Drama in Paris', *New Age*, 10.19 (1912), p. 443; 'Notes from Russia', *Athenaeum*, 4402 (1912), p. 279.
12. Viacheslaf, 'The Theatre of the Future', trans. Stephen Graham, *English Review*, 10 (1912), pp. 634, 640.
13. Brooker and Thacker, 'General Introduction', in *The Oxford Critical and Cultural History of Modernist Magazines*, p. 2.
14. Parton, *Goncharova: The Art and Design of Natalia Goncharova*, pp. 173–8.
15. See Petrova et al., *Natalia Goncharova: The Russian Years*, cat. 244. I am grateful to Anthony Parton for pointing this out.
16. [Mansfield], 'Two Poems of Boris Petrovsky', trans. Mansfield, *Rhythm*, 1.4 (1912), p. 30. See Edward Marsh, ed., *Georgian Poetry, 1911–1912* (London: Poetry Bookshop, 1912).

17. Hastings, 'Present-Day Criticism', *New Age*, 10.22 (1912), p. 519.
18. Przerwa-Tetmajer, 'Song of the Night Mists', trans. Paul Selver, *New Age*, 10.13 (1912), p. 292; [Mansfield], 'Two Poems of Boris Petrovsky', p. 30.
19. Hastings, 'Present-Day Criticism', p. 519.
20. Harris, 'The Holy Man', *Rhythm*, 2.5 (1912), pp. 3, 7.
21. Tolstoy, 'The Three Hermits', in *Walk in the Light and Twenty-Three Tales*, trans. Louise and Aylmer Maude, p. 260; Harris, 'The Holy Man', p. 10.
22. Binckes, *Modernism, Magazines, and the British Avant-Garde*, p. 102.
23. [Murry], 'Notes', *Rhythm*, 2.5 (1912), p. 36.
24. Mansfield, 'Green Goggles', *New Age*, 11.10 (1912), p. 237.
25. Mansfield, 'Tales of a Courtyard', *Rhythm*, 2.7 (1912), pp. 99–105.
26. Andreieff, 'The Present', *Rhythm*, 2.9 (1912), p. 213.
27. Carter, 'The Russian Ballets in Paris and London', *New Age*, 9.9 (1911), p. 211.
28. Banks, 'Pétrouchka – The Russian Ballet', *Rhythm*, 2.2 (1912), pp. 57–63 (italics in original).
29. Rice, 'Les Ballets Russes', *Rhythm*, 2.3 (1912), pp. 108, 107.
30. [Murry], 'What We Have Tried To Do', *Rhythm*, 1.3 (1911), p. 36.
31. *Catalogue to the Second Salon of the Allied Artists' Association* (London, 1909), nos 1068–9, 1923.
32. See Hardiman, 'Infantine Smudges of Paint . . .', pp. 133–47. Hardiman also unravels the identity of the three paintings Kandinsky submitted in 1910.
33. Sadleir, *Michael Ernest Sadler, 1861–1943*, p. 237.
34. Gruetzner Robins, *Modern Art in Britain*, p. 12. Kandinsky, Postcard to Rutter, 22 August 1911, in Kandinsky, *Concerning the Spiritual in Art*, appendix B, letter 1, p. 115.
35. See Glew, '"Blue Spiritual Sounds"', *Burlington Magazine*, 139.1134 (1997), p. 602. Glew's article gives a thorough account of the relationship between the Sadlers and Kandinsky, including their visit to Kandinsky's house in Murnau in 1912.
36. Kandinsky to Michael T. H. Sadler, 6 October 1911, in Kandinsky, *Concerning the Spiritual in Art*, appendix B, letter 2, p. 115. Glew points out that Rupert Brooke met Kandinsky while learning German in Munich in January to May 1911: see Glew, '"Blue Spiritual Sounds"', p. 602 n20.
37. Kandinsky to Michael T. H. Sadler, 7 December 1911, in Kandinsky, *Concerning the Spiritual in Art*, appendix B, letter 3, p. 116.
38. Binckes, *Modernism, Magazines, and the British Avant-Garde*, p. 142.
39. Sadler, 'After Gauguin', p. 24. The words 'inneres klang' should read 'innerer Klang' and translates as 'inner sound' or 'inner resonance'.
40. Kandinsky, *Concerning the Spiritual in Art*, pp. 6, 7, 40, 41, 49, 56.
41. Besant and Leadbeater, *Thought-Forms*, p. 11.

42. Ringbom, *The Sounding Cosmos*, p. 87.
43. Besant and Leadbeater, *Thought-Forms*, pp. 64, 74.
44. Aleksandra Unkovskaia, 'Metoda tsveto-zvuko-chisel', *Vestnik teosofii*, I, 3 (1909); see Carlson, '*No Religion Higher Than Truth*', pp. 197, 246 n12.
45. Ringbom, *The Sounding Cosmos*, pp. 37, 62, 21.
46. 'Invisible: Art About the Unseen 1957–2012', Hayward Gallery Exhibition (June to August 2012).
47. Ringbom, *The Sounding Cosmos*, p. 50.
48. Sadler, 'The Letters of Vincent Van Gogh', *Rhythm*, 1.2 (1911), p. 19; Sadler, 'Fauvism and a Fauve', *Rhythm*, 1.1 (1911), p. 16.
49. Sadler, 'After Gauguin', p. 26.
50. Quoted in Bullock, 'Russian Music in London', in Beasley and Bullock, eds, *Russia in Britain*, p. 125.
51. Noguchi, 'From a Japanese Ink-Slab', *Rhythm*, 2.14 (1913), p. 450.
52. Sadler, 'Kandinsky's Book on Art', *Art News* (9 March 1912), p. 45.
53. Sadler, 'Introduction', in Kandinsky, *Concerning the Spiritual in Art*, p. xxviii.
54. Sadler, 'Kandinsky's Book on Art', p. 45.
55. Murry, 'Art and Philosophy', p. 12.
56. Sadler, 'After Gauguin', p. 25.
57. Bergson, *Creative Evolution*, authorised trans. Arthur Mitchell (1911), pp. 186, 192, 24, 27.
58. Murry, 'Art and Philosophy', p. 9.
59. Kandinsky, *Concerning the Spiritual in Art*, pp. 22, 69.
60. Kandinsky, *Concerning the Spiritual in Art*, p. 41.
61. Fry, 'Post Impressionism', in Bullen, ed., *Post-Impressionists in England*, p. 174.
62. D. S. MacColl, 'A Year of Post-Impressionism', in Bullen, ed., *Post-Impressionists in England*, p. 274.
63. Binyon, *The Flight of the Dragon*, p. 13.
64. MacCarthy, 'The Post-Impressionists' (1910); [Robert Ross?], 'A Post-Impressionist Exhibition: Matisse and Picasso', *The Times*, 4 October 1912, p. 9; P. G. Konody, *The Observer*, 16 July 1911, p. 7, all in Bullen, ed., *Post-Impressionists in England*, pp. 98, 363, 24.
65. Rutter, *Art in my Time*, p. 132.
66. Holmes, 'Stray Thoughts on Rhythm in Painting', *Rhythm*, 1.3 (1911), p. 1.
67. Carter, *The New Spirit in Drama and Art*, pp. 4, 24, 25.
68. Banks, 'The New Spirit in Art and Drama', *Rhythm*, 2.12 (1913), p. 339; Glew, 'Introduction', in Kandinsky, *Concerning the Spiritual in Art*, p. xxi.
69. Carter, *The New Spirit in Drama and Art*, pp. 221–2, 223.
70. Carter, 'New Books on Art', *Egoist*, 1.12 (1914), pp. 235, 236.

71. Marks, *How Russia Shaped the Modern World*, p. 231.
72. Eagle, 'Current Literature, Books in General', *New Statesman*, 3.56 (1914), p. 118; 'Art's Enigma', *Saturday Review* (15 August 1914), p. 202; Kandinsky, *Concerning the Spiritual in Art*, p. 76; [Murry?], 'The Art of Spiritual Harmony', *Athenaeum*, 4523 (1914), p. 24; Rutter, 'Round the Galleries: Twentieth Century Art', *The Sunday Times* (24 May 1914), quoted in Gruetzner Robins, *Modern Art in Britain*, p. 134.
73. Wadsworth, 'Inner Necessity', *Blast*, 1 (1914), p. 119.
74. Lewis, 'A Review of Contemporary Art', *Blast*, 2 (1915), p. 40.
75. Gaudier-Brzeska, 'Allied Artists' Association Ltd', *Egoist*, 1.12 (1914), p. 228.
76. Michael E. Sadler to Kandinsky, 11 March 1913, Michael Ernest Sadler Collection, 8221/2/50, Tate Gallery Archive; Roger Fry, 'The Allied Artists', in Bullen, ed., *Post-Impressionists in England*, p. 459.
77. [Murry], 'Aims and Ideals', p. 36.
78. Polonsky, 'Chekhov and the Buried Life of Katherine Mansfield', in Cross, ed., *A People Passing Rude*, p. 202.
79. Sadleir wrote a number of romance and historical novels, all of which were published by Constable in London: *Hyssop: A Novel* (1915), *The Anchor: A Love Story* (1918), *Privilege: A Novel of the Transition* (1921), *Desolate Splendour* (1923), *The Noblest Frailty* (1925), *These Foolish Things* (1937), *Forlorn Sunset* (1947) and *Fanny By Gaslight* (1956). Sadleir is now better known for his work as a publisher and for his collection of nineteenth-century fiction, bought by the University of California, Los Angeles (UCLA) in 1951.
80. See Ernest Griffin, *John Middleton Murry* (1969), and Sharron Greer Cassavant, *John Middleton Murry: The Critic as Moralist* (1982).
81. Mansfield, review of *The Triumph of Pan* by Victor Neuburg, *Rhythm*, 2.2 (1912), p. 70.
82. See *Katherine Mansfield Notebooks*, ed. Scott, I, pp. 140, 145.
83. Jackson, *The Eighteen Nineties*, p. 160.
84. Owen, *The Place of Enchantment*, pp. 21, 20, 28, 22.
85. Owen, *The Place of Enchantment*, p. 49.
86. Underhill, *Mysticism*, p. x.
87. Murry, 'Art and Philosophy', p. 12; Underhill, *Mysticism*, pp. 90, 91.
88. Murry, *Between Two Worlds*, p. 370; Murry, *Still Life*, p. 220. Subsequent references appear as page numbers in the text.
89. Eagle, 'Current Literature, Books in General', p. 118.
90. Kandinsky, *The Art of Spiritual Harmony*, pp. 8, 32.
91. Antliff and Leighten, *Cubism and Culture*, p. 25.
92. Sadleir, 'After Gauguin', p. 23.
93. Sadleir, 'After Gauguin', p. 24.
94. Child, 'Still Life', *Times Literary Supplement*, 21 December 1916, p. 623.

95. Bergson, *Creative Evolution*, p. 108; Underhill, *Mysticism*, p. 24.
96. We know that Murry was interested in Underhill's work from their correspondence in *The Spectator* in the late 1920s and Underhill's reviews of Murry's 'Life of Jesus' in *The Spectator*, 29 January 1927 and *The Betrayal of Christ by the Churches* in *Time and Tide*, 30 November 1940.
97. Murry, *Fyodor Dostoevsky*, p. 21.
98. Kaye, *Dostoevsky and English Modernism*, pp. 6, 14, 15.
99. Evgeny Soloviev, *Dostoievsky: His Life and Literary Activity*, trans. Hogarth, pp. 22, 18, 228.
100. See Maguire, 'Crime and Publishing: How Dostoevskii Changed the British Murder', for an account of the early reception of *Crime and Punishment*, in Cross, ed., *A People Passing Rude*, pp. 149–61.
101. Murry, 'The Honesty of Russia', in *Evolution of an Intellectual*, p. 29.
102. Murry, *Between Two Worlds*, p. 368.
103. Murry, *Fyodor Dostoevsky*, pp. 31, 33–4, 43.
104. Murry, 'Poetry, Philosophy, and Religion', *Adelphi*, 2.8 (1925), pp. 656, 657.
105. *Katherine Mansfield Notebooks*, I, p. 104.
106. Woods, *Katerina* (2001); *Katherine Mansfield Notebooks*, II, p. 316.
107. *Journal of Katherine Mansfield*, ed. Murry, p. 226 (8 December 1920, 12 December 1920).
108. *Collected Letters*, IV, p. 176 (Mansfield to Constance Garnett, 8 February 1921).
109. See Claire Tomalin, *Katherine Mansfield: A Secret Life* (1987); W. H. New, *Reading Mansfield and Metaphors of Form* (1999), for accounts of Elizabeth Schneider's query in 1935 and E. M. Almedingen's famous accusations of plagiarism in a letter to *The Times Literary Supplement* in 1951.
110. *Collected Letters*, I, p. 112 (12 April 1912).
111. Woods, *Katerina*, p. 130
112. Mansfield, 'Prelude', in *Collected Stories of Katherine Mansfield*, p. 27. 'Prelude' was first published by the Hogarth Press in July 1918. Subsequent references appear as page numbers in the text.
113. *Collected Letters*, I (1984), p. 339 (Mansfield to Murry, 25 November 1917).
114. *Katherine Mansfield Notebooks*, I, p. 255.
115. Majumdar, 'Katherine Mansfield and the Fragility of Pakeha Boredom', p. 131.
116. *Katherine Mansfield Notebooks*, I, p. 151.
117. *Collected Letters*, II (1987), p. 97 (Mansfield to Murry, 28 February 1918). 'Bliss', in *The Collected Short Stories*, pp. 91–105. 'Bliss' was first published in the *English Review* in August 1918. Subsequent references appear as page numbers in the text.
118. *Collected Letters*, I (1984), p. 330 (Mansfield to Dorothy Brett, 11 October 1917).

119. M. B. Oxon was a pseudonym for Lewis Alexander Richard Wallace, a sheep-farmer, banker, philanthropist and expert on social credit and psycho-Egyptology.

120. *Collected Letters*, V (2008), p. 8 (Mansfield to Violet Schiff, 8 January 1922).

121. Woods, *Katerina*, p. 231.

122. Webb, *The Harmonious Circle*, p. 220.

123. *Collected Letters*, V (2008), p. 311 (Mansfield to Murry, 27 October 1922).

124. Owen, 'The "Religious Sense" in a Post-War Secular Age', p. 167.

125. *Collected Letters*, V (2008), p. 312 (Mansfield to Murry, 28 October 1922).

CHAPTER 3

Voices of Stones:
Mary Butts and Petr Ouspensky's
Fourth Dimension

The image of an object being temporarily rescued from a commodi-
fied world is a familiar modernist trope: Stephan Dedalus clutching
his ashplant, Prufrock's teacups, Woolf's politician who becomes so
enamoured of a piece of glass that he devotes his life to pieces of china,
metal and stones. Recent versions of modernism have placed material
objects at their core, blurring the boundary between Huyssen's great
divide[1]: Douglas Mao notes modernists' 'extraordinarily generative
fascination' for objects, as neither commodities nor symbols, but as
solid *objects*: 'as not-self, as not-subject, as most helpless and will-less
of entities', free from human thought and ideology. In rejecting the
consumption of objects, Mao's coterie of modernists turn to their production, and in doing so they emphasise 'making instead of absorbing,
recording instead of experiencing, the enduring instead of the ephemeral, and the solid instead of the fluid'.[2] Bill Brown's alternative version
of object-based modernism advocates a new approach to the way we
think about the history of things. Acting on William Carlos Williams's
well-known maxim, 'No ideas but in things', Brown's method is to
unearth the ideas 'in' things, as well as our ideas 'of' them.[3] He offers
the analogy of a child tearing apart its toy to demonstrate our early, yet
misguided, sense that the ideas *in* things can be easily retrieved. Brown
traces the modernist merging of ideas and things in a historiographi-
cal or anthropological approach; in Brown's version of modernism
thoughts are things and things have thoughts.[4]

The British novelist Mary Butts would not usually be associated with
these material modernisms. Critical attention on her work tends to
focus on her interest in the occult.[5] Butts was intellectually interested
in automatic writing, astral journeys, magical thinking and (of particular interest here) hyperspace philosophy. And yet these investigations
into the unseen relied upon explorations of the material world, and

her work orbits around small objects – buttons, gloves, stones and glass. Butts's connection to a central object-led modernist paradigm has not gone unnoticed. Jane Garrity has argued that Butts's objects resonate with ancestral meaning, and Rochelle Rives has asserted that Butts advocates an empathetic connection with things that lies some-where between private possession and de-commodification: an argu-ment that can be positioned between Brown's dissolution and Mao's maintenance of the solid object.[6]

My purpose here, with reference to both Butts's published and her full unpublished journals, as well as her 'Taverner' novels, *Armed with Madness* (1928) and *Death of Felicity Taverner* (1932), is to reveal how Butts's lifelong interest in the fourth dimension, and in particular her engagement with the Russian theosophical text *Tertium Organum*, signified her ongoing investigation into new modes of perception and expression of the material world.[7] I am not suggesting that Butts was solely interested in Russian versions of the fourth dimension; indeed, her interest in the idea predates her reading of Ouspensky by about ten years. However, Butts's fascination for Russian culture and her interest in occultism were brought together when she read *Tertium Organum* and it is instructive to read her 'Taverner' novels in this light. Jacqueline Rose suggests 'coming at modernism's relationship to history' through the 'problem of perception, that is, by taking the issue of what can and can't be seen'.[8] Rose's emphasis on the seen and unseen highlights the unusual point of intersection between two strains of current investigation in modernist studies: modernism and the occult and modernist materiality, strains that perhaps have more in common than is typically assumed.

The 'fourth dimension'

The 'fourth dimension' as an alternative space was readily available as a concept to modernists in Britain in the first few decades of the twenti-eth century. Linda Dalrymple Henderson has thoroughly investigated its origins in *The Fourth Dimension and Non-Euclidean Geometry in Modern Art* (1983, reprinted 2013) and this brief overview draws on her account.[9] The genesis of the 'fourth dimension' can be traced through non-Euclidean and n-dimensional geometry of the nineteenth century, and was taken up by scientists, philosophers, theosophists, artists and writers in the early twentieth century. Henderson defines hyperspace philosophy as underpinned by the idea that 'the answer to the evils of positivism and materialism is for man to develop his powers of intuition, in order to "perceive" the fourth dimension of our world, the true reality' (*FD*, 25). British mathematician and philosopher Charles Howard Hinton, Russian theosophist Petr Ouspensky and American theosophist and architect Claude Bragdon were influential hyperspace philosophers connected by their faith in the existence of the fourth dimension with no empirical evidence.

Henderson's work moves between North America, France, Italy, Holland and Russia, and she summarises the range of artists attracted to fourth-dimensional space: 'Analytical and Synthetic Cubists as well as Duchamp, Picabia, and Kupka, to Russian Futurists and Suprematists, American modernists in the Stieglitz and Arensberg circles, Dadaists, members of De Stijl, and even certain Surrealists'.[10] For these artists, 'non-Euclidean geometry signified a new freedom from the tyranny of established laws' (*FD*, 339). The idea of an alternative dimension liberated early twentieth-century artists from traditional conventions of representation and the dominance of one-point Renaissance perspective. Or, in Bruce Clarke's words, 'these pre-Einsteinian allegories of space and time provided dynamic models for the aesthetic transition from mimesis to abstraction'.[11] Henderson offers a list of authors who wrote about the fourth dimension, including Fedor Dostoevsky, P. G. Wodehouse, H. G. Wells, Oscar Wilde, Joseph Conrad, Ford Madox Ford, Marcel Proust and Gertrude Stein. To this list we might add Mary Butts, May Sinclair, Henry James, Ezra Pound and E. M. Forster. Interest in the importance of the fourth dimension to British writers of the early twentieth century is growing.[12]

The fourth dimension was not a static concept. One of the first written records of the fourth dimension can be found in Cambridge Platonist Henry More's *Enchiridion Metaphysicum* (1671), in which it represented the Platonic ideal. In the eighteenth century, the fourth dimension was predominantly associated with the concept of time by the French mathematician, physicist and philosopher Jean le Rond d'Alembert in an article 'Dimension' in the *Encyclopédie ou dictionnaire raisonné des sciences, des arts et des métiers* (1754), edited by himself and Denis Diderot. In the nineteenth century, mathematicians began to question Euclid's fifth axiom, the parallel postulate, written in around 300 BC. Euclid's axiom states that two straight lines, intersected by a third so that the inner angles add up to less than 180 degrees, will eventually intersect. In the early nineteenth century, Hungarian mathematician Janos Bolyai and Russian mathematician Nikolai Ivanovich Lobachevsky published their theories around the same time, giving rise to what became known as hyperbolic geometry. And Georg

Friedrich Bernhard Riemann (pupil of Johann Carl Friedrich Gauss) argued, in a famous lecture of 1854 in Germany, that space was curved and, drawing the analogy of a sphere, he claimed that parallel lines would intersect at the 'poles' of space, which became known as elliptic geometry. Thus Riemann was one of the first mathematicians to disprove Euclid's 'parallel postulate'. Fierce debate ensued about whether axioms of geometry were synthetic or analytic, created or true. But if non-Euclidean geometry 'shook the foundations of mathematics and science, branches of learning that for two thousand years had depended on the truth of Euclid's axioms', it also opened up new possibilities of space (*FD*, 17). Scientific discoveries like Wilhelm Conrad Röntgen's discovery of X-rays in 1895, Ernest Rutherford's work on the structure of atoms, and wireless telegraphy in the 1890s based on electromagnetic waves discovered by Heinrich Hertz, all contributed to the changing perception of space.

N-dimensional geometry, related to non-Euclidean geometry, was crucial to the development of the concept of a fourth dimension of space. It was developed in the nineteenth century by, among others, mathematicians Arthur Cayley in England and W. I. Stringham in America. The idea of an unseen dimension of space became more popular than the idea of curved space. N-dimensional geometry was theoretical, but the idea of a real fourth dimension of space became popular, particularly amongst spiritualists. Johann Karl Friedrich Zöllner, Professor of Astronomy at the University of Leipzig, attempted to prove the existence of the fourth dimension through empirical research. Working with the medium Henry Slade between 1877 and 1878 in England, Zöllner conducted a number of experiments in the presence of colleagues, which 'proved' the existence of the fourth dimension. For example, Slade was apparently able to untie a knotted cord whose ends were sealed together and to obtain writing on paper that was placed between two slates sealed together. Kandinsky wrote in *Concerning the Spiritual in Art* in 1912 that 'various learned men, among them ultra-materialists, dedicate their strength to the scientific research of doubtful problems, which can no longer be lied about or passed over in silence'. Zöllner and 'Wagner, Butleroff (Petersburg), Crookes (London) etc.' were Kandinsky's examples of such 'learned men'.[13] Kandinsky did not refer to the fourth dimension explicitly in his aesthetics, but his reference to Zöllner indicates that he was aware of his experiments.

Charles Howard Hinton was central to the popularisation of the concept of the fourth dimension in Britain. Having studied mathematics and physics at Oxford, Hinton taught at Uppingham school and, following a trial and conviction for bigamy in 1886, went to Japan before settling in America in the early 1890s, where he invented a baseball-pitching machine. One of Hinton's earliest accounts on the subject was his article 'What is the Fourth Dimension?', published in the *University Magazine* of Dublin in 1880. The article appears between an article on the failings of the Beaconsfield Administration and one on Keats. Mark Blacklock has traced the republication of the article in the magazine of the Cheltenham Ladies' College (1883) and again in pamphlet form published by William Swan Sonnenschein in 1884, triggered by the interest generated by Edwin Abbott Abbott's *Flatland: A Romance of Many Dimensions by a Square*, published that same year.[14] In the original article, Hinton questions the limits of human perception and knowledge, but highlights human intellectual potential with the analogy of a stream that 'flings itself into the greater river down some precipitous descent, exhibiting at the moment of its union the spectacle of the utmost beauty of which the river system is capable'. With this image of a waterfall Hinton connects the fourth dimension with a natural romantic landscape. In this early account, Hinton claims that 'this flickering consciousness of ours' will evolve from its 'narrow space', and when we finally experience the fourth dimension it will be like one of 'those solemn Egyptian statues' that is 'immersed to their ears in a smooth mass of stone which fits their contour exactly'.[15] The image of an Egyptian statue invokes a silent space that is aesthetically pleasing, ancient and cultured.

A New Era of Thought (1888) and *The Fourth Dimension* (1904) set out Hinton's work with the tesseract, or fourth-dimensional cube. Hinton devised a system of coloured cubes, very like children's building blocks, with detailed instructions of how to make them and complicated sets of exercises in order to achieve visualisation of the fourth dimension (Fig. 8). In addition to painting cubes, Hinton employed painting metaphors in his text. In *A New Era of Thought* he wrote that

> we must form the habit of mental painting, that is, of putting definite colours in definite positions, not with our hands on paper, but with our minds in thought, so that we can recall, alter, and view complicated arrangements of colour existing in thought with the same ease with which we paint on canvas.

The visual, as opposed to the mathematical, interpretation of the fourth dimension was key to its take-up by artists and writers at the turn of the twentieth century. But equally important is Hinton's spiritual or

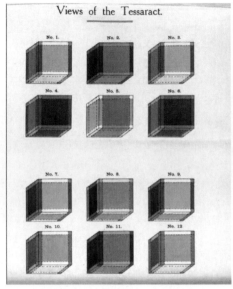

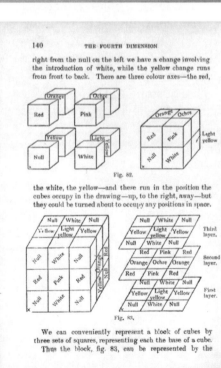

Fig. 8 *Views of the Tessaract*, fold-out frontispiece and page 140 from Charles Howard Hinton, *The Fourth Dimension*, 2nd edn (London: George Allen & Unwin, 1906). © The British Library Board.

quasi-religious language. His work is loaded with phrases like 'spiritual light', 'effortless wonder' and the 'awakening light of this new apprehension'. For Hinton the material world is insubstantial compared to the new reality of the fourth dimension: 'the flimsy world quivers and shakes, rigid solids flow and mingle, all our material limitations turn into graciousness, and the new field of possibility waits for us to look and behold'.[16]

Given the emphasis on new perception and a reality behind the appearance of things, it is not surprising that the fourth dimension was popular among spiritualists, theosophists, occultists and mystics. Although Helena Petrovna Blavatsky referred to unseen worlds in *Isis Unveiled* (1877), she mocked the idea of dividing space into dimensions in *The Secret Doctrine* (1888), referring to the 'superficial absurdity of assuming that Space itself is measurable in any direction'.[17] British theosophist Charles Leadbeater, however, did much to promote Hinton's theories. He recommended Hinton's *A New Era of Thought* in *Clairvoyance*, published in 1899: 'I can at any rate bear witness that the tesseract or fourth-dimensional cube which he describes is a reality, for it is quite a familiar figure upon the astral plane.' Hinton's tesseract provided Leadbeater with objects to visualise in alternative space. Leadbeater wrote that seeing in the fourth dimension enables one to see 'not only the inside as well as the outside of every object, but also its astral counterpart'.[18] Ouspensky translated Hinton's *The Fourth Dimension* into Russian in 1915, and his work, which is discussed later in the chapter, was very much indebted to the British mathematician.[19] Artists and writers drawn to theosophy would therefore have had exposure to theories of the fourth dimension.

Visual interpretations of the fourth dimension found their logical conclusion in cubism. Henderson has successfully revived the spatial fourth dimension as opposed to its temporal incarnation, which evolved with the publicity around Einstein's theories during the period of the British Eclipse expeditions of 1919. It is worth reiterating the important claim made by Henderson in 1971 in *Art Quarterly*, that the 'mistake of art historians anxious to explain references to the fourth dimension and non-Euclidean geometry has been to read back into Cubist writings of 1911 and 1912 a breakthrough in physics which was not published until 1916', when Einstein published his Theory of General Relativity.[20] Henderson points out that *n*-dimensional geometry rather than relativity inspired cubists to think about the fourth dimension. She has written at length about the popularisation of the concept in Paris, via the translation of Leadbeater's *The Other*

Side of Death into French in 1910, as well as the visual n-dimensional geometry of E. Jouffet and the theories of Guillaume Apollinaire, Albert Gleizes and Jean Metzinger. In 1911 Apollinaire wrote that 'the fourth dimension represents the immensity of space externalised in all directions at a given moment. It is space itself, or the dimension of infinity.'[21] Although no causal connection can be made between Picasso and n-dimensional geometry, the formal language that grew up around cubism was certainly written in the aftermath of the new geometries. Picasso's intellectual peers included Maurice Princet and Jean Metzinger (both of them interested in non-Euclidean geometry), and so it is 'highly unlikely' that 'Picasso did not hear some talk of the fourth dimension and non-Euclidean geometry' (*FD*, 69). No such connection has been made between the visual arts and the fourth dimension in Britain and Henderson notes that British vorticists were not interested in the concept. And yet it is worth pursuing the idea that some of the artists involved in Roger Fry's 'Post-Impressionist Exhibition' of 1912 were interested in fourth-dimensional space.

Mikhail Larionov promoted the fourth dimension via rayism or rayonnism, launched in Moscow in March 1913. In June 1912 Larionov wrote that a rayonnist picture will seem 'to glide' and have the appearance of being 'outside time and space', and in this way it will evoke 'the sensation of a fourth dimension through its length, its breadth and the thickness of the colour layer which have to do duty as the sole indices of the concrete world'.[22] It is likely that Larionov would go on to read Mikhail Matiushin's article about cubism and the fourth dimension in the journal *Soyuz Molodezhi* (The Union of Youth) in March 1913, published in response to two Russian translations of Albert Gleizes and Jean Metzinger's *Du 'cubisme'*, published in Paris in 1912.[23] In October 1912, Larionov exhibited *Soldiers* (1910) in Roger Fry's 'Second Post-Impressionist Exhibition'. Although it was not obviously a rayonnist painting, we can track how Hinton's theories filtered into Larionov's understanding of the fourth dimension via Ouspensky. Anthony Parton points out the similarity between Larionov's rays, which are depicted on canvas as coloured lines emanating from objects (as opposed to emanating from a light source) and Hinton's technique of generating hypersolids, which involved drawing lines in an unknown direction from 'every point of a cube interior as well as exterior'.[24]

Tom Gibbons has argued that spiritualism and theosophy, rather than geometry, were key to the early twentieth-century understanding of the fourth dimension, which, he argues, accounts for the delay between the advent of non-Euclidean geometry of the 1880s and the general excitement about the fourth dimension amongst artists and writers by 1910.[25] Gibbons argues that the fourth dimension was not connected to non-Euclidean geometry in the minds of most people because in the *Scientific American* international competition of 1909 for the best popular explanation of the fourth dimension, only one of the essays referred to Bolyai, Lobachevsky and Riemann. However, in the introduction, the editor Henry Manning explains that in

> the same way that we have curved surfaces in ordinary space to which we can apply the non-Euclidean geometries of two dimensions, so in space of four dimensions we have curved spaces or hypersurfaces to which we can apply the non-Euclidean geometries of three dimensions.[26]

Henderson has warned against the misinterpretation of the fourth dimension 'as purely mathematical or purely mystical' (*FD*, xx) and its popularisation must be indebted to a mix of theosophy, spiritualism, mathematics, philosophy, science and religion.

Although there was clearly a shift in emphasis from a spatial to a temporal fourth dimension after the publicity around Einstein's theories, the boundaries were often blurred. The term 'dimension' itself evokes the idea of space and it is likely that Einstein's theories of relativity reignited an interest in unseen space, even if it was tied to time. James Jeans, who promoted Einstein's theories of relativity in his popular science books, discussed relativity in terms common to fourth dimensionalists. In *The Mysterious Universe* (1930), which sold 1,000 copies a day in its first month, he wrote that it 'is harder to pass from three to four [dimensions] because we have no direct experience of a four-dimensional space'.[27] And American theosophist, architect and stage designer Claude Bragdon, who was involved in the translation of Ouspensky's *Tertium Organum* in 1922, had no qualms about bringing together non-Euclidean geometry and Einstein's relativity. He wrote in *Four-Dimensional Vistas* (1923):

> These two ideas, of curved time and higher space, by their very nature are bound to modify human thought profoundly. They loosen the bonds within which advancing knowledge has increasingly labored, they lighten the dark abysses of consciousness, they reconcile the discoveries of Western workers with the inspirations of Eastern dreamers; but best of all, they open vistas, they offer 'glimpses that may make us less forlorn.[28]

There is no anxiety here about Einstein's theories existing in parallel with hyperspace philosophy; indeed, together they generate a

considerable optimism, offering us Wordsworthian 'glimpses' to make
us less forlorn. Together they create a new creed like Proteus rising
from the sea or 'old Triton' blowing his horn.

The fourth dimension served as a useful trope in religious literature
of the period. A. T. Schofield, a doctor from Mayfair, wrote a book
called *Another World: or The Fourth Dimension*, published in 1888,
and, very like Hinton and Edwin Abbott Abbott, created dimensional
kingdoms. Schofield's text claims to reveal the hidden presence of the
fourth dimension in the Bible: 'Angels come and go at will' and 'God
Himself is seen in Old Testament times in human form, and in New
Testament times, when our Lord takes a spiritual body, He appears or
disappears in this world of ours at will.'[29] The fourth dimension as sal-
vation was propagated by Charles Brodie Patterson in *A New Heaven
and a New Earth or The Way to Life Eternal: Thought Studies of the
Fourth Dimension:* (1909), in which he wrote that the

> perception of a Fourth Dimension is dawning on man's consciousness
> through his interior feelings, and through such perception will come Life
> Eternal. If to know God it is necessary to be like God, and God is the Spirit
> of Love, then through Love shall we enter into the full knowledge of the
> Fourth Dimension, and there shall be no death in this New World.[30]

A pamphlet called 'The Fourth Dimension', written by an 'Officer
of the Grand Fleet', claimed that in the third dimension we merely
acknowledge God as the creator but in the fourth dimension we shall
'know God's purpose in creating us'.[31] In his essay 'Reflections on
the Death of a Porcupine' (1925), D. H. Lawrence made a distinction
between merely existing in 'time and space' and attaining a 'fullness of
being' in 'the fourth dimension, the heaven of existence, and there it is
perfect, it is beyond comparison'.[32]

The fourth dimension was famously borrowed for political satire
by Edwin Abbott Abbott in *Flatland: A Romance of Many Dimensions
by a Square* (1884). In 'Flatland', it is forbidden to talk about the third
dimension, and in the third dimension it is forbidden to talk about the
fourth. Abbott's narrator, a square, is imprisoned for trying to explain
the third dimension to his planar companions. In one of his essays in
Scientific Romances Hinton complained that he

> wished to be able to refer the reader altogether to that ingenious work,
> 'Flatland.' But on turning over its pages again, I find that the author has
> used his rare talent for a purpose foreign to the intent of our work. For evi-
> dently the physical conditions of life on the plane have not been his main

object. He has used them as a setting wherein to place his satire and his lessons. But we wish, in the first place, to know the physical facts.[33]

Hinton's purpose was to persuade his readers of the existence of alternate dimensions whereas Abbott's purpose was political. Joseph Conrad and Ford Madox Ford's collaborative novel, *The Inheritors* (1901), continued the trend of borrowing the fourth dimension for political purposes: the concept served as a narrative device to criticise contemporary politics obliquely.[34] In *The Inheritors*, the fourth-dimensional characters represent a kind of über race, without emotion, having plans for world domination. They have 'no feeling for art and no reverence for life; free from any ethical tradition; callous to pain, weakness, suffering and death, as if they had been invulnerable and immortal'.[35] The *Manchester Guardian* described it in 1901 as forging a new genre: 'a ghost story of a new kind, with the vulgar thrills eliminated for a strange quality of mental disturbance'.[36] The fourth dimension pops up in popular fiction of the period too, as in Horace Annesley Vachell's *The Fourth Dimension* (1920), in which a young actress shocks her mother by revealing her discussions about the fourth dimension with her director.[37]

Oscar Wilde's ghost of Canterville slips into the fourth dimension when he needs to make a quick exit: 'hastily adopting the Fourth Dimension of Space as a means of escape, he vanished through the wainscoting, and the house became quite quiet'.[38] Dorothy Scarborough's *The Supernatural in Modern English Fiction* (1917) analysed the use of the fourth dimension in ghost stories. She wrote:

> The Fourth Dimension is another motif that seems to interest the writers of recent ghostly tales. They make use of it in various ways and seem to have different ideas concerning it, but they like to play with the thought and twist it to their whim.[39]

Virginia Woolf reviewed Scarborough's book, praising it for its lack of categorisation and concluding that 'in any discussion of the supernatural suggestion is perhaps more useful than an attempt at science'.[40]

The fourth dimension as both time and space occurs in much of Wells's fiction. In 'The Case of Davidson's Eyes', the protagonist is physically in London but can see a ship on the other side of the world. The explanation is 'a kink in space' where 'two points might be a yard away on a sheet of paper, and yet be brought together by bending the paper round'.[41] In 'The Plattner Story', a school teacher finds himself 'altogether out of space' for nine days, and when he returns his heart is on his right side: 'the curious inversion of Plattner's right and left sides is proof that he has moved out of our space into what is called the Fourth Dimension, and that he has returned again to our world'.[42] In 1930 James Jeans described how the 'combined distortions of the four-dimensional continuum produced by all the matter in the universe causes the continuum to bend back on itself to form a closed surface, so that space becomes "finite"'.[43] After reading Jeans, Woolf wrote to Ethel Smyth: 'I read about the Stars, and try to imagine what is meant by space bending back. Eliz[abeth Williamson]: must take me to her telescope.'[44] Time bends in May Sinclair's 'The Finding of the Absolute', published in her collection, *Uncanny Stories*, in 1923. Kant, in heaven, explains how he did not 'anticipate this multiplicity of spaces and times' in which 'the plane turns on itself to form the cube, so past-present and present-future double back to meet each other and form cubic time, or past-present-future all together'.[45]

In the late summer of 1927 Woolf wrote a short piece called 'Evening over Sussex: Reflections in a Motor Car' (the Woolfs had bought a car earlier that year). It is a description of the Sussex landscape as seen from the moving vehicle. The sun is setting, the beauty is overwhelming and the narrative collapses: 'I cannot hold this – I cannot express this – I am overcome by it.'[46] The inability to express, the anxiety and exhilaration have been rightly connected to the sublime and a way to circumvent the failure of the sublime by replacing it with what Andrew Thacker calls a 'modernist representational space – fluidity captured in form'. Makiko Minow-Pinkney has connected it to modern notions of nervous shock, but I think it is also significant that it was written just after the total solar eclipse in June 1927, the first eclipse visible in Britain for over 200 years.[47]

The self within the text is divided into four. The first two selves, one 'eager and dissatisfied' and the 'other stern and philosophical', are holding forth about 'the wise course to adopt in the presence of beauty'. These two selves notice everything, 'a hay stack; a rust red roof; a pond, an old man coming home with his sack on his back'. The third self is 'aloof and melancholy' and listens to the discussion, adopting both a first person and a third person narrative space 'I (a third party now declared itself)'. The first two selves are located in the present but the third is drawn to the past, feeling that 'life' is left behind 'even as the road is left behind'. Then, out of nowhere:

suddenly a fourth self (a self which lies in ambush, apparently dormant, and jumps upon one unawares. Its remarks are often entirely disconnected with what has been happening, but must be attended to because of their very abruptness) said: 'Look at that.' It was a light; brilliant, freakish; inexplicable. For a second I was unable to name it. 'A star'; and for that second it held its odd flicker of unexpectedness and danced and beamed. 'I take your meaning,' I said. 'You, erratic and impulsive self that you are, feel that the light over the downs there emerging, dangles from the future. Let us try to understand this. Let us reason it out. I feel suddenly attached not to the past but to the future. I think of Sussex in five hundred years to come. I think much grossness will have evaporated. Things will have been scorched up, eliminated. There will be magic gates.[48]

And the vision continues with electric light and machinery from the future. This fourth self (unlike the first three, who are, in turn, dissatisfied, stern and aloof) is shocking and uplifting, and shifts the perspective to space by saying '"Look at that". It was a light.' The third self is speechless for a moment and then unable to name the star, calling it 'brilliant, freakish; inexplicable'. The third self, or perhaps the philosophical stern second self, wants to 'reason it out' and try to understand. This self imagines the 'feeling' of the fourth self – that the emerging light 'dangles from the future'. The dangling gives weight to the light, perhaps a reference to Einstein's theory that light had mass.

Holly Henry and Michael Whitworth give full accounts of the British Eclipse expeditions in 1919 by scientists from the Royal Observatory at Greenwich to photograph the Hyades stellar group in order to assess Einstein's calculations about the deflection of star light passing near the sun.[49] Woolf's light 'dangles from the future' and so compresses different time periods into the same space. Edwin Hubble had discovered that the Milky Way was one of many galaxies by photographing stars from Andromeda nebula in the mid-1920s. It is no accident that the erratic fourth self in Woolf's strange inconclusive text is pointing to a star. In Woolf's story 'Searchlight', a middle-aged woman recounts her grandfather's fascination for stars as a child: 'what are they? Why are they? And who am I?' Looking at the stars leads to the questioning of the self. And time is compressed again as the woman recounts her tale at a party in London, 'a hundred years seemed nothing. They felt that the boy was looking at the stars with them.' In 'Reflections in a Motor Car', the fourth self shifts the narrative away from the material world and marks the moment when ordinary perception is inadequate and space and time begin to behave in unusual ways.

In November 1935 Woolf wrote that

> I have now reached a further stage in my writer's advance. I see that there
> are 4? dimensions; all to be produced; in human life; and that leads to a far
> richer grouping and proportion. I mean: I; and the not I; and the outer and
> the inner – no I'm too tired to say; but I see it: and this will affect my book
> on Roger. Very exciting, to grope on like this.[50]

The potentially unlimited (four?) dimensions are 'produced', according to Woolf, in 'human life' and it is not obvious whether that production is in a textual space or the material world, or if such a distinction
is possible. Woolf turns the self inside out, a laying out of dimensions:
'I and the not I; and the outer and the inner'. The tiredness brought on
by the spatialisation of the self is compensated by her vision ('I'm too
tired to say; but I see it'): four dimensions are more easily imagined
than articulated.

I have outlined just some of the ways in which fourth-dimensional
space was deployed in fiction and fictional practices, but there are
other avenues for further research: for example, in the works of
Algernon Blackwood and H. P. Lovecraft. The popularity of the
concept of the fourth dimension via mathematics, spiritualism, theosophy, religion, fiction and the visual arts is apparent in Leadbeater's
throwaway comment about the 'much-vexed question of the fourth
dimension – a question of the deepest interest',[51] and indeed Woolf's
note about '4? dimensions; all to be produced; in human life'. The rest
of this chapter is an in-depth study of Mary Butts's engagement with
fourth-dimensional space in her life and work.

Mary Butts

Mary Butts's literary reputation is being exhumed. The publication
of her biography (1998) and journals (2002), and the reprinting of
the six novels she published in her lifetime have inspired new interest in her work.[52] In 1998 Lawrence Rainey described Butts's second
novel, *Armed with Madness*, as a 'masterpiece of Modernist prose' and
within a decade, he argued, it 'will assume its rightful place within the
canon'.[53] During her lifetime, Butts's work elicited a mixed response,
as indicated by reviews of her short story 'Speed the Plough', which
was included in a volume of Georgian writing in 1922. It was singled
out by *The Times Literary Supplement* as the 'best of all' the stories in
the volume, but by *The Clarion* as 'nasty and sticky', evoking 'madness

and badness and Bolshevism'.[54] However, Ezra Pound, H.D., May Sinclair and T. S. Eliot all admired Butts's work during her lifetime and if, as Eliot had planned in 1937, a selection of her short stories had been published by Faber, Butts would perhaps already occupy a more central position in critical discussions of modernism.[55]

Butts's preoccupation with things she could not see and could not explain grew out of her disillusionment with, first, religion and then empirical science. In her last years at school she read Darwin's *On the Origin of Species by Means of Natural Selection* (1859) and declared in her autobiography that this 'began a new epoch', during which she went to church less, in part because it 'had nothing to say about the things that were happening outside'. Butts found the structures in both religion and science stifling, observing that if

> we had not all suffered by [religion] in our most delicate years, fewer of us would have 'theorized ourselves silly,' so as to stand now, paralyzed and hypnotized, in the name of Science, into incapacity for any objective contact with reality.

Butts argued that her access to both the material and the immaterial world was blocked by the overly empirical theorisation of science, and yet it was her interest in science and the 'real' world that introduced her to and enhanced her investigations into the unknown.[56]

Having discarded both religion and positivism, as had her contemporaries Yeats, Pound and Lawrence, Butts turned to the occult as a way of creating what she called a 'new synthesis or vision or fact' in her writing. The fourth dimension was one of the ideas that interested her throughout her writing career. The first recorded instance of Butts's interest in the fourth dimension is on 10 October 1916. Aged twenty-five, Butts was living in London and volunteering at the National Council for Civil Liberties, an organisation set up in response to conscription in July 1916. She remarked in her diary:

> At the office talked about the 4th dimension. Mr Francis [unidentified] interesting. He holds that all our consciousnesses are piercing into this new dimension. As a matter of fact, mine is. We went out, & there was a high moon & wind, & light fast-travelling clouds. On the pavement off the Fulham Rd waiting for a 31 Bus I nearly came through. Letter from John. Saw Nevinson's pictures.[57]

The mix of pedestrian detail and hyperspace philosophy is typical of Butts; her grand claim that 'all our consciousnesses are piercing into this new dimension' is undermined by her casual remark that she 'nearly came through' as she waited for a 31 bus. And the reference to receiving a letter from John (Rodker) and seeing (Christopher) Nevinson's art turns the experience of the fourth dimension into an everyday event. Although there is no record of Butts having read any hyperspace philosophy as early as 1916, her account shares its attitude that access to the fourth dimension was a matter of mental application, a theory advocated by Hinton. By 1920 Butts declared that she was 'in love with the 4th dimension' (*Journals*, 144), a sentiment that was not so unusual for the period; as Henderson notes, it had become 'almost a household word by 1910' (*FD*, 43).

Butts's introduction to the idea of a fourth dimension coincided with a period in which she was deliberately searching for new forms of expression. She developed a theory in which the relationship between language and perception was transparent and co-dependent: a theory in which a new way of seeing would lead to a new way of writing. In November 1917 she argued that, in order to write differently, writers must see differently:

> Up to now we have had writers who have been marvelously close, with complete realism of detail. What we want is a new way of seeing – a complete new attitude of approach. In fact a new imagination. The analysis has been made, now for a new synthesis. Joyce, Eliot, Lewis? (*Journals*, 95)

Butts clearly felt part of a new synthesis, or the wider modernist project of finding new ways of conveying one's experience of the world. Rather than describing the world in close-up or details such as 'the curl of the eyelash', as she put it in her journal, she aimed to stand back and build a model of a new world, a world of four dimensions. During this early phase of her career, the fourth dimension became a shorthand for good fiction for Butts; she created lists of 'literature of the 4th Dimension' in her diaries, by which she meant work that could sharpen the mind. Donne, Yeats, 'Anywhere in' Dostoevsky, de la Mare and Hogg were among the writers whom Butts decided had the potential to expand consciousness (*Journals*, 124, 144–5).

The fourth dimension was one part of Butts's general interest in the occult, albeit a concept that has been largely ignored in critical readings of her work. Butts's diaries are saturated with descriptions of her spiritual experiences and references to occult books she had read. From the late teens and throughout the 1920s Butts recorded séances, instances of clairvoyance, attempts at automatic writing, and meetings with her 'daimon' or guardian spirit. In 1921 she and Cecil Maitland began to practise astral journeys, or out-of-body experiences, achieved through meditative visualisation. In the summer of 1921, Maitland and Butts visited Aleister Crowley's retreat in the 'Abbey of Thelema' in Cefalù, Sicily, where she helped to edit and shape an early draft of Crowley's *Magick in Theory and Practice* (1929). However, like her attitude towards science, Butts's relationship with occult studies was not straightforward. As early as February 1920 Butts had discarded the methodology of institutionalised magic; she wanted to 'throw away' the tools of investigation and concentrate on 'direct enquiry' (*Journals*, 142). And she was not impressed by Crowley, writing on her return from Cefalù 'I'd sooner be the writer I am capable of becoming than an illuminated adept, magician, magus master of this temple or another' (*Scenes*, 106).

The boundaries between science and occultism were less fixed during this period. Although spiritualism and theosophy defined themselves in direct opposition to the orthodoxy of science, the Society for Psychical Research employed scientific methodologies, or as Roger Luckhurst puts it, 'procedures of experiment, observation, and induction of general laws' to investigate psychical phenomena.[58] As with her early rejection of scientific systems, Butts rejected the methodologies that grew around magical, spiritual and psychical institutions. She rejected any process of investigation that she decided would destroy the spirituality of the 'material world' because she was convinced of the 'terrific and absolute importance of phenomena' (*Journals*, 142). Noumena and phenomena were held in a delicate balance; emphasis on either could destabilise the equilibrium. Books that dealt solely with magic or occultism were pointless to Butts, and her diary reveals the strength of her distaste for their 'bastard words, credulities, falsities on facts, emotion and aesthetic falsities', which 'inwardly revolt me'.[59] She condemned *The Occult Review* for being 'as milky a slosh as ever I read' (*Journals*, 149, 190). By the mid-twenties Butts felt in a position to analyse her experience of the occult, explaining in her diary that she 'had studied "occultism" & found it stirring', but that it had become 'unsatisfactory, a maze of blind alleys'. She pointed out that although Cecil Maitland inspired her early interest in the occult, Aleister Crowley almost convinced her that 'there was nothing in it' (*Journals*, 214).

By 1926, the year she wrote most of her novel, *Armed with Madness*, Butts had rejected any form of both institutionalised science and occultism, and turned instead to the philosophy of the Russian theosophist Petr Ouspensky. In late 1924 and throughout 1925, when she began to plan *Armed with Madness*, Butts was reading James Breasted's *History of Egypt* (1906), Roger Fry's *The Artist and Psychoanalysis* (1924), *Studies in Dreams*, edited by Mary Arnold-Forster (1921), and Arthur Edward Waite's *The Holy Grail* (1909). She also read Bury's *History of Freedom of Thought* (1913) and Ethel Colburn Mayne's short story collection *Inner Circle* (1925). Although between 1924 and 1927 Butts had periods where she was not writing due to depression, we know that in 1926, the year she wrote the majority of *Armed with Madness*, she was reading Ouspensky's *Tertium Organum* (1911), his follow-up to *The Fourth Dimension* (1909), to the exclusion of almost anything else.[60] Butts quoted from many of the books she was reading in her journals, and some of them at length, but Ouspensky's *Tertium Organum* is the one she most carefully transcribed, filling over thirty single pages of her diary with notes from his work, with little mention of her daily life.[61]

Like so many of her contemporaries, Butts's fascination for Russia began with Dostoevsky. She read *The Brothers Karamazov* (1880) in 1916 and recorded having 'new sensations . . . quite in the Russian mode' (*Scenes*, 38). And in January 1917, while reading *The Possessed* (1872), she noted that 'I don't believe our life differs so much from that depicted as Russian. Our angle of approach is different, but the events and temperamental agonies are much the same. All these days could be written in the Russian mode' (*Journals*, 75–6). For Butts the 'Russian mode', similar to her 'literature of the 4th Dimension', signalled an acute awareness of thoughts and emotions. Her enthusiasm for Russian literature spilled into her personal relationships. Having married John Rodker in May 1918, Butts wrote to her aunt and described him as Russian. This, as Blondel notes, was 'pure whimsy' in order to avoid describing his true Jewish heritage, although Ian Patterson notes that Rodker's parents had fled from 'Russia or Eastern Europe'.[62] On meeting Cecil Maitland in 1920, she described him in her diary as a 'Russian character' with 'a ferocity in him' (*Journals*, 133). As she was writing *Armed with Madness*, Butts met the Russian interior designer and refugee Sergei Maslenikov, who became the inspiration for Boris, the White Russian in the Taverner novels and *Imaginary Letters* (1928). Robert Medley described Maslenikov as 'extremely talented [. . .] always broke, but a very sweet and charming man' (*Scenes*, 168). Russian exiles from pre-Revolutionary Russia appear in many of Butts's novels, characters who have lost their material possessions and their social status, like 'Serge Sarantchoff' in *Ashe of Rings*. In *Death of Felicity Taverner* Boris notes that 'Russian emigration is making a world within this world' (*DFT*, 314–15).

Russian literature and the 'Russian mind' offered a symbolic tran-
scendence for Butts. In 1916 she described a Slavonic 'mental outlook'
as being 'outside time' and in 1917 that she had 'Power' in her as
though 'surcharged with electricity', followed by a sentence fragment –
'The Russian mind' (*Journals*, 71, 77). Three years later she wrote that
the conclusion to *The Possessed* is

> so vital that nothing so important may be said with probability to have been
> imminent before – that a new man is being born, or rather a special kind
> of man is being recognized and developed – the man who not only looks
> into but lives in the timeless world. [. . .] To get rid of the preoccupation
> with 3 dimensional time and space will be the first step – only the first step.
> Everything else will go in its turn. (*Journals*, 151)

We can see, then, how Butts was primed to respond with enthusiasm
to *Tertium Organum*, a Russian mystic's exposition of higher space
with an emphasis on art and perception. Butts would not have read
Ouspensky's *Fourth Dimension* of 1909, which was not translated into
English until it appeared in a revised form as part of *A New Model of
the Universe* in 1931. But access to *Tertium Organum* was not difficult;
as Alex Owen notes, there was already 'a buzz in the air' by the time
Ouspensky arrived in London in 1921 and Lady Rothermere, wife of
the press baron, 'was spreading the word about Ouspensky's own esoteric opus *Tertium Organum*'.[63] It is likely that Butts read the translation of the revised second edition of 1916, first published in English in
the United States in 1920 and then in England in 1923.[64]

Tertium Organum, so called because, according to Ouspensky, 'it is
the *third canon* – third instrument – *of thought* after those of Aristotle
and Bacon', reads as a textbook for those interested in the existence of
more than three spatial dimensions (*TO*, 262). Butts treated *Tertium
Organum* as doctrine, commenting that Ouspensky 'never says a thing
that isn't true', and referred to 'working' with, as opposed to reading,
her copy of the book. However, Butts was also able to criticise what she
saw as weakness in Ouspensky's text and complained that he became
too 'exalted' over 'Blavatsky & the Secret Doctrine & the Kabbalists'
and that he 'should have thrown his net wider' rather than use the
'stock examples' of Lao Tze and Plotinus.[65]

Tertium Organum begins with an outline of Kant's premise that
space and time are functions of our receptivity or categories of our
intellect, the prism through which we regard the world. According to
Ouspensky, although we can conceptualise beyond time and space in
the abstract, we are unable to perceive objects as they truly exist: 'our

cognition of things has nothing in common with the things as they are outside of us – that is, in themselves' (*TO*, 17). Ouspensky rejects empiricist or positivist solutions to this Kantian question and suggests that we are capable of seeing things 'in themselves' by training our intellect to understand and perceive higher dimensions of space: a theory derived from the hyperspace philosophy of Hinton. Butts was immediately drawn to Ouspensky's description of the limitations of human perception. Her first transcribed extract from the book echoes her call for a 'new way of seeing, a new attitude of approach' from the previous decade:

> Furthermore it is necessary to understand that all objects known to us exist not only in those categories in which they are perceived by us, but in an infinite number of others in which we do not & cannot sense them. And we must learn first *to think* things in other categories, and then so far as we are able, to imagine them therein. (*TO*, 57)

In short, if we think differently, we will see differently: a theory that caused Butts to experiment with a new way of writing.

The fourth dimension represents both an idealised space and a concrete reality in which new perceptive capabilities are possible in *Tertium Organum*. However, according to Ouspensky, in our current stage of evolution we catch only glimpses of this new space, due to our limited perception of time; as Henderson neatly summarises, 'the illusion of motion arises out of our incomplete sensation of time, and the idea of time itself results from our incomplete sense of space' (*FD*, 250). Ouspensky likens this limited perception to a flickering flame, 'each spark of which flashes for a moment and disappears, never to appear any more' (*TO*, 40). He argued that a new race of supermen will be capable of perceiving the world in its true dimensions, and that artists are the vanguard of this evolution:

> At the present stage of our development we possess nothing so powerful, as an instrument of knowledge of the world of causes, as art. The mystery of life dwells in the fact that the *noumenon*, i.e., the hidden meaning and the hidden function of a thing, is reflected in its *phenomenon*. . . . Only that fine apparatus which is called *the soul of an artist* can understand and feel the reflection of the noumenon in the phenomenon. In art it is necessary to study 'occultism' – the hidden side of life. The artist must be a clairvoyant: he must see that which others do not see; he must be a magician: must possess the power to make others see that which they do not themselves see, but which he does see. (*TO*, 161–2, italics in original)

The artist as vanguard was not a new notion in cultural or political terms, but Ouspensky's elevation of the perceptive capabilities of artists appealed to Butts, who noted in her diary that the artist is the only person 'who can understand the noumenon through the phenomenon' (*Journals*, 235). Through the language of art, according to Ouspensky, human consciousness will evolve because

> the combination of meaning, rhythm and music; in sounds, colors, lines, forms – men are creating a new world. . . . Thus in art we have already the first experiments in *a language of the future*. Art marches in the vanguard of inner evolution, anticipating the forms it is to assume tomorrow. (*TO*, 83)

Butts began to conceive of her novel *Armed with Madness* before she read *Tertium Organum*. In November 1924 she described the germination of the book as a 'growth – the laboratory where a new idea of human life and relationship is being tried out. A scientific kind of poetry. Waste products. It would have to be rather like a ballet' (*Journals*, 204). The combination of science, waste and ballet is Butts at her most typically eclectic. She referred to the novel variously as 'In the Wood' and later 'People Among Trees', and in 1927 thought that it 'might well have been called "The Wasteland." Eliot always anticipates my titles' (*Journals*, 263). But in January 1926 she was still struggling with the opening, noting that she wished she 'knew how to begin that novel. I know all it is to be about; no plot' (*Journals*, 222).

For a novel with no plot, *Armed with Madness* is full of activity. It tells the story of Scylla and her brother Felix, who are 'handsome and young, always together, and often visited by their friends'. They live for the summer by the sea in a house they cannot afford, in Dorset (like Salterns, where Butts grew up), and have three friends who come and go. Clarence, an artist is described as 'tall and black, with close-set eyes and a walk affected to hide his strength'. Clarence is in love with Picus, who is 'grave as a marsh-bird dancing and as liable to agitation, his colour drawn from the moon's palette, steel gilt and pale', and Ross, also an artist, is 'rougher, shorter, fairer, better bred'.[66] An American, Dudley Carston, is invited to the house and is subsequently accused of stealing a jade cup that the four Englishmen have found in a disused well. We later discover that the cup was stolen by Picus from his father's collection.

The novel is a self-conscious reworking of the Grail myth, but once the cup's history has been established, albeit 'complicated, violent, inconclusive' (*AWM*, 95), the structure of the novel changes. The chapters become short scenes, as opposed to the linear narrative of the first twenty chapters. Towards the end of the book, the characters are drawn together, and the vicar comments that the 'grail knights are gathering it seems'. Either this is 'curiously coincidental', the vicar continues, or 'we are taking part in events, only part of which are happening on the earth we see. Meanwhile, I approve the spacious dust-bin into which you throw most things.' The vicar's comments reflect the novel's poise between potential and waste, the jade cup is both 'an ash-tray in a Cairo club' and the Holy Grail (*AWM*, 140). The characters are reunited for a dramatic finale in which Scylla is almost murdered by Clarence as he binds her to a statue of Picus and shoots arrows at her, and then she is rescued by Carston.

The Grail myth, famously revived by Tennyson in *Idylls of the King* and William Morris's *The Defence of Guinevere*, was given new life in 1907 with a newspaper article that recorded the apparent discovery of the Holy Grail in a well in Glastonbury. The Grail was associated with both space and Russia for Butts. She wrote in September 1927, having reread Jessie Weston's *From Ritual to Romance* (1920), that the Grail Quest is man 'depassing the time and space boundaries, going through the fourth or "astral"' into 'what one can call the Fifth, where the pure forms are'. She had finished writing *Armed with Madness*, and her work, she claimed, was shifting from the 'fourth' and into the 'fifth' dimension. This new search, she continues, 'has expressed itself in Russia' (*Journals*, 264).

The hierarchy of perception in the Taverner novels is political as well as aesthetic. Ian Patterson, Patrick Wright and Jane Garrity have tracked the anti-Semitism, closely tied to anti-Bolshevism, in Butts's work, most obvious in the depiction of Kralin, the Jewish Russian, in *Death of Felicity Taverner*.[67] Kralin represents the modern city, as opposed to the ancient laws of the countryside and the ancestral home. He wants to buy up land belonging to his dead wife's family and build 'a hotel and a row of bungalows along the low cliff, light the sea lane and drain it'.[68] He blackmails the family with Felicity's letters and private journals, which, given his interest in psychoanalysis, he claims will provide plenty of material for an 'erotic classic' (*DFT*, 261). Eventually he is tricked into a cave by Felix's Russian lover, Boris, who knocks him on to a rock, weighs his body down in a rock pool and leaves him to drown in the rising tide. Garrity writes that with 'the sacrifice of Kralin, Englishness is secured and the family is reinstated as the dominant cultural paradigm'.[69]

Outsiders have limited perception in the Taverner novels. Life for

Carston, for example, is 'an elaborate theatre' but once he arrives in Dorset, he begins to 'see in a new way he disliked', he is lost 'in a green transparent world, he was blind' (*AWM*, 12, 23). As Patterson writes, 'to be English, it appears, is to have occult access by genetics and ontology, to sources of virtue inaccessible to strangers'.[70] By contrast to Carston, the 'better bred' Ross is positioned as an Ouspenskian vanguard of the evolution of consciousness. He thinks of the 'shape of each thing he drew'; the earth 'seemed one growing stillness, of innumerable separate tranquilities, for ever moving, for ever at rest'. As he draws, the landscape moves cinematically in front of him; life appears to open 'like the unfolding of a scene. An endless screen of coromandel lacquer, the design traveling with it, fold in, fold out.' Ross picks out particular objects from this moving antique screen; he can 'seize the detail' piece by piece (*AWM*, 92), and so perceives the curl of the eyelash as well as the greater synthesis. Ross's grasp of the landscape echoes Butts's definition of '4th dimension space' as 'the separating of a group of solids, binding them also together into a whole we cannot see' (*Journals*, 233), and it is appropriate for Butts that this whole is an antique coromandel laquer screen.

Like Ross's perception of the folding land or Woolf's spatialisation of the four selves in her reflections in a motor car, the idea of the screen folds time into space. In her poem, 'Avenue Montaigne', Butts described: 'No more time in that house / No time at all / Times and spaces folded in and out / Tenfold on the tall / Coromandel screen that folds the wall.'[71] Butts notes that 'Ouspensky works out: each aspect of each thing real & unreal – a most unusual perception of things as folds of a screen' (*Journals*, 237). Although she is not an artist, Scylla, like Ross, searches for a 'new value, a different way of apprehending everything' and yet she 'wished the earth would not suddenly look fragile, as if it was going to start shifting about'. Scylla is aware that Ross 'knew something that she was only growing conscious of', and indeed Ross is able to think through objects as though they have been X-rayed (*AWM*, 9). He thinks of

the brickness of a brick until he seemed aware of it throughout, not side after side or two or three, but each crumb of its body, and each crumb reduced to its molecular construction, until the brick ceased to be a cube and could as easily be reformed again. (*AWM*, 92)

The shattering of objects into their molecular construction is familiar in modernist texts, like Woolf's 'incessant shower of innumerable atoms', but thinking through a cube until it ceases to be a cube reminds us of Hinton's tesseract exercises, which Butts would have read about at length in *Tertium Organum*.[72]

Understanding the difference between materials, and subtle differences between objects of the same substance is an important step in fourth-dimensional thought. Ouspensky described crossing the Neva, looking up and sensing the '*difference* between the chimneys and the prison walls *with unusual clearness* and like an electric shock I realized *the difference between the very bricks themselves*' (*TO*, 156). Kralin, for example, according to Scylla, is unable to distinguish the 'touch – difference between silk and stone, or glass and jade' (*DFT*, 296) but Ross, by contrast, knows the 'brickness of a brick' and has inhabited Ouspensky's fourth form of consciousness that has a 'knowledge of the hidden substance of things'.[73] Felix and Scylla lay out all of Felicity's possessions to see what they will 'tell us':

> the jay – feather posy, a handful of red rose leaves, paper dry; a ring of grey jade, two anonymous keys, a bundle of orange sticks, a rouge pot, a box of nibs, four french stamps, a bar of green sealing wax, a bar of black; one drawing pin; a sock of the gayest pattern and the softest wool trodden into huge holes. Three curtain rings, an amber cigarette-holder, once a thin gold trumpet, now in half, with a tooth-bitten hole at its mouth. Half a French card-park, a domino, a cribbage-peg, a spellican, a draught piece, two chess men and a halfpenny to play shove ha'penny. (*DFT*, 222)

The assembled fragments of Felicity's life, similar to Butts's list of Gertrude Stein's possessions (*Journals*, 253), continue for a further half-page, until Felix declares 'I shall go mad' (*DFT*, 223). And yet the intimate objects of Felicity's life do tell us something of her character, her writing tools, a tooth-bitten cigarette-holder, odd pieces of games, make-up. The details are set up to contrast with Kralin, who 'overlaid' his 'gear' on to his dead wife's things. Kralin fakes antiques to make money, and his possessions include a typewriter, a row of pipes and a pair of leather slippers, all of which 'wore an air of openness, of un-secrecy' (*DFT*, 240, 241). Felicity's 'treasured and auratic' objects, to borrow Patrick Wright's phrase, have history and meaning.[74]

Scylla and Boris sit outside the inn at the end of *Felicity Taverner*, and as she stares at the stone on the green, Scylla thinks that rocks have personality if 'one has had time to know them, a very long time' (*DFT*, 333). Scylla anticipates an Ouspenskian evolution of consciousness, suspecting 'that an account of their perception might be the means to an incalculable enlargement of human power' (*DFT*, 200–1). In her pamphlet *Traps for Unbelievers*, published in the same year as *Death of*

Felicity Taverner, 1932, Butts described the 'relations between things of a different order; the moon and a stone, the sea and a piece of wood, women and fish', and described how this 'perception has no more died in man than has his sight or any other of his senses; only he does not now try it out'.[75] Perception is linked to evolution for Butts.

Like the perceptual breakdown of objects in the novel, *Armed with Madness* breaks down to form a series of vignettes as opposed to structured chapters. After Chapter 20, the temporal narrative is flattened out and some of the events take place in parallel, as though laid out on a folding screen. In the 'Ross' section we follow him as he finishes a painting, and the next section begins 'On the same night' as we follow Picus to his mother's graveside (*AWM*, 110). The following section opens, 'while Felix was whirling down from Montmartre in a taxi with the boyfriend and the Russian all of them drunk' (*AWM*, 112), indicating the whirling is happening 'while' Ross is painting and Picus is prostrated on his mother's grave. The characters are then brought back to Dorset: as the vicar notes, the Grail knights gathering. As Felix telegraphs to say he is bringing his lover Boris, Carston's consciousness appears to move up a notch: 'more than an approach to wonder. Wonder was the answer, and familiar objects out of their categories' (*AWM*, 140). Carston, Picus and the vicar decide the cup should be replaced in the well at Tollerdown.

Time overlaps during the climactic ending when Scylla visits Clarence, who, in a fit of madness, ties her to a statue of Picus and shoots her with arrows. We are shown Scylla being shot by Clarence but then the baker's van that she is riding in passes Carston on the path as he struggles to reach Tollerdown. The timelessness is linked to Carston's new sense of perception; he 'mounted, into silence. He had never been so well in his life' and he hurries, knowing that 'hanging about an eternity he'd been, up in the air' (*AWM*, 146, 147). And yet ultimately, Carston refuses to remain among 'that poverty and pride, cant and candour, raw flesh and velvet; into that dateless, shiftless, shifting, stable and unstable Heartbreak House' (*AWM*, 159). The reference to Shaw's play sets up the arrival of Boris, who smells the honey and the sea and remembers 'the smell of fruit bubbling in copper pans, in a kitchen – a child with his nurse – in a country-house, in Russia, in a pine forest' (*AWM*, 162). Boris brings the novel to a close by drawing together Dorset and the rural Russian peasant idyll of his childhood.

Reading Butts's prose requires crossing physical and metaphorical breaks in the text, a process echoed in individual sentences. An early description reads: 'naked, the enormous space, the rough earth dressed her. The sparkling sea did not.' It is not immediately clear if the space is naked or if Scylla is naked, standing in the 'enormous space', dressed by the earth, as she watches her brother swim in the sea (*AWM*, 5). Writer Elizabeth Madox Roberts described Butts's technique in *Armed with Madness* as etching 'events and persons with delicate hair lines, leaving to the active mind the process of filling in the color and heft'. By contrast, the reviewer for *The New Age* was fed up with the way the 'words halt and bump each other' and the sentences 'get themselves knotted up, cryptically' (*Scenes*, 206, 207).

The impact of *Tertium Organum* on Butts's writing can be discerned not only in her echo of specific phrases, images and arguments, but also in the representation of language, or non-language and silence, itself. Butts opens *Armed with Madness* with an overtly theosophical concept – the idea that silence has a voice. According to Ouspensky, a poet hears 'the voices of stones', understands the whisperings of ancient walls, of tumuli, of mountains, rivers, woods and plains. He hears '*the voice of the silence*', understands the psychological difference between silences, knows that *one silence can differ from another* (*TO*, 161, italics in original). *Armed with Madness* begins with a description of the 'unpleasantly quiet' house set in the 'marvellously noisy' rural landscape. The 'silence let through by the jays, the hay-cutter, and the breeze, was a complicated production of stone rooms, the natural silence of empty grass, and the equivocal, personal silence of the wood' (*AWM*, 3). The focus on sound rather than image is unconventional for a narrative opening. Blavatsky defined the concept of 'Dhâranâ' in her short theosophical text, *The Voice of the Silence*, as 'the intense and perfect concentration of the mind upon some one interior object', which enables the 'select few' to hear the soundless sound, the voice of the silence.[76] By concentrating on their interiority Butts's narrator hears the silence of the stone rooms, the empty grass and the woods. The noisy silence creates a sense of unease, which is confirmed by the fact that guests 'who had come for a week' were known to 'leave next day' (*AWM*, 3).

True silence, not interrupted by hay-cutters or jays, but rather a physical, audible silence, can be found at the heart of one of Butts's most explicit references to the fourth dimension, which occurs at the beginning of *Death of Felicity Taverner*. Scylla and Felix are narrating the story of the mysterious death of their cousin Felicity to Boris, whom we met at the end of *Armed with Madness*. Scylla's narrative is interrupted by Felix, who shows a photograph of Felicity to Boris that silences the group; the visual image arrests the verbal narrative. In place of the dialogue we hear the 'voice of flames . . . the crack of old panels responding to heat, and behind them the ground-scratch of mice. A door in the kitchen quarters opened and shut.' Behind these sounds the characters begin to hear 'the pulse of the long room in the delicate candle-light beat in time with the house and the wood. In time with its own time, a pace inaudible, yet sensible to each' (*DFT*, 180). The inaudible beat is the overture to a new kind of space opening out. The long room takes 'advantage of their silence' and

> its shadowless walls seemed to move each in its own direction to some uncharted place. . . . In this second silence the walls left them behind, pre-occupied with Felicity's passion and death; aware only that something was happening to the place where they sat. (*DFT*, 181)

The silence and stillness of the characters provide the environment for the fourth dimension to make itself felt. Language fails the narrator, who admits that this is a 'perception not easy to discuss for lack of terms', and who defers to the characters who resort to literary references: Felix offers the story of Alice 'running with the Red Queen on the squares', and Picus provides John Buchan's story about a man 'who died of finding out what space is really like' (*DFT*, 180). The absent protagonist of Buchan's 'Space', a physicist, discovers that space was 'perpetually "forming fours" in some fancy way', and that when sitting in a room full of people he has an 'odd sense of detachment' because he knows that 'nothing there but himself had any relation at all to the infinite strange world of Space that flowed around them'.[77]

Butts shared this connection between silence, stillness and the fourth dimension with Ezra Pound, who concluded 'Canto 49' with the line: 'The fourth; the dimension of stillness.' Ian Bell examines Pound's poetics in relation to the fourth dimension and argues that the mental work required to perceive the Poundian image enacts the struggle to perceive the dimensions of hyperspace. The blank spaces in the early typographical organisation of 'In a Station of the Metro', for example, are a necessary support to this process of fourth-dimensional thought.[78] Momentary and uneasy stillness, silence and blank spaces, immanently interruptible, lie at the heart of Pound and Butts's apprehension of what a fourth dimension of space might look, or sound, like.

Silence was a practical solution to the difficulty of defining a 'fourth dimensional world in terms of three' or, to deploy one of Butts's favourite quotations from Ouspensky, 'that which can be expressed cannot be true' (*Journals*, 233, 234). Ouspensky argued that 'our language is absolutely inadequate to [describe] the *spatial expression of*

temporal relations' and in order to describe space accurately he wanted
to form a language without verbs, avoiding a linear temporal framework and moving closer to the spatialised time of the fourth dimension (*TO*, 122). Ouspensky quoted Richard Maurice Bucke's *Cosmic
Consciousness: A Study in the Evolution of the Human Mind* (1901),
a book that argues that language evolves as a system of signs, similar
to algebra, representing complex concepts, allowing us to think more
quickly and efficiently. Lifting from *Tertium Organum*, Butts noted in
her diary that our consciousness creates 'algebraical signs for things'.
Putting this into practice, she developed a collection of symbols to represent different emotions and experiences in her diary: for example, Ω
signified 'work in progress', Σ signified 'the signatures' and Δ signified
'dreams'.[79] But even visual symbols rely on verbal elucidation and they
became redundant for Butts; she searched for a new margin-sign

> for something for which I have yet to find the words – & this because no
> one yet has found the words, the names for certain new relations between
> things, states; which sometimes flash across my mind, and then I almost
> immediately lose.

Butts was not deterred; she decided to 'wait till the next flash & then
force myself to describe it. While, as our language was not invented to
express these experiences, words will have to be found' (*Journals*, 332).

In rendering her characters speechless and her narrators silent,
Butts gave a voice to the material world: flames speak, woods laugh,
trees have conversations. Butts's animism has been explored by Jane
Garrity and Ruth Hoberman, both of whom read it through her
intellectual encounter with Jane Harrison's work on ritual, myth and
mana.[80] Mana, by which Harrison meant 'a vague force in man and in
almost everything' or the 'unseen power lying behind the visible universe', was central to Butts's animism (in 1929 she noted in her diary
that she wanted to write a book about '"mana" and animism' (*Journals*,
324).[81] However, *Tertium Organum* offered Butts a different inflection
to her approach to the physical world and the 'potency that lives in the
kind of earth-stuff that is hard and coloured and cold'.[82]

Ouspensky's animist philosophy is drawn from Bucke's *Cosmic
Consciousness* and Fechner's theory of an 'earth soul'. Bucke and
Fechner argue that the world is one conscious organism, functioning
along the same principles as a human body. Ouspensky overlays these
evolutionary theories of animism with his concept of spatial dimensions; he argues that the evolution of the collective consciousness of

the universe is tied to the individual's perception of space. His list of experiences exclusive to those who perceive four dimensions includes 'Flashes of cosmic consciousness. The idea and sometimes the sensation of a living universe' (*TO*, 330). Scylla, not unlike Clarissa Dalloway, who has 'odd affinities with people . . . even trees, or barns', has, at times, the idea or sensation of a living universe; she knows that 'the trees and stones and turf were not dumb, and she had their speech' (*DFT*, 300).[83] The language of things is an object to be 'had' and Scylla owns it, unlike Carston who is unable to 'hear' the jade cup: 'why couldn't the thing speak. Just once. Dumb was the word for it' (*AWM*, 123). Scylla sees the land as 'not happening in our kind of time' (*DFT*, 300), similar to Ouspensky's spatialisation of time or J. W. Dunne's *Experiment with Time* (1927), which Butts read in 1928, in which he argued that we are living in two temporal states simultaneously. A certain 'awareness' comes over Picus when he is repairing a boat on the shore; '"right and "left," "before" and "after" became interchangeable' and he 'acted as though he were living in both at once' (*DFT*, 248). Like Fechner's collective consciousness, in which the 'earth-mind' knows the 'contents of our minds together' (*TO*, 211), the minds in Butts's novels drift outside of themselves, to create a cosmically conscious world.

Butts's lifelong investigations into things she could not see or understand masked her intellectual struggle to apprehend the physical world. Butts's engagement with Ouspensky's *Tertium Organum* brought together her fascination with Russia and with the occult, and provided the catalyst for her use of the idea of a fourth dimension both as a writing tool and as a literary device. She took a thorough and sometimes practical approach to the theory behind a fourth dimension of space and the mental processes required to access it. However, in her fiction the fourth dimension was a symbolic space in which connections to, and perceptions of, the material world were at their strongest, a space in which people hear the silence of stone rooms, the 'brickness of a brick'. The intersection of objects and space places Butts's modernism squarely within the context of material modernisms, in that her playful use of unseen space existing in parallel to 'our' (unseen) space, was a way of reflecting life back on itself, an environment from which to view things differently, as neither commodities nor symbols. Butts's texts demand an understanding of the ideas around things, or the silent spaces between them. The fourth dimension appears in Butts's fiction when the world of three dimensions is no longer adequate: the dialogue is disrupted, the characters fall silent and spaces open up in the narrative to reveal the sound of silence.

Notes

1. See Huyssen's *After the Great Divide: Modernism, Mass Culture, Postmodernism* (1986).
2. Mao, *Solid Objects*, pp. 4, 19.
3. 'A Sort of Song', *The Collected Poems of William Carlos Williams*, ed. MacGowan, II, p. 55.
4. Brown, *A Sense of Things*.
5. For largely biographical accounts of Butts's interest in occultism, see: Jascha Kessler, 'Mary Butts: Lost . . . and Found', *Kenyan Review*; Rainey, 'Good Things: Pederasty and Jazz and Opium and Research', *London Review of Books; A Sacred Quest: The Life and Writings of Mary Butts*, ed. Wagstaff; Mary Hamer, 'Mary Butts, Mothers, and War', in *Women's Fiction and the Great War*, ed. Raitt and Tate.
6. See Rives, 'Problem Space: Mary Butts, Modernism, and the Etiquette of Placement'; Garrity, *Step-daughters of England*.
7. Ouspensky, *Tertium Organum*, trans. Bessarabov and Bragdon, 2nd edn, rev. (1923). Further references are abbreviated to *TO* in the text.
8. Rose, *On Not Being Able to Sleep: Psychoanalysis and the Modern World*, p. 90.
9. Henderson, *The Fourth Dimension and Non-Euclidean Geometry in Modern Art*. Further references are abbreviated to *FD* in the text.
10. Henderson, 'Italian Futurism and "The Fourth Dimension"', p. 317.
11. Clarke, *Energy Forms*, p. 12.
12. See Clarke's *Energy Forms* for a discussion of the fourth dimension in relation to D. H. Lawrence, Edward Carpenter, H. G. Wells and Dora Marsden.
13. Kandinsky, *The Art of Spiritual Harmony*, p. 27 n27.
14. See Blacklock, 'The Emergence of the Fourth Dimension', p. 122.
15. Hinton, 'What is the Fourth Dimension?', pp. 34, 32.
16. Hinton, *A New Era of Thought*, pp. 87, 79, 84.
17. Blavatsky, *Secret Doctrine*, I, p. 271.
18. Leadbeater, *Clairvoyance*, pp. 34–5, 35.
19. Henderson points out that the ideas behind Hinton's major texts must have reached Russia in the early years of the twentieth century, even though they were not translated into Russian until 1915 (*FD*, 246).
20. Henderson, 'A New Facet of Cubism', p. 417. See also Richardson, *Modern Art and Scientific Thought*, Chapter 5.
21. Apollinaire, 'The New Painting: Art Notes', p. 222.
22. Larionov, quoted in Ingold, *Rayonnism: Its History and Theory*, p. 21.
23. Lodder and Hellyer, 'St Petersburg/Petrograd/Leningrad. From Aesthetics to Revolutionaries', p. 1268.
24. Parton, *Mikhail Larionov and the Russian Avant-Garde*, p. 133.

25. Gibbons was responding to Henderson's early articles in *Art Journal* and *Art Quarterly*, as opposed to her monograph, which was not published until 1983.

26. Manning, 'Introduction', in *The Fourth Dimension Simply Explained*, p.12. (Essays were submitted from Turkey, Austria, Holland, India, Australia, France, Germany and America, but the collection includes essays almost exclusively from America.)

27. Jeans, *The Mysterious Universe*, p. 87.

28. Bragdon, *Four-Dimensional Vistas*, p. 9.

29. A. T. Schofield, *Another World: or The Fourth Dimension*, p. 71.

30. Charles Brodie Patterson, *A New Heaven and a New Earth or The Way to Life Eternal*, p. 94.

31. An Officer of the Grand Fleet, *The Fourth Dimension*, p. 87.

32. Lawrence, 'Reflections on the Death of a Porcupine', in *Reflections on the Death of a Porcupine and Other Essays*, p. 358.

33. Hinton, 'A Plane World', *Scientific Romances*, 1 (1886), p. 129.

34. David Seed notes that 'Greenland', the fourth-dimensional home of one of the characters, is a 'thinly disguised version of the Belgian Congo'. Seed, 'Introduction', in Conrad and Ford, *The Inheritors*, p. ix.

35. Conrad and Ford, *The Inheritors*, p. 10.

36. *Manchester Guardian*, 10 July 1901, p. 157.

37. Vachell, *The Fourth Dimension* (1920).

38. Wilde, 'The Canterville Ghost', in *The Canterville Ghost and Other Stories*, p. 5.

39. Scarborough, *The Supernatural in Modern English Fiction*, p. 259.

40. Woolf, 'Across the Border', p. 55.

41. Wells, 'The Case of Davidson's Eyes', pp. 282, 283.

42. Wells, 'The Plattner Story', pp. 333, 328. We know Butts read the story because she wrote in her notebook, 'right hand that cannot be the right. Wells's Plattner story'. Mary Butts Papers, General Collection, Beinecke Rare Book and Manuscript Library, Yale University, folder 62 (Writings: Notebooks, volume 12).

43. Jeans, *The Mysterious Universe*, p. 112.

44. Woolf, *Letters*, IV (1978), p. 266 (Woolf to Ethel Smyth, 27 December 1930).

45. Sinclair, 'The Finding of the Absolute', in *May Sinclair's Uncanny Stories*, pp. 239, 243–4.

46. Woolf, 'Evening Over Sussex', p. 204.

47. Thacker, *Moving Through Modernity*, p. 182; Minow-Pinkney, 'Virginia Woolf and the Age of Motor Cars', in *Virginia Woolf in the Age of Mechanical Reproduction*, ed. Caughie, pp. 159–82.

48. Woolf, 'Evening Over Sussex', p. 205.

49. See Whitworth, *Einstein's Wake*, and Henry, *Virginia Woolf and the Discourse of Science*.

50. Woolf, *Diary*, IV (1982), p. 353.
51. Leadbeater, *Clairvoyance*, p. 34.
52. Butts's work was widely available during her lifetime, during which she published three novels: *Ashe of Rings* (1925), *Armed with Madness* (1928), *Death of Felicity Taverner* (1932); one epistolary novel, *Imaginary Letters* (1928); two collections of short stories, *Speed the Plough and Other Stories* (1923) and *Several Occasions* (1932); and two historical narratives, *The Macedonian* (1933) and *Scenes from the Life of Cleopatra* (1935). She also published two pamphlets and numerous poetry and reviews in contemporary journals, including *The Little Review*, *The Dial*, *The Egoist* and *Pagany*. McPherson Press has reprinted all of her novels and most of her short stories.
53. Rainey, 'Good Things', pp. 14, 17.
54. Lubbock, 'Georgian Stories', *Times Literary Supplement*, 6 July 1922, p. 440; *Clarion*, 4 August 1922. Cuttings held in the Beinecke Rare Book and Manuscript Library, Yale University, Mary Butts Papers, box 15, folder 200, press cuttings bound volume 1922–8.
55. See Blondel, *Mary Butts: Scenes from the Life*, p. 426; further references are to *Scenes* in the text.
56. Butts, *The Crystal Cabinet*, pp. 234, 235, 138.
57. *Journals of Mary Butts*, ed. Blondel, p. 60; further references are to *Journals* in the text.
58. Luckhurst, *The Invention of Telepathy*, p. 57.
59. Butts was reading Westcott's translation of Alphonse Louis Constant's *The Magical Ritual of the Sanctum Regum, interpreted by the Tarot Trumps* (1896) and Samuel Liddell MacGregor's *The Book of the Sacred Magic of Abra-Melin the Mage* (1898).
60. In the late teens and early twenties the books that seemed of most importance to Butts were Bertrand Russell's *Problems of Philosophy* (1912), Forster's *The Celestial Omnibus* (1911) and Dostoevsky's *The Possessed* (1872). Butts returned to a number of texts throughout the 1920s, including Jane Harrison's *Prolegomena to the Study of Greek Religion* (1904) and *Themis: A Study of the Social Origins of Greek Religion* (1912), Jessie Weston's *From Ritual to Romance* (1920), Gilbert Murray's *Rise of the Greek Epic* (1907) and James Frazer's *The Golden Bough* (1915). According to her diaries, the only other texts she read in 1926 were T. S. Eliot's *The Hollow Men* (1925), René Crevel's *Mon corps et moi* (1925), some Ralph Waldo Emerson and work by the British classical historian Arthur Weigall.
61. Butts also quoted long passages from Crevel's *Mon corps et moi* (1925) and Waite's *The Holy Grail* (1909). Blondel edits Butts's notes on *Tertium Organum* so that they amount to about four single pages in the published edition of her journals; see pp. 233–6.
62. Patterson, 'The Translation of Soviet Literature: John Rodker and PresLit', p. 189.

63. Owen, *The Place of Enchantment*, p. 232.
64. Henderson notes that the rare 1909 edition of *The Fourth Dimension* was 'an account of nineteenth-century ideas about the fourth dimension' (*FD*, 248). The 1916 second edition of *Tertium Organum* was translated into English by Nikolai Bessarabov and Claude Bragdon, and printed by Bragdon's Press in New York in 1920; it was then revised in 1922 and published by Alfred A. Knopf in the United States and by Kegan Paul in London (1923). Quotations are taken from the British edition.
65. Beinecke, box 3, folder 62, diary, volume 12.
66. Butts, *Armed with Madness*, in *The Taverner Novels: Armed with Madness and Death of Felicity Taverner* (1992), pp. 5, 14; henceforth abbreviated *AWM* in the text. Jane Harrison described Picus as 'an oracular bird, a tree-guardian, a guardian of kings' in *Themis*, p. 104.
67. See Wright, *On Living in an Old Country*; Patterson, 'The Plan Behind the Plan', in *Modernity, Culture and the Jew*, ed. Cheyette and Marcus; and Garrity, *Step-daughters of England*.
68. Butts, *Death of Felicity Taverner*, p. 249; henceforth abbreviated to *DFT* in the text.
69. Garrity, *Step-daughters of England*, p. 234.
70. Patterson, 'The Plan Behind the Plan', p. 137.
71. Butts, *Scenes*, p. 167; 'Avenue Montaigne', *Antaeus*, 12 (winter 1973), p. 151.
72. Woolf, 'Modern Fiction' (1925), in *Essays* (1994), p. 161.
73. Ouspensky, *Tertium Organum*, fold-out table insert.
74. Wright, *On Living in an Old Country*, p. 113.
75. Butts, *Traps for Unbelievers*, p. 25.
76. Blavatsky, *The Voice of the Silence*, p. 73.
77. Buchan, 'Space', pp. 150, 152.
78. See Bell, 'The Poundian Fourth Dimension', *Symbiosis: A Journal of Anglo-American Literary Relations*, 11.2 (October 2007), and 'Ezra Pound and the Materiality of the Fourth Dimension', in *Science in Modern Poetry: New Directions* (2012), pp. 130–50.
79. Beinecke, box 3, folder 62, volume 12, folder 67, diary, volume 16.
80. See Garrity, *Step-daughters of England*, and Ruth Hoberman, *Gendering Classicism*.
81. Harrison, *Themis*, pp. 67, 68.
82. Butts, *Crystal Cabinet*, p. 15.
83. Woolf, *Mrs Dalloway*, p. 230.

CHAPTER 4

'That Magic Force that is Montage':[1] Eisenstein's Filmic Fourth Dimension, *Borderline* and H.D.

In a workshop on montage given in London in 1929, Sergei Eisenstein urged his students to 'choose pieces which do not fit'.[2] Montage, a technique of filmmaking employed by Russian filmmakers of the 1920s, was used by different directors to mean different things. The method was originally developed by Lev Kuleshov's now famous experiments of c. 1920. Although the footage is lost, Kuleshov describes how he juxtaposed three identical copies of a short piece of footage of the actor Ivan Mozzukhin's face with images of a bowl of soup, a dead woman in an open coffin and a girl playing with a toy bear to show how editing changes our visual interpretation; audiences, Kuleshov claimed, perceived hunger, grief and joy in the actor's blank expression.[3] For Kuleshov, montage was 'the same as the composition of the colours in painting or a harmonic sequence of notes in music', in that it was cinema's medium-specific method for making meaning.[4] For Vsevolod Pudovkin, montage was linkage, or the 'requisite order of shots or pieces, and the rhythm necessary for their combination'.[5] But for Eisenstein, montage was an act and product of collision: 'Montage is not an idea recounted by pieces following each other, *but an idea that arises in the collision of two pieces independent of one another*' (italics in original).[6] To cite a well-known example, in his film *Strike* (dir. Eisenstein, 1925), in which politics and aesthetics are united, Eisenstein intercut the image of a bull being slaughtered with images of the suppression of the factory workers so that audiences imagine the strikers being slaughtered like cattle.

Montage has fallen out of fashion as a term employed to discuss literary modernism. David Trotter argues that it is anachronistic to associate high modernist texts like *The Waste Land* with montage filmmaking. The films of Eisenstein, Pudovkin, Dziga Vertov, Grigory Kozintsev and Leonid Trauberg, he argues, were not shown in Britain until the establishment of the Film Society, the main venue for the dissemination of international films in Britain in the 1920s, set up by Ivor Montagu in 1925.[7] And Eisenstein's most famous theories of film were not published in Britain until 1929, when they were translated for *Close Up* (1927–33), the first British journal that claimed to 'approach films from the angles of art, experiment and possibility', and which, as Laura Marcus points out, was set up in Switzerland 'as a response to, or a way of skirting' censorship in Britain.[8] Andrew Shail suggests cross-cutting in place of montage as a more accurate description of the continuity, rather than interruptions, of time and space in texts like *Mrs Dalloway* or *Ulysses*.[9] The relationship between the literary and the cinematic is certainly more complex and specific than the tendency to exchange 'transferable narrative techniques' between writers and film-makers.[10] The relationship is also more complex than the cinematic qualities attributed to modernists' work through their brief encounters with film: for example, Joyce's opening of the Cinematograph Volta in Dublin in 1909, and Woolf's viewing of *The Cabinet of Dr Caligari* (dir. Wiene, 1920) in 1926. The malfunctioning of the projector created a shadow on the screen, which became the subject of her most famous essay on the cinema.[11] The origins of montage, or cross-cutting, as a narrative tool can be traced back to D. W. Griffith, who explored parallel action in *Birth of a Nation* (1915) and *Intolerance* (1916). So, although we can certainly borrow the term montage to discuss modernist texts prior to 1929, Eisenstein's dialectic montage is better discussed in relation to British modernism after the publication of his 'Principles of Film Form' in *Close Up* in 1929.

This chapter builds on recent debates about montage and British modernism. It suggests that Eisenstein's theory of 'overtonal' montage, which he also referred to as the filmic fourth dimension, should be positioned more centrally in discussions of his aesthetics and poli-tics. Scholars have tended to concentrate on his theory of intellectual montage, in which the collision of montage elements functions as a Marxist dialectic between hypothesis and antithesis, producing a synthesis that alerts the audience to the values of communism.[12] Eisenstein's overtonal montage has been neglected but not ignored: Maggie Humm has noted Woolf's prescient account of the concept in her description of connections between scenes by means of 'something abstract, something moving'.[13] And Anne Nesbet has argued that the montage in *Battleship Potemkin* (dir. Eisenstein, 1925) was designed to push the perceptual boundaries of the audience to experience a higher reality, not unlike the fourth spatial dimension defined in Russian in

1909 by Petr Ouspensky.[14] Anne Friedberg and Laura Marcus have discussed the apparently retrospective impact of overtonal montage on the British film *Borderline* (1930), which was written and directed by Kenneth Macpherson, the editor of *Close Up*, with H.D. in a starring role.[15]

Analysis of Eisenstein's overtonal montage reveals that it holds trace elements of both theories of space–time and the theosophical idea of an alternative dimension. Mathematician Hermann Minkowski explored the idea that space and time were two parts of a unified whole in 1908. His article 'Space and Time' led to the idea that time is not a separate, fixed entity, as it was under Euclidean laws. Einstein's Theory of Special Relativity, expanding on Minkowski's theory, argued that time is not independent of motion and that it varies for different events and between reference frames. My claim is that Eisenstein's idea of cinema as a four-dimensional space expressed in *Close Up* draws both on Einstein's theory of relativity and on Ouspensky's theory of the fourth dimension, and offered the projection of a new ideological space. Eisenstein's aesthetics of overtonal montage are borrowed to analyse *Borderline* and its preoccupation with cinematic space. H.D.'s writing on cinema is investigated, and although she wrote most of her reviews of Russian films in *Close Up* before Eisenstein was translated into English, H.D. and Eisenstein shared, to borrow Trotter's phrase, a 'certain aesthetic convergence', which, I argue, evolves into aesthetic cultivation.[16] The chapter begins by putting Eisenstein's theories into a wider context of spirit photography and early cinema.

The 'haunted frame': spirit photography and early cinema

Photography's early associations with an unseen world worked, broadly speaking, on two levels: explicitly, photography that sought to capture evidence of the supernatural on film, and implicitly, in that photographs are images of the world in which we no longer exist. 'Spirit photography' was established in the 1860s by William Mumler in America and became an instant commercial success, particularly after the Civil War, when families wanted to capture images of their deceased loved ones. Mumler discovered that you could take photographs of people and then add images to the negative from other photographs through double exposure. People were willing to pay to ease their grief. Crista Cloutier notes that Mumler charged ten dollars per sitting, when regular photographs sold for a quarter each.[17] The genre was established in Europe by Édouard Isidore Buguet in Paris and Frederick Hudson in London. Charges of forgery and subsequent trials took place on both sides of the Atlantic, and spirit photography began to decline towards the end of the nineteenth century. Mumler was accused and tried after living residents of Boston were recognised as the spirits in his photographs and, although the outcome of his trial was inconclusive, the photography section of the American Institute denounced spirit photography as trickery. Buguet was tried in 1875 in Paris. Owing to his connections with Hudson, spirit photography declined in London, accelerated by the declaration by the Society for Psychical Research that the evidence for capturing spirits on film was not sufficient to warrant further investigation.

The discovery of the X-ray by Wilhelm Conrad Röntgen in 1895 rekindled public interest in spirit photography: if the invisible human form could be photographed, what else might be photographed that is invisible to the naked eye? Allen Grove notes that 'x-rays seemingly legitimated the late Victorian and Edwardian ghost by making invisibility appear feasible'.[18] As well as legitimising ghosts, seeing one's skeleton was a shocking reminder of mortality, captured when Hans Castorp viewed his hand through a fluoroscope in Thomas Mann's *The Magic Mountain* (1924); he saw what 'is hardly permitted man to see', he 'looked into his own grave'.[19]

Early photography created a 'parallel world of phantasmatic doubles alongside the concrete world of the senses'.[20] Freud's notion of the uncanny, in which things from our unconscious surprise us, 'nothing new and foreign, but something familiar and old', captures the disorientating effects of early photography.[21] For example, as Grove notes, a bustling street could be turned into 'an eerie still life' and in a family portrait a mother might stand motionless but disconcertingly hold the faceless blur of a child unable to sit still.[22] Julia Margaret Cameron used this effect in her photography; she welcomed small movements by her sitters and became famous for the haunting, ghost-like qualities of her pictures. Marcus calls *To the Lighthouse* 'a ghost-story of a kind', concerned with presence and absence, and notes that Woolf wrote it during the same period that she was writing an essay of introduction to a volume of Cameron's photographs.[23] Trotter argues that film taught Woolf to imagine the 'world seen without a self' or 'life as it is when we have no part in it'.[24] Indeed, photographs of rooms without people and empty chairs are interspersed in Woolf's photograph albums. In one album she places a photograph in the centre of the page (most have four), that appears to be a spirit photograph showing a woman floating on a landscape, achieved through double exposure.[25]

Like photography, cinema across Europe and America was associated from its earliest days with spectres, magic, dreams, memory and
visions. It is difficult to recapture the sense of excitement and shock
inspired by the first moving images around the turn of the century.
The new magical machine, it was variously believed, could bring the
dead back to life, travel in time and space, arouse sexual desire, speak
(silently) in a universal primeval language, and offer magnified and
telescopic views of reality. Tom Gunning has traced the origins of film
to the magical imagistic traditions of Giulio Camillo's and Giordano
Bruno's theatres of memory, magic lanterns and the camera obscura.
The magic lantern, according to Gunning, never shook off its eerie
associations. For example, it was popular to project images of spirits
of the dead, or ghoulish images in kinetoscope peepshows and phan-
tasmagorias. Early film, then, was magical in both content and form.
Trick photography was popular: for example, spirits or ghosts appeared
on screen, figures disappeared in vanishing acts, and devils, magicians
and sorcerers with transformational powers were common figures.[26]
Iurii Tsivian notes that Russian films of the 1910s frequently made use
of mirrors and portraits to create mystical or uncanny effects.[27] Early
cinema screenings were regularly held in magic lantern venues, emphasising the cinema's magical inheritance. Although the 'phantasmagoria
of the trick film with its magical metamorphoses' is interesting, the
unexplained, magical quality of film is more relevant for this study.[28]

Like photography, cinema shows us things that are no longer there,
within what Tsivian calls the 'haunted frame'.[29] The interest in spiritualism, the occult and magic in the late Victorian period was easily translated on to this strange new medium, in which images from the past were
brought to life. French and Russian symbolists and British decadents
cultivated mystery and suggestion, as in Jean Moréas's famous hostility
to 'l'enseignement, la déclamation, la fausse sensibilité, la description
objective'.[30] Ian Christie has noted that both the Parisian newspapers
reporting on the first Lumière brothers' show in 1896 concluded their
reviews with the idea that cinema would bring the dead back to life.[31]

In Nizhny Novgorod, Maxim Gor'ky, having attended a screening of
the Lumière brothers' first films in the summer of 1896, famously drew
a parallel between the new medium and symbolism:

Last night I was in the kingdom of the shadows.
    If you only knew how strange it is to be there. It is a world without sound,
without colour. Everything there – the earth, the trees, the people, the water
and the air – is dipped in monotonous grey. Grey rays of the sun across the

grey sky, grey eyes in grey faces, and the leaves of the trees are ashen grey. It is not life but its shadow, it is not motion but its soundless spectre.

Here I shall try to explain myself, lest I be suspected of madness or indulgence in symbolism. I was at Aumont's and I saw Lumière's *cinématographe* – moving photography (italics in original).[32]

Gorky emphasises the monotonous 'grey' and an overriding sense of gloom. The prose focuses on the lack of sound and colour, which creates death-like 'shadow[s]' and 'spectre[s]' on the screen. It is life devoid of colour, sound and movement; the camera is motionless. However, as Marcus points out, Gorky is shaken out of this gloom by 'a gay chatter and a provoking laughter of a woman', and the grey motionless images are replaced by a scene of a family having breakfast.[33]

The experience of seeing a film at the turn of the twentieth century in Russia was not unrelated to the experience of attending a séance or an occult ritual. Tsivian notes that the half-illuminated faces in a dark auditorium, concentrating in silence on a rectangle of light, 'evoked images of occult circles, in particular the rituals of secret sects'. He argues that the 'end of history, the death of culture, and a mystical fear of the future were central to the Symbolist universe', which is why cinema with 'its flickering, vibrating, unstable image was a perfect symbol for such a representation of the world'.[34] Unlike in Europe, Tsivian argues, Russian film theatres were kept very dark, and the vibration of the flickering image would have held strong associations with the popular theosophy of the turn of the century, because vibration was considered to be a means of telepathic or clairvoyant communication. This is evident if we turn to the British theosophist Charles Leadbeater, who argued that 'like so many other things in nature' clairvoyance is a question of 'vibrations'.[35] And in 1895, in a text on astral planes that was translated into Russian in 1908, he argued that access to the unseen world of higher astral planes was a matter of our consciousness responding to a 'higher and more refined order' of vibrations.[36] The level of vibration on screen would also have depended on the condition of the equipment and the skill of the projectionist, who turned the reel by hand.

Early silent film was associated with a pure, pre-linguistic, hieroglyphic, primordial condition. Hieroglyphs, notes Marcus, were popular because they were both 'esoteric script and populist communication'[37] and film, according to Armstrong, offered modernists a solution to their 'language crisis' through direct access to the body. He highlights the linguistic metaphors associated with film, from

Shklovsky's definition of film as 'conversation prior to an alphabet', to Louis Haugmard's claim that film was 'a form of notation by image' and Ernest Betts's implication that film was 'gestural language'.[38] The potential for a visual language of film underpins Woolf's essay, 'The Cinema', in which she described the moment when the projector malfunctioned during her viewing of *The Cabinet of Dr Caligari*. A dark shadow appeared, 'like a tadpole' at the corner of the screen, and then 'swelled to an immense size, quivered, bulged, and sank back again into nonentity'. For Woolf this signalled the moment she realised film could make emotion visible. A Russian critic described a momentary obstruction of a projector beam in another screening, so the actors 'remained motionless and grew dimmer in the semi-gloom', creating a '*chill of death emanating from the screen*' (italics in original). This, he claimed, made 'a deeper impression on me than anything else I had ever seen in the cinematograph'.[39] In the same way that Besant and Leadbeater believed thoughts could produce forms, Woolf argued that thought 'could be conveyed by shape more effectively than by words'. Film, Woolf argued, had the potential to create 'something abstract, something moving, something calling only for the very slightest help from words', and so it might become some 'new symbol for expressing thought'.[40]

Eisenstein at the Film Society

Known by Ivor Montagu's family as 'Ivor's Sunday afternoons of gloom', the aim of the Film Society was to show films of interest 'in the study of cinematography' that were not easily accessible elsewhere.[41] The early programmes were dominated by German films, but by the fourth season (1928) it was showing Soviet films that had been banned from public distribution by the British Board of Film Censors. Laura Marcus has discussed the ways that negotiations with and around censorship shaped film aesthetics and film theory in Britain in the 1920s.[42] Even before the screenings of Soviet films, founder member Sidney Bernstein described how the first screenings 'made quite a splash', and the gossip columnists commented on 'the big cars, the women in striking hats, the well-known Bloomsbury figures making themselves conspicuous in the audience with their unconventional dress and loud conversation'.[43] A draft history of the film society by David Robinson, held at the British Film Institute, remains unpublished because founder member Iris Barry felt that it gave the 'unfair and incorrect impression that the F. S. was largely some sort of organ of Soviet propaganda and its members a horde of rough-necks'. Barry points out that between 1925 and 1930, of 179 films shown, only 12 were Russian, although she admits that they were 'striking' and 'explosive'.[44] Between 1925 and 1939, the entire lifespan of the Film Society, 41 Russian and Soviet films were shown out of a total of about 500, including about 100 each of German, French and British films, as well as works from Japan, India, Sweden, Belgium and America. Mainstream British films were exhibited elsewhere, and so the Film Society screened mostly scientific, experimental and, in the later years, documentary British films. Although Soviet works did not dominate the programme, their exhibition inspired the most extreme press coverage.

The first Russian film to be shown at the Film Society in February 1927 was a series of extracts from Iakov Protazanov's *Father Sergius* (1917). During the third season (1927–8), scenes from Tolstoy's daily life were shown, fuelling the appetite for details of his personal life. The fourth season opened in October 1928 with Pudovkin's *Mother* (1926), which, as *Film Weekly* (launched that same month) stated, was the first time that a Soviet film of 'uncompromisingly political hue' was shown to a British audience.[45] In the programme notes, Montagu commented that Pudovkin

> makes special use of alternation of rhythm by long and short cutting; of groups of successive very short shots, each a few inches only in length, to express violent movements; and, peculiar to him, of scenes only remotely connected in external logic with his subject, cut in with others to express the essential significance of the latter.[46]

Montagu's early analysis draws Pudovkin's editing in line with Eisenstein's montage of collison. *Film Weekly* picked up on Montagu's analysis and noted the film's 'telegraphic style' and how its 'exalted and rapid rhythm is deliberately employed to give not an exact picture of all that happened, but a series of vivid impressions which tell more'.[47]

Robert Herring wrote of *Mother* in the *London Mercury* that the 'spiritual reality it breathes is reflected by the actual reality of the sets, the *real* woods and factories among which these *real* people move – a material reality possible only to the cinema'.[48] The emphasis on the 'spiritual' and the 'real' implicitly contrasts with the 'phony' qualities of Hollywood, but also parallels the British reception of Russian arts and literature, where fiction was often considered as fact. By contrast, *The Times* complained that Pudovkin drew a picture of revolution with a 'brush dipped quite frankly in the pot of propaganda'.[49] The

subsequent screening of Pudovkin's *The End of St Petersburg* (1927),
accompanied by his talk about montage principles in February 1929
('Types as Opposed to Actors', translated from Russian by Montagu),
upstaged the response to *Mother*. The *Sunday Express* described the
admiration as 'hysteria' and the *Daily Sketch* claimed that a cheer broke
out when 'All Power to the Soviets' appeared on the screen. Hisses
were heard during the playing of the National Anthem, according to
the same review, and many of the 'bearded youths and crop-haired
girls' remained seated.[50] The reports of cheers by the audience led to
questions being asked in the House of Commons but Montagu later
noted that the presence of a Conservative Member of Parliament in
the audience saved them from a 'knuckle-rapping in the Commons'.[51]
Other critics referred to Pudovkin's film as a 'supreme work of art' and,
writing for *Close Up*, Hellmund-Waldow argued that it was not 'in any
way biased, and constitutes a document of quite impartial interest'.[52]
Macpherson, editor of *Close Up*, referred to *The End of St Petersburg*,
Bed and Sofa (dir. Room, 1927) and *Jeanne Ney* (dir. Pabst, 1927) as
'superb' because they are 'true to life, because they say something we
know, because they move us, because their beauty is a beauty we recognise, and their greatness a greatness we can comprehend'.[53] Realism
signalled 'beauty' and 'greatness' for Macpherson, as it did for Herring.

By the time Eisenstein's *Battleship Potemkin* was eventually screened
at the Film Society in 1929, hostility to Soviet films had peaked. The
film was first banned in 1926 but Montagu secured a print from the
Soviet film delegation in Berlin. The programme note referred to the
'use of non-acting material and the incitement to hysteria by means
of rhythmic cutting'.[54] The term 'hysteria' curiously echoed the words
of the film's detractors.[55] The *Evening Standard* described *Potemkin*
as a 'strange blend of brilliant technique and naïve melodrama'. The
reviewer was less concerned that 'it would harm the British public'
than that it would 'bore them'.[56] Bryher anticipated the apathy of a
British audience in *Film Problems of Soviet Russia*, published only
months before *Potemkin* was screened in Britain. She expressed her
concern that as soon as the auditorium lights came up audiences would
be wondering about which bus to catch, and think 'wasn't it queer' the
way those women on the steps 'got hysterical' about something that
did not concern them. Like *Close Up*, Bryher's book was a way to dis-
seminate information about Soviet film to a wider audience.[57] For the
Times journalist, *Potemkin* was no better than 'the average Soviet film',
and it certainly did not live up to the hopes created by the censor's
ban.[58] Other conservative papers like *The Morning Post* agreed that as

'propaganda' the film was 'singularly ineffective', and the *Evening News* felt that it was 'childish' in its fervour against law and order.

By contrast, the *Daily Mail* praised both the photography and the film's 'lively rhythm' but attacked it for having too much sympathy with the 'mutineers'. And the *Daily Sketch* called it the most 'appalling film in the horror and terror it inspires that London has yet seen', and declared that the Odessa Steps sequence 'is almost beyond bearing'.[59] In fact, the programme note stated that the Odessa Steps scene was 'easily excisable' if the British Board of Film Censors had decided to release the film.[60] Bryher captured the polarised response to Soviet film in Britain: 'Either, it appears, you must be prepared to bayonet your aunt because she wont [sic] read Karl Marx, or else you must leave the room because *Potemkin* is mentioned.'[61]

In the early 1930s, the Film Society screened Pudovkin's *Storm over Asia* (1928), Eisenstein's *General Line* (1929) and Dovzhenko's *Earth* (1930). The *Daily Express* argued that the Film Society was intent on 'furthering the subversive propaganda of the Bolsheviks'.[62] Bryher referred to *The General Line* as 'never quite a story nor quite a document', and although it did not have 'the rhythm and power of *Potemkin* and *Ten Days*', it was 'the finest educational film ever made'.[63] Eisenstein was 'disagreeably surprised' by the review, indicating the close attention he paid to the journal.[64] The Film Society's final screening was Eisenstein's *Alexander Nevsky* in April 1939. Avant-garde film and Left politics were united, according to Annette Michelson, in 'a certain euphoria' surrounding early film-making and film theory, in which Marxism and modernism would converge 'in the hopes and promises, as yet undefined, of the new medium'.[65]

The British journal *Close Up* was founded by novelist Annie Winnifred Ellerman (Bryher) and her husband, the Scottish artist Kenneth Macpherson, with H.D. agreeing to provide regular contributions. *Close Up* positioned itself as an international journal with correspondents in Moscow, Berlin, Paris, Geneva, London, New York and Los Angeles, and it devoted special issues to Japanese and 'Afro-American', as well as to Russian cinema. The first issue came out in July 1927 and it was published monthly until January 1931, then quarterly until December 1933. Austrian director G. W. Pabst told Bryher that *Close Up* was the 'thing we all desire[;] the paper expresses our inmost psychological thoughts'. Pabst's surprise was that 'an English man should have written it'. Eisenstein wrote to Macpherson, describing him as the editor of the 'Closest Up to what cinema should be'.[66]

The journal published articles about film and education, montage, censorship, spectatorship, film in relation to psychoanalysis, dreams, performance, socialism, gender and the transition to sound.

The September 1928 issue was the 'Russian number' and Macpherson's editorial noted that 'Russia has imposed – without knowing it – a difficult task on *Close Up*. For we cannot begin where Russia begins. The ground is not yet ready.' Russian films, unlike films from elsewhere, he continued, are on a 'level of intellect, spiritual value and truth which has never been approached in any medium'. Rather than use the camera as a passive recording instrument, the camera, for Russian filmmakers, argued Macpherson, functioned as a brain: 'It darts surely and exactly from one vital thing to another vital thing. Its penetration is acute and deep.'[67] Again, this captures the dual response to Russian art as both authentic or true and carefully constructed. In the first issue of the journal Macpherson had complained of being 'sick of Russian novels and Russian plays' but that 'Potemkin and [Protazanov's, 1924] Aelita put an end to that. Russia was getting its finger on something.'[68] By January 1928 Macpherson argued that Russia was the 'foremost country to deal with the cinema artistically and educationally on a wide scale'.[69] Iris Barry had referred, two years earlier, to the 'wiser' and 'paternal' Soviet government that took 'great care' of the 'mental food' given to its subjects in the cinemas.[70]

Eisenstein's overtonal montage

Coinciding with the first British screening of *Battleship Potemkin* in November 1929, Eisenstein gave a series of six two-hour workshops to a group of about twenty members of the Film Society at a cost of five guineas each. From the BFI archive we know that the documentary filmmaker Basil Wright, academic Jack Isaacs, film critic Robert Herring and playwright Lionel Britten were among the attendees. From Marie Seton's biography we can add Anthony Asquith, Arthur Elton, Ivor Montagu, Thorold Dickinson, H. P. J. Marshall and John Grierson, who was 'darting in and out'. Grierson had just finished *Drifters* (1929), his documentary, which was shown with *Potemkin* at the Film Society on 10 November and caused what Eisenstein referred to as a 'creative explosion'.[71] According to the leaflet inviting applicants, the subjects for the workshops were to include the 'technique of perception', 'montage of attractions', 'theory of conflict' and 'three forms of expression', including psychological, classical and ideological cutting.[72]

The British Film Institute holds a transcript of reminiscences by two of the attendees, Basil Wright and Jack Isaacs, which were broadcast on BBC radio in 1949. Wright's account offers an evocative physical description of Eisenstein as 'chubbily built, plump in face; a pliable and expressive nose; a shock of dark hazel-coloured curly hair rising briskly above an imposingly extensive brow'. Isaacs noted Eisenstein's interest in mysticism and the occult, describing him as 'dissipating his energies into the occult, into studies in the synchronization of the senses, into colour audition, into graphology'. The key to Eisenstein's film aesthetics, continued Isaacs, was the 'overriding logical cohesion of his view'. Wright referred to Eisenstein's eclectic tastes, noting that he talked about 'Japanese Kabuki plays, about William James, Darwin, Toulouse Lautrec, Daumier; about Kenyon's proposition that "two opposite reactions can be provoked by the same stimulus"'. Wright noted that Eisenstein's montage was a 'synthesis' or 'putting together of material in such a way that the sum of the various units produces an entirely new quality, an unknown, an X'. 'There he stood', chalk in hand, Wright continued, ready 'to expound the inner, the Eleusinian mysteries of Film Art'.[73] Hakan Lövgren has detailed Eisenstein's initiation into a Rosicrucian order in 1920 during his period as a volunteer with a Red Army engineering unit, and the development of his interest in occultism, theosophy, the Cabala, alchemy and astrology. However, like many of his contemporaries, Eisenstein later declared that he had tried to 'put as much ground as possible between myself and the Rosicrucians, Steiner, and Madame Blavatskaya'.[74]

Of the nine articles Eisenstein published in *Close Up*, six were the first English translations from the original Russian and one was translated from Eisenstein's German original. Two interviews and a report of one of Eisenstein's lectures at the Sorbonne (1930) were also published in the journal between 1929 and 1933. In their first published piece for *Close Up* in October 1928, Eisenstein, Pudovkin and Aleksandrov made an assertive claim for the technique of montage: 'the fundamental (and only) means, by which cinematography has been able to attain such a high degree of effectiveness, is the *mounting* (or cutting)'. Sound, they argued, must be used in opposition to the image: '*The first experiments with sound must be directed towards its pronounced non-coincidence with the visual images*' (italics in original).[75]

Eisenstein argued that cinema must create a new language, distinct from literary language. In his first solo piece for the journal, published in May 1929, 'The New Language of Cinematography', he argued that 'cinematography is for the first time availing itself of the experience of literature for the purpose of working out *its own language, its own speech, its own vocabulary, its own imagery*' (italics in original).[76] On 2 January 1930, Eisenstein sent Macpherson a manuscript for two articles originally written for the Russian newspaper, *Kino*, warning him that they would be 'very difficult to translate' because 'they are very complicated being of big theoretical importance'. This became the two-part essay 'The Fourth Dimension in the Kino', published in the March and April 1930 issues of *Close Up*.[77] The essay was based on the workshops Eisenstein had given to Film Society members the previous autumn. Eisenstein suggested to Macpherson that he should ask Robert Herring to explain the ideas in the essay, because he had heard the 'whole thing' in the lectures.[78] After the workshops Herring wrote to H.D. that Eisenstein had put 'into new, crystal terms all one knew (nothing else); but surprising one that what one knew was so complicated'.[79]

'The Fourth Dimension of the Kino' concentrates on the overall effects of montage as opposed to individual moments of collision. It begins, in communist idiom, with the claim that each shot in *The General Line* (1929) was treated democratically so that 'all the stimulants' could be 'viewed together as a complex'. Without obvious segue Eisenstein claims that secondary resonances are thus created, because 'overtones' and 'undertones' collide with one another.[80] Eisenstein noted that it was 'the first film to be edited on the principle of visual overtone' because the montage within it 'takes the sum of *stimuli* of all the stimulants as the dominant'. The stimuli vary, but are 'bound together in an iron unity through their reflex-physiological essence'. Although his meaning is not obvious here, he goes on to describe the re-editing of the religious procession sequence, when he realised that the 'creative ecstasy' he experienced during the assembly and montage of 'hearing and feeling' the shots, akin to altered consciousness, was no longer apparent: 'Cutting and shortening do not require inspiration, only technique and skill.'[81] The montage of icons in *October* (1927) from baroque Christ to Eskimo Idol, began to approach the film language he sought: 'achieving direct forms for ideas, systems, and concepts' without need for transitions and paraphrases. According to Seton, this was the beginning of his synthesis of 'art and science'.[82]

Macpherson interpreted Eisenstein's theory of montage as concentrating on a 'unified, orchestrated whole', on 'mass grandeur' rather than 'niggling detail'.[83] In the second part of the two-part article, Eisenstein set out his scientific array of montage principles, including 'metric', 'rhythmic', 'tonic', 'overtonal' and 'intellectual'. 'Metric montage' referred to a pattern of varied shot duration, and Eisenstein noted that tension could be built through 'mechanical acceleration' or the repeated 'shortening of the lengths of the shots' in terms of the actual length of the celluloid pieces. 'Rhythmic montage' might be defined as the perceived length of a shot and is concerned with the movement within the frame, as opposed to the length of the celluloid. Wright records that 3 feet of close-up is, relatively, different from 3 feet of a long shot, by which he meant that shots of the same length appear to last for different periods of time, depending on their content. In fact, Eisenstein nearly always used pieces that were cut to about the same length, and so the rhythm was made by *changing the subject of the pieces* (italics in original).[84] 'Tonal montage' might typically be concerned with the emotional content of the frame, emphasised, for example, by the focus of the shot.[85] Wright notes that in tonic montage 'we get what may be called VIBRATION: effects of *light* and *shape* and *form*' (italics in original).[86] Or in Eisenstein's words, the chief 'indicator' for the assembly of shots in relation to tonal montage was 'their basic element – optical light vibrations (varying degrees of "haze" and "luminosity"). And the organization of these vibrations reveals a complete identity with a minor harmony in music.'[87]

Overtonal montage, Eisenstein's fourth type of montage, was closely connected to the vibrations of tonal montage, and the idea of fourth-dimensional space and time. Overtonal montage was physical, the indefinable sensation that you experience when watching a film or the 'particular "feeling" of the shot that the shot as a whole produces'. It was 'the furthest organic development of tonal montage' that takes full account 'of all the stimulants in the shot'.[88] In his lecture notes, Wright described 'overtonic' montage as 'the point at which montage passes beyond the confines of the cutting-room and becomes a dominating factor in the total conception of film-making'. 'Overtonic' montage, continued Wright, was the 'unanalysable element – that rare and wonderful aesthetic impact which comes to us only too seldom from the screen'.[89] Like Clive Bell's 'Significant Form', Kandinsky's 'inneres klang' or Epstein's 'photogénie', Eisenstein's 'fourth dimension' of the cinema is not easily iterated.[90] One way to define it is that the first four types of montage are 'methods' that become constructions when in conflict with one another, but overtonal montage emerges out of the conflict 'between the principal tone' and 'the overtone' of the piece.[91]

The impact on the spectator is perhaps more easily defined: the fourth dimension of the cinema transports the experience of the spectator from a merely emotional response to '*a direct physiological sensation*' (italics in original). Marcus notes that Eisenstein's emphasis on the physiological, evident in the rhythmic editing, was one of the reasons the British censors feared the 'dangers of sexual and political "arousal"', which were 'more intertwined than they might at first appear'.[92] Like Kandinsky's 'stimmung' of a picture, which produces a 'corresponding thrill' in the spectator, or his description of being 'tossed about like a tennis ball' when listening to Debussy or Skryabin, Eisenstein's 'overtonal montage' had the '*physiological* quality of Debussy or Scriabin' as opposed to the '*classicism* of Beethoven' (italics in original). The 'theory and methodology' of the musical overtone have been elaborated and made known by Debussy and Skryabin, but *Old and New*, argued Eisenstein, was the first instance of visual overtone.[93]

Eisenstein defined the fourth dimension of cinema in both temporal and spatial terms. In the same way that a symphony creates musical 'overtones' when an orchestra performs it, a film, he argued, has a 'visual overtone' only when run through a projector. Leigh Wilson makes a useful distinction between kinds of movement or animation in relation to Eisenstein's politics. The right kind of movement, for Eisenstein, is linked to revolution and shifting the political status quo whereas the wrong kind simply 'repeats the inertia of the world as it is according to bourgeois capitalism'.[94] The fourth dimension, for Eisenstein, represented a new ideological space. Things that are 'spatially unrepresentable' in three-dimensional space emerge in the 'fourth dimension (three plus time)'. The 'visual overtone' proves to be 'a real piece, a real element . . . of the fourth dimension'. Eisenstein was not alone in connecting cinema with the idea of the fourth dimension. American poet Vachel Lindsay wrote in 1922 that he tried 'to find that fourth dimension of architecture, painting, and sculpture, which is the human soul in action, that arrow with wings which is the flash of fire from the film'.[95]

Eisenstein feigned reluctance for the fourth dimension for dramatic effect by pausing ('a real element . . . of the fourth dimension'). He imagined his reader's incredulity: 'The fourth dimension?!' and responds: 'Einstein? Mysticism?', simultaneously drawing out the scientific and theosophical heritage of the term. About two months before he wrote the article, he met Einstein briefly in Berlin, just before he left for Paris in the autumn of 1929. Eisenstein urged his readers to 'stop being frightened of this "beast", the fourth dimension'. Although one might be 'seized' by a 'mysterious shuddering', Eisenstein reassured his readers that the idea that we live in a 'four-dimensional space–time continuum' is 'common-place'; and soon we shall feel just as much at home in the fourth dimension as if 'we were in our bedsocks!'[96] Eisenstein's fourth dimension of the cinema was not fixed to space or time. He referred to a 'space–time continuum' in the Russian original of the essay and the English translation includes a quotation from Einstein's *Relativity: The Special and the General Theory* to add further scientific authority. The Russian phrase for the 'fourth dimension', 'Chetvertoe izmerenie', can translate as 'fourth measurement', emphasising precision over mysticism.[97] The combination of mystical and scientific language is typical of Eisenstein's writing, itself a form of verbal montage. The fourth dimension was a creative and political space both on and off the screen for Eisenstein.

Eisenstein offered the gods sequence in *October* as an example of intellectual montage because the gods were assembled in accordance with 'a descending intellectual scale – pulling back the concept of God to its origins, forcing the spectator to perceive this "progress" intellectually'. But, he continued,

> this is not yet the intellectual cinema, which I have been announcing for some years! The intellectual cinema will be that which resolves the conflict-juxtaposition of the physiological and intellectual overtones. Building a completely new form of cinematography – the realization of revolution in the general history of culture; building a synthesis of science, art, and class militancy.

Although intellectual montage fits with our understanding of Eisenstein's political aesthetics, its existence relies on overtonal montage. 'In my opinion,' stated Eisenstein, 'the question of the overtone is of vast significance for our film future.'[98]

Borderline

These theories are reflected in one of the cornerstones of British modernist film. In October 1930, POOL, the production arm of *Close Up*, released their fourth film, *Borderline*.[99] It was written and directed by Kenneth Macpherson, with Paul and Eslanda Robeson, H.D., Gavin and Charlotte Arthur, Bryher, Blanche Lewin and Robert Herring all acting in the film. An accompanying programme note explained that Adah (Eslanda Robeson) has been 'involved in an affair' with Thorne (Gavin Arthur) and is staying with the white couple, Thorne and Astrid (H.D.). Adah's husband Pete (Paul Robeson) comes to win back his wife and is staying in the same town in a hotel-café run by the apparently lesbian manager (Bryher). Blanche Lewin plays the fun-loving barmaid at the hotel, and Robert Herring is the piano player. A fight between Astrid and Thorne results in Astrid's 'accidental death'. Thorne is acquitted of her death, Adah leaves town and Pete is also asked to leave by a note from the mayor. Pete is 'a scapegoat for the unresolved problems, evasions and neuroses for which the racial "borderline" has served justification'.[100] H.D.'s essay on the film describes Pete and Adah as a 'borderline couple' of 'dominant integrity'. Astrid and Thorne are, by contrast, 'borderline social cases, not out of life, not in life; the woman is a sensitive neurotic, the man, a handsome, degenerate dipsomaniac'.[101]

Anne Friedberg has written of the film's alliance of the psychoanalyst Hans Sachs's 'Freud-driven theories of the figurational processes of the unconscious and Eisenstein's theories of intellectual montage'.[102] Marcus notes Bryher's meetings and subsequent analysis with Sachs during this period.[103] Judith Brown has read the film through Bertrand Russell's *The Analysis of the Mind* and his theory of a 'sensational space, the space of the unconscious', which is 'obscure, chaotic, and cloaked in mystery'.[104] Others have written extensively on the treatment of homosexuality and race in the film. They note, for example, both the limitations of its racial representations (Paul Robeson is turned into a 'modernist ideal of the Negro male, outside of history') and its experimental methods, which 'draw into radical relief the very processes by which racist fantasies are installed'.[105]

While race, homosexuality and psychoanalysis are significant themes in *Borderline*, Eisenstein's overtonal montage is an underexamined influence. Macpherson wrote in the November 1930 issue of *Close Up*:

> *Borderline* began to be composed about eighteen months ago. It was finished in June of this year. Eighteen months ago Europe was unaware, and so was I, of Eisenstein's now commonly accepted, though little understood, theory of over-tonal montage. Eighteen months ago I decided to make *Borderline* with a 'subjective use of inference.' By this I meant that instead of the method of externalised observation, dealing with objects, I was going to take my film into the minds of the people in it, making it not so much a film of 'mental processes' as to insist on a mental condition. To take the action, the observation, the deduction, the reference, into the labyrinth of the human mind, with its queer impulses and tricks, its unreliability, its stresses and obsessions, its half-formed deductions, its glibness, its

occasional amnesia, its fantasy, suppressions and desires. . . . *Borderline*, then, whether you like it or not, is life. To a mind unaware of *nuance*, to a one-track mind, it would naturally appear chaotic. I do not deny for a moment that it is chaotic. It was intended to be. But over this chaos rings and reverberates one pure, loud, sullen, note. I had no specific name for it, but now we know it is overtone.[106]

Although Macpherson is keen to assert his independence from Eisenstein's 'commonly accepted, though little understood' theory of overtonal montage, Friedberg notes that the planning for *Borderline* began in May 1929, the same month that Eisenstein's first essay was translated for *Close Up*. More importantly, in January 1930, two months before filming commenced, Eisenstein sent Macpherson the manuscript of 'The Fourth Dimension of the Kino', the first part of which was published in March, as the filming started. Marcus notes that Eisenstein's fourth dimension essays 'seem to have been central to Macpherson's conception of the workings of association and the connections between shots in *Borderline*'.[107] She also cites a review from the period that analysed the '"overtonal" mounting' in the film by which an impression from the first scene was carried over to the next.[108] Although Macpherson claimed to have made his film in isolation, the planning and shooting of the film coincided with his coordination of the translations of Eisenstein's montage principles. It is clear that overtonal montage was connected, for Macpherson, with his theories of the subconscious in film. I want to suggest that overtonal montage also released the film from the conventions of two-dimensional representation. Projection was confined to the screen, but the possibilities of space are explored in the film.

Borderline begins with an image that by 1930 was already a cliché in the cinema: a train speeding past the viewpoint and into off-screen space. The film quickly disrupts conventional narrative. A thin disembodied arm (Astrid's) lunges for a telephone, not to answer it, but to ring Pete (Figs 9a and 9b) at the hotel. The telephone conventionally indicates the present moment's continuing in two separate locations, but in this scene the telephone disrupts the continuity of time and space. After Astrid dials we are shown a door swinging (Fig. 9c), a picture falling (Fig. 9d), and then a fight between Thorne and Adah (Figs 9e and 9f); and then finally we are shown the hotel manager picking up Astrid's telephone call. Pete refuses to speak to Astrid, and Astrid stops mid-sentence when she tells Adah where Pete is: 'At the – .' The redundancy of words is replaced by a rapid montage

Fig. 9(a)–(f) Stills from the opening shots of *Borderline*, film, directed by Kenneth Macpherson, GB: Pool Films, 1930.

sequence at the bar of the hotel. H.D. argued that Macpherson was not interested in abstract film, but that he treated everyday things as abstract: 'A telephone receiver of usual form and literacy, is dealt with, as abstraction.'[109] Macpherson himself celebrated the complexity or 'unexplainedness' of the film, likening it to 'something seen through a window or a key-hole'.[110]

Space is treated unconventionally in the film. At the time of the film's release, H.D. argued that 'film montage as *per se*, an art, stands at the moment, with a few brilliant exceptions, almost unexploited'.[111] In the rapid montage sequence that depicts the 'accidental' death of Astrid, space is turned upside down and runs backwards, and so the spectators are not guided through it, as they might have been through the shot-reverse-shot spatial conventions of a contemporary Hollywood film.[112] Just as Astrid reaches towards the knife (Fig. 10a), the shot flips upside down, and the knife, hand and table appear to hover momentarily on the ceiling (Fig. 10b). The recently restored six-minute short, *Monkey's Moon* (1929), made by Macpherson, Bryher and H.D., also uses an 'upside-down' shot of one of the monkeys walking down a dusty path just before it is caught. The disorientating effect closes down the space, setting up the imminent capture.[113] In *Borderline* the shadowy ink bottle that will later be spilled, a cigarette and some papers also appear in this topsy-turvy strip of film. When Astrid brings the knife to slash Thorne's hand, the weight from its new height is intensified (Fig. 10c). H.D. described the 'jagged lightning' effect, which was characterised as 'double exposure' or 'clatter montage' by Eisenstein, achieved in the scene:

> The white woman is here, there, everywhere, the dagger is above, beneath, is all but in her heart or in the heart of her meretricious lover. This effect of immediacy is not achieved by a facile movement of a camera; that would be impossible. It is attained by the cutting and fitting of tiny strips of film, in very much the same manner that you would fit together a jig-saw puzzle.[114]

This 'instantaneous' effect, argued H.D., was Eisenstein's 'innovation' in *Ten Days* (also known as *October*, 1928), in which he cut and fitted together 'minute strips of soldier, gun, gun-fire, soldier, gun'. The sequence appears as superimposition, continued H.D., but was in fact created by the 'meticulous cutting of three and four and five inch lengths of film and pasting these tiny strips together'.[115] H.D. was in a position to understand the editing techniques at first hand. She wrote in her autobiographical notes: 'finished shooting, K develops a bad throat and Bryher and I work over the strips doing the montage as K indicates'.[116] So, because of a sore throat H.D. found herself as editor of the first film to use Eisenstein's theory of overtonal montage in British cinema.

The death scene employs Eisenstein's 'metric montage', in which the shots are accelerated. Objects take on significance beyond their materiality. The vibrating knife held by Astrid signals the tiny cuts of the film strip (Fig. 10d), and when Thorne brings down the knife, instead of witnessing the fatal wound, we are shown a hat with drops of blood (Fig. 10e), the pages of a book closing (Fig. 10f), a table toppling over and a bottle of black ink that spills, like blood, into an ashtray (Fig. 10g). If books and ink signal death, cinema, we can only assume, is life. H.D. argued that for film to become art of 'another dimension', it must

Fig. 10 (a)–(g) Stills from the fight scene in *Borderline*, film, directed by Kenneth Macpherson, GB: Pool Films, 1930.

combine the everyday with the 'super-normal'. The curtain, the stuffed gull and the crowded mantelpiece, wrote H.D., were 'more obviously out of the world than any pantomime effect of cloud spook'.[117] The self-referential quality of the film, which began with the arrival of the train, is sealed by the final shot of the bar manager (Bryher) closing her account book and putting down her pen; Bryher was the financial backer for both POOL and *Close Up*.

H.D. and Eisenstein

Critics disagree about whether H.D. met Eisenstein.[118] The biographical evidence suggests that it is possible that they met in late August or early September of 1928, when H.D. joined Macpherson and Bryher in Berlin and met with the 'great minds' of the 'Russians and Germans', which certainly included Pabst and may have included Eisenstein.[119] Eisenstein's theories of film were, however, an important influence on H.D.'s work. Marcus notes that Eisenstein's 'intellectual montage' was clearly a 'crucial influence on H.D.'s film-writings' and that H.D.'s lifelong interest in hieroglyphics was stimulated by the writings of both Eisenstein and Freud.[120] Rachel Connor draws out a shared sense of the spiritual qualities of cinema spectatorship between Eisenstein and H.D., arguing that H.D.'s construction of the image was grounded in the concepts of collectivity and community from her Moravian upbringing.[121] According to Helen Carr's group biography, the Moravian Brethren 'had a gentle and tolerant way of life' and were 'cultured, valued learning and had a strong musical tradition'.[122] The spheres of influence were mutual: we know that Eisenstein was an avid reader of *Close Up*, and that his friend Pera Attasheva (whom he married in 1934) became the Moscow correspondent of the journal in 1929.[123] This section argues that the shared interest in cinema spectatorship between Eisenstein and H.D. can be further broken down into theories of a physiological response to cinema, and cinema as a new ideological spatial dimension.

H.D.'s interest in alternative narratives and unseen spaces evolved from a young age. Carr documents her early love of the Greek myths, which began when her schoolteacher in Bethlehem read *Tanglewood Tales*, Hawthorne's retelling of Greek myths for children, on Friday afternoons.[124] When H.D. was nine, her family moved to Philadelphia because her father was offered a professorship at the University of Pennsylvania, and in 1905 H.D. passed the entrance examinations to the prestigious women's college Bryn Mawr, where she took courses in Latin, English and Chemistry. Even before she started at Bryn Mawr, H.D. began to teach herself Greek. Her fascination with Greek myths had also been inspired by a student production of Euripides' *Iphigenia in Aulis* at the University of Pennsylvania, in which Pound, in the chorus, was dressed in 'a togalike ensemble topped by a great blond wig at which he tore as he waved his arms about and heaved his massive breasts in ecstasies of emotion'. By the autumn of 1905, H.D. and Pound had embarked on a relationship and he introduced her to the works of William Morris, Ibsen, Shaw and, as she wrote later, 'the *Séraphita* and a volume of Swedenborg – *Heaven and Hell*? Or is that Blake?' and a 'series of Yogi books, too'.[125] Like Pound, H.D. was engaged with non-Western modernity and esotericism.

Initial readings of H.D.'s film theories appear to diverge from Eisenstein's. She was concerned with the 'blur of half tones and hypnotic vibrant darkness' and he with 'Collision. Conflict between two neighbouring fragments. Conflict. Collision'.[126] Closer analysis reveals that their language and their theories of spectatorship and filmic space overlap. In her review of the first Russian film she saw, Kuleshov's *Po Zakonu* (1926), H.D. referred to one of the shots as a hieroglyph, a symbol favoured by Eisenstein. The principle of montage, argued Eisenstein, 'can be identified as the basic element of Japanese representational culture [. . .] The hieroglyph.' Two hieroglyphs form an ideogram, which is 'exactly what we do in cinema, combining shots that are *depictive*, single in meaning, neutral in content – into *intellectual* contexts and series' (italics in original).[127] Describing the female lead, Aleksandra Khokhlova, H.D. wrote that 'she has a way of standing against a sky line that makes a hieroglyph, that spells almost visibly some message of cryptic symbolism. Her gestures are magnificent. If this is Russian, then I am Russian.' The hieroglyph vibrates for H.D., connecting her body with the image of the body on the screen. The heroine's 'mind, her soul, her body, her spirit, her being, all vibrate, as I say, almost audibly' and H.D. is 'attuned to certain vibration'. Rachel Moore has analysed the shift from the personal to the collective experience of watching films and experiencing rituals. For H.D. the moment has moved from the collective to the personal, it is 'psychic, compelling, in a way destructive' and she feels that she could not 'see many of these Russian films if there are others like this. This is my first.'[128]

'Cinema begins', argued Eisenstein, when 'vibration begins'. Metric montage produced the crudest kind of vibration for Eisenstein; he 'really laughed' when he witnessed the more 'impressionable' members of the audience beginning to rock 'slowly from side to side' with increasing acceleration as the shots grew shorter. 'Tonal' montage, by contrast, caused an 'emotional *vibration*' (italics in original) and the overtonal or fourth-dimensional montage sparked the 'kinds of vibrations that once again cease to be perceived as tones but are perceived rather as purely physical "parallaxes" on the part of the perceiver'. The vibrations created by overtonal montage are likened to the effects of 'very large Turkish drums, bells, organs'.[129] Eisenstein's use of parallax in connection with music is obscure, given that sound is not visual. Parallaxes occur when an observer shifts position and an object appears to have moved. Although an image on screen does not move if the spectator moves, Eisenstein is describing the perception of movement. For Slavoj Žižek, subject and object become 'inherently mediated' through parallax and 'the subject's gaze is always-already inscribed into the perceived object itself . . . "Sure the picture is in my eye, but I, I am also in the picture".'[130] Borrowing Žižek's inherent mediation of parallax, we might regard Eisenstein's overtonal parallaxes as binding the spectator to the screen, as experienced by H.D. when she saw Khokhlova against the Yukon landscape.

The word used by Eisenstein for 'vibration' in his essay on the fourth dimension is '*kolebaniia*', which translates as a fluid and irregular movement, like a leaf blowing in the breeze, unlike the small movements around a fixed point implied by 'vibration'.[131] *Kolebaniia* also can suggest wavering or hesitation, satisfying Eisenstein's reluctance to make concrete assertions.[132] In her autobiographical text, *The Gift*, written between 1941 and 1944, H.D. connected a kind of loose vibration and the fourth dimension. She argued that dreams must be allowed to 'sway backward and forward, as if the sheet or screen upon which they are projected, blows and is rippled in the wind'. And later in the text, one of her dreams is 'four-dimensional'; it could not be relegated to a 'collection of dried memories'. If you shut the doors, she argued, you create 'a neat flat picture', but if you 'leave all the doors open', you are 'almost within the un-walled province of the fourth-dimensional'.[133] Like Mary Butts's walls that move to uncharted territory, open doors inspire new ideas about space and visual narrative for H.D. The 'picture-writing, the hieroglyph of the dream' create a universal language, wrote H.D., because they are outside time and space.[134]

H.D. called film an 'art of another dimension', and she made explicit connections between the fourth dimension, cinema, dreams, visions and psychoanalysis.[135] Marcus has analysed H.D.'s transformations of the 'unwalled' fourth wall in Freud's consulting room (a wall with glass

doors) and the room in which she experienced her life-changing projections, or 'picture writing', in Corfu in April 1920. Both spaces, argues
Marcus, become 'sites of projection', turning psychoanalysis into 'a cinematographic arena' with both analyst and analysand 'facing towards a
surface – wall or screen – onto which memories and imaginings could
be projected'.[136] And indeed, it is the depth and not the surface that is
important here. The visions or 'psychic or occult' experiences began as
'colourless transfers', a 'silhouette cut of light, not shadow'; then she
saw the outline of a goblet 'suggesting the mystic chalice', and then
an abstract pattern of two circles joined by lines giving the suggestion
of perspective. These lines evolved into moving pictures, echoing, as
Marcus notes, the history of optics, the evolution from photography
to the moving images of film. We can also map H.D.'s visions on to
Eisenstein's montage principles. The early images reflect metric, rhythmic and tonal montage, and so the final part of the vision, the image
of Nike, represents overtonal montage. The image of Nike is 'not flat
or static, she is in space, in unwalled space, not flat against the wall'.
Nike is released from the wall/screen and freed from the boundaries
of cinematic projection. This freedom connects the image of Nike both
with the psychoanalytic projections on the unwalled wall of Freud's
consulting room and with Eisenstein's theory of parallax and overtonal
montage. During the vision H.D. imagines that one day she too will be
able to travel to 'another, a winged dimension'.[137]

Film critic Robert Herring wrote to Bryher in 1929 that 'my next
article for *Close Up* will be on *Magic*, & will treat of the elimination of
the screen from projection'. He continued the theme in another letter:

> I do not see why, as voice is sound waves, in time we could not do the same
> with light waves, and keep and bring the images of cinema, moving people
> into a room in the same way. Give them depth and all roundness. No screen.[138]

Herring enjoyed playing on the physicality of the medium. By walking
in front of the projectionist's beam, the images created by the 'magic
fingers writing on the wall' are absorbed, and the spectator has the
power to 'hold them' or 'let them go'. In the same way that the voice
can be separated from the body in film, Herring argued that it is
'absurd to be tied down to a screen'.[139]

Herring was not alone in this theory. In December 1929, an article
about Vertov's *Man with a Movie Camera* in *Close Up* noted Vertov's
outlandish theory that films would one day be projected by thought
rather than through a projector. But if Herring wanted to do away with

the screen, the French correspondent for *Close Up*, Jean Lenauer, was interested in Vertov's removal of the projector. The article described Vertov's 'remarkable' theory of cinema in which 'film *thought*[s]' will be projected 'telepathically' and will 'appear simultaneously upon all the screens in the world'. He added that screens would most likely be installed in private dwellings rather than public cinemas.[140] Vertov's theory was perhaps not as outlandish as Lenauer described. 'Kino-eye is a kind of telepathy,' argued Vertov, because it catches people 'without masks, without makeup, to catch them through the eye of the camera in a moment when they are not acting, to read their thoughts, laid bare by the camera'. And as Wilson notes in her chapter on Vertov and telepathy, close-ups were particularly suited to reading thoughts.[141]

While Eisenstein was undoubtedly a propagandist, and described his method of filmmaking in such terms, the subtler and less easily articulated strand to his aesthetics, which he defined in 'The Fourth Dimension in Cinema', is, I think, an important strand of H.D.'s later aesthetics. Overtonal montage releases images from two dimensions into the space in between because a new kind of cinema requires a new perception of space. By appearing to liberate images and blurring the boundaries between spectator and screen, fact and fiction, H.D. and Eisenstein sought to create a new space, a filmic space of four dimensions.

Notes

1. Eisenstein, 'The Dinamic Square', *Close Up*, 8.1 (1931), p. 15.
2. British Film Institute (hereafter BFI), Film Society Collection, Item 6c, Film Society Projects, 'Eisenstein's Lectures in London: A Reconstruction by Basil Wright and J. Isaacs', Saturday 17 December 1949, Third Programme 10.05–10.45 p.m. Transcript.
3. The exact date of Kuleshov's experiments is unclear. Pudovkin's address to the Film Society, 'Types as Opposed to Actors', on 3 February 1929 indicates that he was involved in the experiments when he met Kuleshov in 1920. See *Film Technique and Film Acting: The Cinema Writing of V. I. Pudovkin*, trans. Montagu (London: Vision Press, 1954), pp. 137–41. Kuleshov's description of the experiments does not mention Pudovkin and indicates that they took place in 1918 or 1919. See *Kuleshov on Film*, ed. Levaco, p. 200.
4. Kuleshov, 'Iskusstvo Svetotvorchestva', *Kino*, 12 (1918), quoted in Taylor, *The Politics of the Soviet Cinema*, p. 135.
5. BFI, Film Society Collection, Item 6b, Copy of Pudovkin's Address to the Film Society, 6 February 1929.

6. Sargeant calls the differences between Pudovkin and Eisenstein's theories of montage a 'supposed controversy', arguing that it was defined wholly by Eisenstein because Pudovkin took a practical as opposed to a theoretical approach to filmmaking; see Sargeant, *Vsevolod Pudovkin*, p. xi; Eisenstein, 'Principles of Film Form', p. 173.

7. Trotter, *Cinema and Modernism*, p. 2.

8. Cover wrapper, *Close Up*, 1.4 (1927); see Marcus, 'The Tempo of Revolution', p. 227.

9. Shail, *The Cinema and the Origins of Literary Modernism*, p. 108.

10. Trotter, *Cinema and Modernism*, p. 1.

11. Woolf, 'The Cinema', in *Essays*, IV (1994), pp. 348–54.

12. Eisenstein, 'Perspectives' (1929), in Taylor (ed. and trans.), *Sergei Eisenstein: Selected Works*, I (1988), p. 158. For a useful discussion about the shift of Eisenstein's theories from overtonal towards intellectual montage, see Edmunds, *Out of Line*, p. 202 n35.

13. Humm, *Modernist Women and Visual Cultures*, p. 190.

14. Nesbet, *Savage Junctures*, pp. 48–75.

15. See Friedberg, 'Borderline and the POOL films', pp. 212–20; Marcus, *Tenth Muse*, p. 393.

16. Trotter, *Cinema and Modernism*, p. xi. Even though Bazin argues that the 'question of borrowing' is of 'secondary importance', he notes that 'the way things are' makes it seem that 'the cinema was fifty years behind the novel' and that '*Citizen Kane* would never have existed if it had not been for James Joyce'. Bazin, *What is Cinema?*, I, pp. 63, 64.

17. Cloutier, 'Mumler's Ghosts', p. 21. The essays in this catalogue to the 2005 exhibition of the same name at the Metropolitan Museum of Modern Art inform the history of spirit photography outlined here.

18. Grove, 'Röntgen's Ghosts', p. 142.

19. Mann, *The Magic Mountain*, I, p. 279.

20. Gunning, quoted in *Uncanny Modernity*, ed. Collins and Jervis, p. 5.

21. Freud, 'The Uncanny', in *Literary Theory: An Anthology*, p. 429. Marcus notes that Freud rejected cinema as part of the 'technological uncanny' in the essay through his repression of the identification of the uncanny and the automatic doll in Hoffmann's 'The Sandman': *The Tenth Muse*, p. 43.

22. Grove, 'Röntgen's Ghosts', pp. 145, 149.

23. Marcus, *Tenth Muse*, p. 157.

24. Woolf, *The Waves*, p. 314; Woolf, 'The Cinema', in *Essays*, IV (1994), p. 349.

25. Monks House Photo Albums, volume two, Harvard Theatre Collection, Houghton Library.

26. Georges Méliès was probably the most famous filmmaker who made use of trick photography in his hundreds of fantastical films: for example, *A Vanishing Lady* (1896) or *Journey to the Moon* (1902).

27. Tsivian, *Early Cinema in Russia*, p. 4.

28. Gunning, 'Tracing the Individual Body', p. 16.
29. Tsivian, *Early Cinema in Russia*, p. 6.
30. 'Meanings, declamations, false sentimentality and objective description'. Jean Moréas, 'Manifeste du Symbolisme', *Le Figaro*, 18 September 1886, <http://www.ieeff.org/manifestesymbolisme> [accessed 20 May 2014].
31. Christie, *The Last Machine*, p. 111.
32. Gorky, 'The Kingdom of Shadows', p. 10.
33. Marcus, *Tenth Muse*, p. 74.
34. Tsivian, *Early Cinema in Russia*, pp. 18, 150.
35. Leadbeater, *Clairvoyance*, p. 7.
36. Leadbeater, *The Astral Plane*, p. 17. (The pamphlet was translated from French into Russian as *Astral'nyi plan* by A. V. Troianovskii (St Petersburg: V. L. Bogushevskii, 1908).)
37. Marcus, *Tenth Muse*, p. 365.
38. Armstrong, *Modernism, Technology, and the Body*, pp. 226, 227, 228.
39. Tsivian, *Early Cinema in Russia*, p. 111.
40. Woolf, 'The Cinema', in *Essays*, IV (1994), pp. 350, 351.
41. BFI, Film Society Collection, Item 45b, David Robinson manuscript, 'The Career and Times of the Film Society'. Further references abbreviated to 'Career and Times'; *The Film Society Programmes 1925–1939*, p. 32 (8th performance, 30 May 1926).
42. Marcus, 'The Tempo of Revolution', pp. 225–40.
43. Quoted in Marcus, *Tenth Muse*, p. 265.
44. BFI, Film Society Collection, Item 45a, Correspondence regarding commission to write a history of the Film Society 1959–63, Iris Barry letters. Film critic for the *Daily Mail*, *The Spectator*, *The Adelphi* and *Vogue*, Barry was also a published poet, founding member of both the London and the New York Film Societies, and Curator and then Director of the Film Library of the Museum of Modern Art in New York.
45. BFI, Robinson, 'Career and Times', p. 280.
46. *Film Society Programmes*, p. 98 (25th performance, 21 October 1928).
47. BFI, Robinson, 'Career and Times', p. 281.
48. Herring, 'The Movies', *London Mercury*, 19.110 (1928), p. 201.
49. 'The Film Society: "Mother"', *The Times*, 22 October 1928, p. 12.
50. BFI, Robinson, 'Career and Times', p. 286.
51. Montagu, 'The Film Society: London', *Cinema Quarterly*, 1.1 (1932–3), quoted in Marcus, *Tenth Muse*, p. 273.
52. Simpson, 'The Cinema', *The Spectator*, 9 February 1929, p. 191; Hellmund-Waldow, Review of *The End of St Petersburg*, *Close Up*, 2.4 (1928), p. 32.
53. Macpherson, 'As Is', *Close Up*, 2.4 (1928), p. 10.
54. *Film Society Programmes*, p. 131 (33rd performance, 10 November 1929).
55. Marcus, *Tenth Muse*, p. 270.
56. BFI, Robinson, 'Career and Times', p. 297.
57. Bryher, *Film Problems of Soviet Russia*, p. 33.

58. 'The Film Society: "The Battleship Potemkin"', *The Times*, 12 November 1929, p. 14.
59. BFI, Robinson, 'Career and Times', pp. 298, 297.
60. *Film Society Programmes*, p. 130 (33rd performance, 10 November 1929).
61. Bryher, *Film Problems of Soviet Russia*, p. 11.
62. BFI, Robinson, 'Career and Times', p. 312.
63. Bryher, 'Pre-View of *The General Line*', *Close Up*, 6.1 (1930), pp. 38, 39.
64. BFI, Marie Seton Collection, Item 35, Eisenstein to Macpherson letter, 27 January 1930.
65. Michelson, *New Forms in Film* (exhibition catalogue), Montreux (1974), p. 10, quoted in Marcus, *Tenth Muse*, p. 274.
66. Bryher to H.D. (28 October 1927, Beinecke), quoted in Marcus, *Tenth Muse*, p. 334; frontispiece, *Close Up*, 4.1 (1929).
67. Macpherson, 'As Is', *Close Up*, 3.3 (1928), pp. 5, 8, 13.
68. Macpherson, 'As Is', *Close Up*, 1.1 (1927), p. 7.
69. Macpherson, 'As Is', *Close Up*, 2.1 (1928), pp. 5–6.
70. Barry, *Let's Go to the Pictures*, p. 216.
71. Seton, *Sergei M. Eisenstein*, p. 144.
72. BFI, Film Society Collection, Item 6c, 'Pamphlet for Eisenstein's Study Groups'.
73. BFI, Film Society Collection, Item 6c, Film Society Projects, Wright and Isaacs transcript. Basil Wright's notes are printed in full as appendix two in Seton's biography, pp. 482–5.
74. Lövgren, 'Sergei Eisenstein's Gnostic Circle', p. 278.
75. Eisenstein, Pudovkin and Alexandrov, 'The Sound Film: A Statement from U.S.S.R.', *Close Up*, 3.4 (1928), pp. 11, 12. This manifesto was first published in an authorised German translation as 'Achtung! Goldgrube!! Gedanken über die Zukunft des Hörfilms' in *Die Lichtbildbühne* on 28 July 1928. The Russian original was first published as 'Zayavka' in *Zhizn' iskusstva*, 5 August 1928.
76. Eisenstein, 'The New Language of Cinematography', *Close Up*, 4.5 (1929), p. 11.
77. Eisenstein, 'The Fourth Dimension in the Kino', parts I and II, *Close Up*, 6.3–4 (1930).
78. BFI, Marie Seton Collection, Item 35, Eisenstein to Macpherson letters, 2 January 1930.
79. Quoted in Marcus, *Tenth Muse*, p. 343.
80. Eisenstein, 'The Fourth Dimension in Cinema', p. 182.
81. Eisenstein, 'The Fourth Dimension in Cinema', pp. 183, 184.
82. Seton, *Sergei M. Eisenstein*, p. 102.
83. Macpherson, 'Introduction', in 'The Fourth Dimension in the Kino', *Close Up*, 6.3 (1930), p. 177.
84. Seton, *Sergei M. Eisenstein*, p. 484.
85. Eisenstein, 'The Fourth Dimension in Cinema', p. 186.

86. Seton, *Sergei M. Eisenstein*, p. 484.

87. Eisenstein, 'Methods of Montage', p. 76.

88. Eisenstein, 'The Fourth Dimension in Cinema', pp. 183, 191.

89. BFI, Film Society Collection, Item 6c, Film Society Projects, Wright and Isaacs transcript. It is unclear at which point 'overtonal' became 'overtonic' in Wright's account, either in his own notes from Eisenstein's lectures or in the transcript of the radio programme.

90. Bell, *Art*, p. 11; Kandinsky, *Concerning the Spiritual in Art*, p. 52. French film theorists of the 1910s and 1920s were fascinated by Epstein's concept of 'photogénie', which referred to the shock of seeing ordinary things as if for the first time; see Ray, *How a Film Theory Got Lost*.

91. Eisenstein, 'Methods of Montage', pp. 78, 79.

92. Marcus, 'The Tempo of Revolution', p. 232.

93. Kandinsky, *The Art of Spiritual Harmony*, pp. 8, 34; Eisenstein, 'The Fourth Dimension in Cinema', pp. 183, 186. Henderson notes that Skryabin, 'who had a strong mystical orientation that was stimulated by Theosophy and, very likely, Ouspensky's writings', recorded his 'interest in a "many-measured space" beyond three dimensions in 1915, the year of his death'; quoted in Henderson, *The Fourth Dimension*, p. 240.

94. Wilson, *Modernism and Magic*, p. 141.

95. Quoted in *Tenth Muse*, p. 197.

96. Eisenstein, 'The Fourth Dimension in Cinema', p. 185.

97. Eisenstein, 'Chetvertoe izmerenie v kino', p. 49.

98. Eisenstein, 'Methods of Montage', in *Film Form*, pp. 82, 83.

99. *Borderline* was shown at a limited number of film society and *ciné-club* screenings, and at the Academy Cinema in London in October 1930. It was also later screened in Brussels, Catalonia and Berlin. See *Close Up 1927–1933*, ed. Donald, Friedberg and Marcus, p. 220. The first three films were the short films *Wing Beat* (1927), *Foothills* (1929) and *Monkey's Moon* (1929).

100. *Borderline* programme note, Beinecke Rare Book and Manuscript library, Yale University, quoted in Friedberg, 'Borderline and the POOL films', p. 218.

101. H.D., '*Borderline*: A Pool Film with Paul Robeson', p. 221.

102. Friedberg, '*Borderline* and the POOL films', p. 218.

103. Marcus, *Tenth Muse*, p. 27.

104. See Brown, '*Borderline*, Sensation and the Machinery of Expression', p. 694.

105. Carby, *Race Men*, p. 68; McCabe, 'Borderline Modernism', p. 639. See also Walton, 'White Neurotics, Black Primitives, and the Queer Matrix of *Borderline*', pp. 243–70.

106. Macpherson, 'As Is', *Close Up*, 7.5 (1930), in *Close Up 1927–1933*, ed. Donald, Friedberg and Marcus, pp. 236, 237.

107. Marcus, *Tenth Muse*, p. 393.

108. 'Mercurius', 'Act, Fact and Abstraction', *Architectural Review*, 68 (1930), p. 258, quoted in Marcus, *Tenth Muse*, p. 393.

109. H.D., '*Borderline*', p. 223.

110. Macpherson, 'As Is', *Close Up*, 7.5 (1930), in *Close Up 1927–1933*, ed. Donald, Friedberg and Marcus, p. 238.

111. H.D., '*Borderline*', p. 228.

112. For descriptions of Hollywood editing conventions of the period, see Bordwell, Staiger and Thompson, *The Classical Hollywood Cinema* ([1985] 1996).

113. *Monkey's Moon* has been restored and digitized, and can be viewed at beinecke.library.yale.edu/collections/highlights/monkeys-moon-pool-films [accessed 20 May 2014].

114. Eisenstein, 'A Dialectic Approach to Film Form', in *Film Form*, p. 55; H.D., '*Borderline*', p. 230.

115. H.D., '*Borderline*', p. 230.

116. H.D., 'Autobiographical Notes', quoted in *Close Up 1927–1933*, ed. Donald, Friedberg and Marcus, p. 334 n26.

117. H.D., '*Borderline*', pp. 232, 235, 236.

118. Edmunds claims that Eisenstein may have been one of the 'great minds' that H.D. spoke to in Berlin in 1928, referred to in H.D.'s September 1928 essay in *Close Up*, 'Russian Films' (Edmunds, *Out of Line*, p. 203 n51). Connor argues that it is unlikely that they ever met (*H.D. and the Image*). Guest does not refer to a meeting in her biography of H.D., *Herself Defined*. Marie Seton claims that Eisenstein went to Berlin in 1929: Seton, *Sergei M. Eisenstein*, p. 125.

119. H.D., 'Russian Films', p. 136.

120. Marcus, *Tenth Muse*, p. 365.

121. Connor, *H.D. and the Image*, p. 14.

122. Carr, *The Verse Revolutionaries*, p. 9.

123. Eisenstein requested copies of previous issues of *Close Up* on at least two separate occasions and asked Macpherson for a copy of Frederick Carter's *D. H. Lawrence and the Body Mystical*, which had been advertised in the journal. BFI, Marie Seton Collection, Item 35, Eisenstein/Macpherson Letters.

124. Carr, *The Verse Revolutionaries*, p. 43.

125. Carr, *The Verse Revolutionaries*, pp. 43, 56, 59.

126. H.D., 'The Cinema and the Classics III', p. 120; Eisenstein, 'Beyond the Shot', p. 144.

127. Kuleshov's *Po Zakonu* (1926) is now translated as *By the Law* but referred to as *Expiation* or *Sühne* in H.D.'s article. Eisenstein, 'The Cinematographic Principle and the Ideogram', pp. 28, 30.

128. H.D., 'Expiation', pp. 126, 127. See Moore, *Savage Theory*.

129. Eisenstein, 'The Fourth Dimension in Cinema', p. 192. Eisenstein's theory of overtones was likely to have been influenced by the acoustic

theory of the German physicist Hermann von Helmotz, who worked on the sensation of tone and perception of sound.
130. Žižek, *The Parallax View*, p. 17.
131. I am grateful to Dunja Popovic for pointing out this nuance.
132. *Oxford Russian Dictionary*, ed. Marcus Wheeler and others, 4th edn (Oxford: Oxford University Press, 2007), p. 182.
133. H.D., *The Gift*, pp. 83, 84.
134. H.D., *Tribute to Freud*, p. 71.
135. H.D.'s analysis with Freud and the impact on her work is discussed in Edmunds's *Out of Line* and Susan Stanford Friedman's *Psyche Reborn*. Marcus argues that H.D. saw her sessions with Freud as a way 'of continuing or perhaps replacing, the work of film' because analysing dreams and using symbolic interpretation were an extension of the interpretation of silent cinema; *Tenth Muse*, p. 365.
136. Marcus, *Tenth Muse*, pp. 366–7.
137. H.D., *Tribute to Freud*, pp. 45, 56.
138. Herring to Bryher, Beinecke, quoted in Marcus, *Tenth Muse*, p. 378.
139. Herring, 'A New Cinema', pp. 54, 56.
140. Lenauer, 'Vertoff: His Work and the Future', p. 465.
141. Quoted in Wilson, *Modernism and Magic*, pp. 109, 132.

Epilogue

In *Orlando* Woolf mocks the Russophilia of the previous decade, describing how in Russia the 'sunsets are longer, the dawns less sudden, and sentences often left unfinished from doubt as to how best to end them – '.[1] More recently, foreign ministers Sergei Lavrov and William Hague declared 2014 the 'Russia–UK Year of Culture', just before political events in Crimea and Ukraine began to put bilateral relations under considerable stress. This is not unusual, as Donald Rayfield observed; the cultural relationship between Russia and Britain has 'typically been out of sync with the political'.[2] In fact, conflict inspires cultural curiosity, as revealed, for example, by the mutual interest triggered by the Crimean War. And the urge to draw the two nations together has persisted over time. Just as Winifred Stephens wrote in *The Soul of Russia* (1916) that her volume might 'knit more closely those bonds of mutual interest and friendship which unite us to our heroic Ally', almost a century later the 'Russia–UK Year of Culture 2014' aims to 'foster cultural exchange, increase the flow of ideas and develop stronger relationships between people, institutions and governments'.[3]

The interest in the unseen was one of the many strands that made up the widespread appeal for Russia, a place unknown to most people in modernist Britain. Russia offered a full range of imagined possibilities, from high-brow intellectualism to rural peasant idyll, from pure authentic realism to highly constructed aesthetics, from radical revolutionaries to exiled white Russians devoid of all possessions. Russia, in short, offered most things that anyone could imagine. And so, whilst it is not new to think through the appeal, or indeed the distaste for Russia in modernist Britain, the focus here has been the specifically occultist discourse through which Russomania and Russophobia were mediated.

There is clearly scope for further research on the cultural exchange and reciprocal influence on both cultures, building, for example, on the work of Rachel Polonsky.[4] My research has revealed that ideas about Russia and Russians, and ideas about the unseen were not static, but were shaped and reshaped by both East and West. As Dostoevsky wrote in 1876, 'We Russians' 'have two motherlands: our Rus, and Europe'. He continued:

> Much of what we have taken from Europe and translated to our country has not merely been copied by us . . . but has been grafted into our organism, into our flesh and blood . . . every European poet, thinker and philanthropist is always most fully and intimately understood and accepted in Russia in all the countries of the world apart from his own . . . [5]

It would be worth exploring the repatriation of British versions of Russia and how ideas of the 'Russian soul', which emerged from eighteenth-century European romanticism, were reconfigured in Russia, in terms of twentieth-century British mysticism. Some of the cultural interchange discussed here includes Ouspensky's introduction of, to Russian readers, the work of Charles Howard, from whom he quoted extensively in *Tertium Organum* (1911) before Hinton's books were translated into Russian in 1915.[6] Ouspensky also borrowed from texts by Richard Maurice Bucke and Edward Carpenter. Theosophical works by Helena Blavatsky and Annie Besant, as well as work by the psychical researchers Frederic Myers and Edmund Gurney, were translated into Russian and widely read.[7] Lev Tolstoy admired Edward Carpenter, calling him a 'worthy heir of Carlyle and Ruskin', and enabled the translation of Carpenter's *Civilisation* into Russian in 1899.[8] In turn, Tolstoy's *What is Art* became central to Fry's distinction between an active and imaginative life in 'An Essay on Aesthetics' (1909). The research has highlighted some of the networks of ideas that may have originated in the West, but gained intellectual authority by being rerouted through the East.

An unexpected outcome of my research has been that, by concentrating on the contribution of occultism via Russia to the forms of British modernism, the research has challenged formalist readings of modernist aesthetics. In other words, unpicking the forms has dismantled the formalism. The study contributes to the broader project within modernist scholarship that challenges the notion that formalism and abstraction during the early twentieth century were solely concerned with the shapes and structures of works of art, primarily a legacy of the criticism of Clement Greenberg and Alfred H. Barr in the 1930s and 1940s. Early modernist scholarship provided a model that did not look at the esoteric traditions of artists and writers, but concentrated on the rationality and ordering of formal qualities of art, epitomised by Eliot's famous essay of 1923 in which he set out Joyce's use of myth as 'a way of controlling, of ordering, of giving a shape and a significance to the immense panorama of futility and anarchy which is contemporary history'.[9] There was also a very real sense of political danger associated with mystical and occult ideas. Maurice Tuchman notes, for example, that the Nazi theory of Aryan supremacy was indebted to strands of theosophy, including ariosophy, which fused ideas of karma, the ether and sun worship with the idolatry of Aryan ancestry.[10] And so, rather than deny the unseen to avoid the politics, it is now possible and unavoidable to recognise that spirituality and abstraction, or mysticism and modernism, were inextricable. And indeed, as I have indicated, further research is needed into the relationship between Russian occultism, politics and aesthetics. Rather than refer exclusively to those modernists who were explicit about their intellectual engagement with esoteric traditions, the book has sought to locate a particularly Russian-inflected mysticism within the mainstream of British modernist aesthetics: the post-impressionism of Fry and Woolf, the romanticism of Murry and Mansfield, the materialism of Mary Butts and the film writing of H.D.

In his essay on the 'Aetiology of Hysteria', written in 1896, Freud argued that in order to cure a hysteric, one must lead the patient to the place in which his symptoms arose, and recreate the traumatic scene in order to correct the course of events. He likens this to an archaeologist's digging amongst ruins, which may, with 'good luck', reveal 'an alphabet and a language, and, when they have been deciphered and translated' may 'yield undreamed-of information about the events of the remote past [. . .] *Saxa loquntur!*' [stones talk!].[11] The current emphasis on the things of modernism in modernist studies is not at odds with a study that foregrounds the unseen. Modernism, mysticism and materiality should be examined in relation, not in opposition, to each other. Objects, or – in their de-commodified state – things, come alive, stones talk, and unseen forces lurk in discarded pieces of china or in a fourth dimension of space.

Notes

1. Woolf, *Orlando*, p. 21.
2. Rayfield, 'False Teeth and Frozen Fish', p. 11.
3. Stephens, *The Soul of Russia*, pp. v–vi. See also Hellberg-Hirn, *Soil and*

Soul (1998), for a cultural studies approach to ideas of Russianness and the Russian soul; www.ukrussia2014.ru [accessed 20 May 2014]

4. Polonsky, *English Literature and the Russian Aesthetic Renaissance.*

5. Dostoevsky, *Polnoe sobranie sochinenii*, 12 vols (St Petersburg, 1894–5), vol. x, pt 1, pp. 204–5. Quoted in Polonsky, *English Literature*, p. 1.

6. Hinton's works included *Vospitanie voobraheniia i chetvertoe izmerenie* [Training the imagination and the fourth dimension], with an introduction by Ouspensky (Petrograd: M. Pirozhkov, 1915), and *Chetvertoe izmerenie i era novoi mysli* [The fourth dimension and an era of new thought] (Petrograd: Novyi chelovek, 1915).

7. See Kasinec and Kerdimun, 'Occult Literature in Russia', in *The Spiritual in Art*, pp. 361–5.

8. Tolstoy, 'Modern Science', *New Age*, 31 (1898), quoted in Tsuzuki, *Edward Carpenter 1844–1929*, p. 2.

9. Eliot, '*Ulysses*, Order and Myth', p. 177.

10. Tuchman, 'Hidden Meanings in Abstract Art', p. 18.

11. Freud, 'The Aetiology of Hysteria', p. 192.

Bibliography

Archives (showing abbreviations)

Beinecke Rare Book and Manuscript Library, Yale University.
  Mary Butts Papers.
British Film Institute (BFI) Special Collections.
  Film Society Collection.
  Marie Seton Collection, Eisenstein / Macpherson Correspondence.
Harry Ransom Humanities Research Center (HRHRC), University of Texas at Austin.
  Mary Hutchinson Papers, Series II, Correspondence 1910–77.
  Ottoline Morrell Collection, Series II, Correspondence 1894–1938.
Harvard Theatre Collection, Houghton Library, Harvard College Library.
  Monks House Photo Albums, volume two.
King's College Archive Centre (KCAC), Cambridge.
  Papers of Roger Eliot Fry (REF).
National Art Library (NAL) Special Collections, UK.
  Boris Anrep Papers.
Tate Gallery Archive (TGA), London.
  Correspondence between Kandinsky and the Sadlers.

Bibliography

Aitken, Charles, discussion following Anrep's paper 'Mosaics', *Journal of the Royal Institute of British Architects*, 34.6 (1927), pp. 203–11.
Allied Artists' Association Catalogue (London, 1908).
Allied Artists' Association Catalogue (London, 1912).
Alpers, Anthony, *The Life of Katherine Mansfield* (London: Jonathan Cape, 1980).
Andreieff, Léonide, 'The Present', *Rhythm*, 2.9 (1912), pp. 207–13.
Anrep, Boris, 'Anrep's Speech at Opening of East Vestibule of National Gallery' (13 November 1933), NAL, Manuscript, MSL/1974/16160.
—, 'Mosaics', *Journal of the Royal Institute of British Architects*, 34.6 (1927), pp. 203–11.

—, 'Po Povodu Londonskoi Vystavki s "Uchastiem' Russkikh" Khudozhnikov Salon' ['Report of an Exhibition in London in which Russian Artists Participated'], *Apollon*, 2 (1912), pp. 39–48.

—, 'The Russian Group', *Catalogue of the Second Post-Impressionist Exhibition* (1912), pp. 18–21, in Bullen, ed., *Post-Impressionists in England*, pp. 356–8.

—, 'Works by Boris von Anrep', *Chenil Gallery Catalogue* (London: Charles Chenil, 1913).

Antliff, Mark, 'The Fourth Dimension and Futurism: A Politicized Space', *The Art Bulletin*, 82.4 (2000), pp. 720–33.

—, *Inventing Bergson: Cultural Politics and the Parisian Avant-Garde* (Princeton: Princeton University Press, 1993).

Antliff, Mark and Patricia Leighten, *Cubism and Culture* (London: Thames & Hudson, 2001).

Apollinaire, Guillaume, 'The New Painting: Art Notes' (1912), in *Apollinaire on Art: Essays and Reviews 1902–1912*, ed. LeRoy Breunig and trans. Susan Suleiman (New York: Viking, 1972).

Apraxine, Pierre and Sophie Schmit, 'Photography and the Occult', in *The Perfect Medium: Photography and the Occult*, ed. Clément Chéroux et al. (New Haven, CT: Yale University Press, 2005), pp. 12–17.

Ardis, Ann, 'Staging the Public Sphere: Magazine Dialogism and the Prosthetics of Authorship at the Turn of the Twentieth Century', in *Transatlantic Print Culture, 1880–1940: Emerging Media, Emerging Modernisms*, ed. Ann Ardis and Patrick Collier (Basingstoke: Palgrave Macmillan, 2008), pp. 30–47.

—, *Modernism and Cultural Conflict: 1880–1922* (Cambridge: Cambridge University Press, 2002).

Armstrong, Tim, *Modernism: A Cultural History* (Cambridge: Polity Press, 2005).

—, *Modernism, Technology, and the Body: A Cultural Study* (Cambridge: Cambridge University Press, 1998).

Arnold, Matthew, *The Works of Matthew Arnold*, 15 vols (London: Macmillan, 1903–4), IV (1903).

'Art at Moscow', *The Times*, 3 October 1882, p. 4.

'Art's Enigma', *The Saturday Review*, 15 August 1914, pp. 202–3.

'An Art Victory: Triumphant Exit of the Post-Impressionists', *Daily Graphic*, 16 January 1911, p. 15, in Bullen, ed., *Post-Impressionists in England*, pp. 183–4.

Banfield, Ann, *The Phantom Table: Woolf, Fry, Russell and the Epistemology of Modernism* (Cambridge: Cambridge University Press, 2000).

Banks, Georges, 'The New Spirit in Art and Drama', *Rhythm*, 2.12 (1913), p. 339.

—, 'Pétrouchka', *Rhythm*, 2.2 (1912), pp. 57–63.

Banta, Martha, *Henry James and the Occult: The Great Extension* (Bloomington: Indiana University Press, 1972).

Baring, Maurice, *Landmarks in Russian Literature* (London: Methuen, 1910).

Barry, Iris, *Let's Go to the Pictures* (London: Chatto & Windus, 1926).

Bazin, André, *What is Cinema?* 2 vols (Berkeley: University of California Press, 1967).

Beasley, Rebecca, 'Reading Russian: Russian Studies and the Literary Canon', in Beasley and Bullock, eds, *Russia in Britain*, pp. 162–87.

—, 'Russia and the Invention of the Modernist Intelligentsia', in *Geographies of Modernism: Literatures, Cultures, Spaces*, ed. Peter Brooker and Andrew Thacker (Abingdon: Routledge, 2005), pp. 19–30.

Beasley, Rebecca and Philip Ross Bullock, 'Introduction Against Influence: On Writing about Russian Culture in Britain', in *Russia in Britain*, pp. 1–18.

—, eds, *Russia in Britain, 1880–1940: From Melodrama to Modernism* (Oxford: Oxford University Press, 2013).

—, eds, *Translating Russia, 1890–1935*, special issue of *Translation and Literature*, 20.3 (2011).

Beer, Patricia, 'Very like Poole Harbour', *London Review of Books*, 5 December 1991, pp. 16–17.

Bell, Clive, *Art* (London: Chatto & Windus, 1914).

—, 'The English Group', *Catalogue of the Second Post-Impressionist Exhibition* (1912), pp. 9–12, in Bullen, ed., *Post-Impressionists in England*, pp. 349–51.

Bell, Ian, 'Ezra Pound and the Materiality of the Fourth Dimension', in *Science in Modern Poetry: New Directions* (Liverpool: Liverpool University Press, 2012), pp. 130–50.

—, 'The Poundian Fourth Dimension', *Symbiosis: A Journal of Anglo-American Literary Relations*, 11.2 (October 2007).

Benstock, Shari, *Women of the Left Bank* (Austin: University of Texas Press, 1986).

Bergson, Henri, *Creative Evolution*, authorised trans. Arthur Mitchell (London: Macmillan, 1911).

—, *L'Évolution créatrice* (Paris: Félix Alcan, 1907).

Besant, Annie and C. W. Leadbeater, *Thought-Forms* (London: Theosophical Publishing Society, [1901] 1905).

Binckes, Faith, *Modernism, Magazines, and the British Avant-Garde* (Oxford: Oxford University Press, 2010).

Binyon, Laurence, *The Flight of the Dragon: An Essay on the Theory and Practice of Art in China and Japan, Based on Original Sources* (London: Murray, [1911] 1935).

—, *Painting in the Far East* (London: Arnold, 1908).

—, 'The Return to Poetry', *Rhythm*, 1.4 (1912), pp. 1–2.

Blacklock, Mark, 'The Emergence of the Fourth Dimension: A Cultural History of Higher Space, 1869–1909' (unpublished doctoral thesis, University of London, 2013).

Blakesley, Rosalind and Susan Reid, eds, *Russian Art and the West: A Century of Dialogue in Painting, Architecture, and the Decorative Arts* (DeKalb: Northern Illinois University Press, 2007).

Blavatsky, Helena, *Isis Unveiled: A Master-Key to the Mysteries of Ancient and Modern Science and Theology* (Pasadena: Theosophical University Press, [1877] 1972).

—, *Secret Doctrine: The Synthesis of Science, Religion, and Philosophy*, 3 vols (London: Theosophical Society, [1888] 1905).

—, *The Voice of the Silence* (London: Theosophical Publishing Society, 1889).

Blondel, Nathalie, *The Journals of Mary Butts* (New Haven, CT: Yale Univeristy Press, 2002).

—, *Mary Butts: Scenes from the Life* (Kingston, NY: McPherson, 1998).

Bordwell, David, Janet Staiger and Kristin Thompson, *The Classical Hollywood Cinema: Film Style and Mode of Production to 1960* (London: Routledge, [1985] 1996).

Bragdon, Claude, *Four-Dimensional Vistas* (London: Routledge, 1923).

Brewster, Dorothy, *East–West Passage: A Study in Literary Relationships* (London: George Allen & Unwin, 1954).

Brooke, Rupert, *Cambridge Magazine*, 23 November 1912, pp. 125–6, and 30 November 1912, pp. 158–9, in Bullen, ed. *Post-Impressionists in England*, pp. 403–8.

—, 'Choriambics – I', *Collected Poems with a Memoir by Edward Marsh* (London: Sidgwick & Jackson, [1918] 1947).

Brooker, Peter, and Andrew Thacker, 'General Introduction', in *The Oxford Critical and Cultural History of Modernist Magazines* (Oxford: Oxford University Press, 2009).

Brown, Bill, 'The Secret Life of Things (Virginia Woolf and the Matter of Modernism)', *Modernism/Modernity*, 6.2 (1999), pp. 1–28.

—, *A Sense of Things: The Object Matter of American Literature* (Chicago: University of Chicago Press, 2003).

Brown, Judith, '*Borderline*, Sensation and the Machinery of Expression', *Modernism/Modernity*, 14.4 (2007), pp. 687–705.

Bryher, *Film Problems of Soviet Russia* (Territet, Switzerland: Pool Publishing, 1929).

—, 'Pre-View of *The General Line*', *Close Up*, 6.1 (1930), pp. 34–9.

Buchan, John, 'Space' (1911), in *The Best Supernatural Stories of John Buchan*, ed. Peter Haining (London: Robert Hale, 1991), pp. 145–59.

Bullen, J. B., 'Byzantinism and Modernism 1900–1914', *Burlington Magazine*, 141 (1999), pp. 665–75.

—, *Byzantium Rediscovered: The Byzantine Revival in Europe and America* (London: Phaidon, 2003).

—, ed., *Post-Impressionists in England* (London: Routledge, 1988).

Bullock, Philip, *Rosa Newmarch and Russian Music in Late Nineteenth and Early Twentieth-Century England* (Farnham: Ashgate, 2009).

—, 'Russian Music in London', in Beasley and Bullock, eds, *Russia in Britain*, pp. 113–28.

Burkdall, Thomas, *Joycean Frames: Film and the Fiction of James Joyce* (London: Routledge, 2001).

Burwick, Frederick and Paul Douglass, eds, *The Crisis in Modernism: Bergson and the Vitalist Controversy* (Cambridge: Cambridge University Press, 1992).

Butts, Mary, *Armed with Madness* (1928), in *The Taverner Novels: Armed with Madness and Death of Felicity Taverner* (Kingston, NY: McPherson, 1992).

—, *Ashe of Rings* (Paris: Three Mountains Press, 1925).

—, 'Avenue Montaigne', *Antaeus*, 12 (Winter 1973), pp. 151–2.

—, *The Crystal Cabinet: My Childhood at Salterns* (London: Methuen, 1937).

—, *Death of Felicity Taverner* (1932), in *The Taverner Novels: Armed with Madness and Death of Felicity Taverner* (Kingston, NY: McPherson, 1992).

—, 'Ghosties and Ghoulies: Uses of the Supernatural in English Fiction', *The Bookman*, 83 (1933), pp. 386–9.

—, 'Mappa Mundi', in *From Altar to Chimney-Piece: Selected Stories of Mary Butts* (New York: McPherson, 1992), pp. 218–33.

—, *Traps for Unbelievers* (London: Desmond Harmsworth, 1932).

—, 'With and Without Buttons', in *From Altar to Chimney-Piece*, pp. 22–38.

Carby, Hazel, *Race Men* (Cambridge, MA: Harvard University Press, 1998).

Carlson, Maria, 'Fashionable Occultism: Spiritualism, Theosophy, Freemasonry, and Hermeticism in Fin-de-Siècle Russia', in Rosenthal, ed., *The Occult in Russian and Soviet Culture*, pp. 135–52.

—, *'No Religion Higher Than Truth': A History of the Theosophical Movement in Russia, 1875–1922* (Princeton: Princeton University Press, 1993).

—, and Robert H. Davis, 'Russian Occult Journals and Newspapers', in Rosenthal, ed., *The Occult in Russian and Soviet Culture*, pp. 423–43.

Carpenter, Edward, *Angels' Wings: A Series of Essays on Art and its Relation to Life* (London: Swan Sonnenschein, 1898).

Carr, Helen, *The Verse Revolutionaries: Ezra Pound, H.D. and the Imagists* (London: Jonathan Cape, 2009).

Carter, Huntly, 'Art and Drama', *The New Age*, 10.4 (1911), p. 84.

—, 'Art and Drama', *The New Age*, 10.10 (1912), p. 227.

—, 'Art and Drama in Paris', *The New Age*, 10.19 (1912), p. 443.

—, 'The "Blue Bird" and Bergson in Paris', *The New Age*, 9.2 (1911), pp. 43–5.

—, 'New Books on Art', *The Egoist*, 1.12 (1914), pp. 235–6.

—, *The New Spirit in Drama and Art* (London: Frank Palmer, 1912).

—, 'The Russian Ballets in Paris and London', *The New Age*, 9.9 (1911), pp. 209–11.

'Cases for Binding Rhythm', Advertising Section, *Rhythm*, 1.4 (1912), p. iv.

Cassavant, Sharron Greer, *John Middleton Murry: The Critic as Moralist* (Tuscaloosa: University of Alabama Press, 1982).

Catalogue to the Second Salon of the Allied Artists' Association (London, 1909), nos 1068–9, 1923.

Certeau, Michel de, *The Mystic Fable: The Sixteenth and Seventeenth Centuries*, trans. Michael Smith (Chicago: University of Chicago Press, 1992).

Chadd, David and John Gage, eds, *The Diaghilev Ballet in England* (Norwich: Sainsbury Centre for Visual Arts [n. pub.], 1979).

Chamot, Mary, Dennis Farr and Martin Butlin, *Tate Gallery Catalogue: The Modern British Paintings, Drawings and Sculpture*, 2 vols (London: Oldbourne Press, 1964).

Child, Harold Hannyngton, 'Still Life', *The Times Literary Supplement*, 21 December 1916, p. 623.

Christie, Ian, *The Last Machine: Early Cinema and the Birth of the Modern World* (London: BBC Educational Developments, 1994).

Clarke, Bruce, *Energy Forms: Allegory and Science in the Era of Classical Thermodynamics* (Ann Arbor: University of Michigan Press, 2001).

Clarke, Stuart, ed., *Translations from the Russian by Virginia Woolf and S. S. Koteliansky* (Banks, Southport: Virginia Woolf Society of Great Britain, 2006).

Cloutier, Crista, 'Mumler's Ghosts', in *The Perfect Medium: Photography and the Occult*, ed. Clément Chéroux et al. (New Haven, CT: Yale University Press, 2005), pp. 20–3.

Collins, Jo and John Jervis, eds, *Uncanny Modernity: Cultural Theories, Modern Anxieties* (Basingstoke: Palgrave Macmillan, 2008).

Conant, Oliver, 'Countryside Modern', *New York Times Book Review*, 26 July 1992, p. 23.

Connor, Rachel, *H.D. and the Image* (Manchester: Manchester University Press, 2004).

Conrad, Joseph and Ford Madox Ford, *The Inheritors: An Extravagant Story*, introduction by David Seed (Liverpool: Liverpool University Press, 1999).

Cook, Ebenezer Wake, 'The Post-Impressionists', *The Morning Post*, 19 November 1910, p. 4, in Bullen, ed., *Post-Impressionists in England*, pp. 117–20.

Cornwell, Neil, *James Joyce and the Russians* (Basingstoke: Palgrave, 1992).

Cover wrapper, *Close Up*, 1.4 (1927).

Cover wrapper, *Close Up*, 3.4 (1928).

Cross, Anthony, ed., *A People Passing Rude: British Responses to Russian Culture* (Cambridge: OpenBook, 2012).

Crossthwaite, Arthur, 'Ennui', *Rhythm*, 1.1 (1911), p. 22.

Csengeri, Karen, 'Introduction', in *The Collected Writings of T. E. Hulme* (Oxford: Oxford University Press, 1994).

Curle, Richard, 'Joseph Conrad', *Rhythm*, 2.10 (1912), pp. 242–55.

Dalgarno, Emily, *Virginia Woolf and the Visible World* (Cambridge: Cambridge University Press, 2001).

Demoor, Marysa, 'John Middleton Murry's Editorial Apprenticeships: Getting Modernist "Rhythm" into the *Athenaeum*, 1919–1921', *English Literature in Transition 1880–1920*, 52 (2009), pp. 123–43.

Diaghilev, Sergei, 'Principles of Art Criticism', trans. Olive Stevens, in *The Ballets Russes and its World*, ed. Lynn Garafola and Nancy Van Norman Baer (New Haven, CT: Yale University Press, 1999), pp. 84–93.

Diment, Galya, *A Russian Jew of Bloomsbury: The Life and Times of Samuel Koteliansky* (Montreal: McGill-Queen's University Press, 2011).

Dixon, Joy, *Divine Feminine: Theosophy and Feminism in England* (Baltimore: Johns Hopkins University Press, 2001).

Donald, James, Anne Friedberg and Laura Marcus, eds, *Close Up 1927–1933: Cinema and Modernism* (London: Cassell, 1998).

Dorontchenkov, Ilia, ed., and Charles Rougle, trans., *Russian and Soviet Views of Modern Western Art 1890s to Mid-1930s* (Berkeley: University of California Press, 2009).

Drey, O. Raymond, 'Introduction', in *Anne Estelle Rice: Paintings*, ed. Malcolm Easton (exhibition catalogue) (Hull: University of Hull [n. pub.], 1969).

Eagle, Solomon, 'Current Literature, Books in General', *New Statesman*, 3.56 (1914), p. 118.

Edmunds, Susan, *Out of Line, History, Psychoanalysis, and Montage in H.D.'s Long Poems* (Stanford: Stanford University Press, 1994).

Eisenstein, Sergei, 'Beyond the Shot' (1929), in *Sergei Eisenstein: Selected Works*, ed. and trans. Richard Taylor, 4 vols (London: BFI Publishing, 1988), I, pp. 138–50.

—, 'Chetvertoe izmerenie v kino' ['The Fourth Dimension in Cinema'], in *Izbrannye proizvedeniya* ['Selected Works'] (Moscow: Iskusstov, 1964), II, pp. 45–59.

—, 'The Cinematographic Principle and the Ideogram', in *Film Form: Essays in Film Theory* ed. and trans. Jay Leyda (London: Dennis Dobson, 1963), pp. 28–44.

—, 'A Dialectic Approach to Film Form', in *Film Form*, ed. and trans. Jay Leyda (London: Dennis Dobson, 1963), pp. 28–44.

—, 'The Dinamic Square', *Close Up*, 8.1 (1931), pp. 3–16.

—, 'Eisenstein on Eisenstein: the Director of "Potemkin"' (1926), in *Selected Works*, I (1988), pp. 74–6.

—, 'The Fourth Dimension in Cinema' (1929) in *Selected Works*, I (1988), pp. 181–94.

—, 'Methods of Montage', in *Film Form*, ed. and trans. Jay Leyda (London: Dennis Dobson, 1963), pp. 72–83.

—, 'The New Language of Cinematography', *Close Up*, 4.5 (1929), pp. 10–13.

—, 'Perspectives' (1929), in *Selected Works*, I (1988), pp. 151–60.

—, 'Principles of Film Form' (1929), trans. Ivor Montagu, *Close Up*, 8.3 (1931), pp. 167–81.

Eisenstein, Vsevolod Pudovkin and Grigori Alexandrov, 'The Sound Film: A Statement from U.S.S.R.', *Close Up*, 3.4 (1928), pp. 10–13.

Eliot, T. S., '*Ulysses*, Order and Myth', in *Selected Prose of T. S. Eliot*, ed. Frank Kermode (London: Faber & Faber, 1975), pp. 175–8.

'Exhibition of Russian Art', *The Times*, 1 November 1910, p. 11.

Faivre, Antoine, *Access to Western Esotericism* (Albany, NY: State University of New York Press, 1994).

Falkenheim, Jacqueline, *Roger Fry and the Beginnings of Formalist Art Criticism* (Ann Arbor: UMI Research Press, 1980).

Farjeon, Annabel, 'Mosaics and Boris Anrep', *Charleston Magazine*, 7 (1993), pp. 15–22.

'The Film Society: "The Battleship Potemkin"', *The Times*, 12 November 1929, p. 14.

'The Film Society: "Mother"', *The Times*, 22 October 1928, p. 12.

The Film Society Programmes 1925–1939 (New York: Arno Press, 1972).

Flint, Kate, 'Introduction', in *Jacob's Room* (1922) (Oxford: Oxford University Press, 2000), xii–xxviii.

—, 'Introduction', in *The Waves* (1931) (London: Penguin, 1992), xii–xxviii.

'Foreign Pictures at Munich', *The Times*, 31 August 1928, p. 10.

Foster, Roy, *W. B. Yeats: A Life. I: The Apprentice Mage 1865–1914* (Oxford: Oxford University Press, 1997).

—, *Words Alone: Yeats and his Inheritances* (Oxford: Oxford University Press, 2011).

Freud, Sigmund, 'The Aetiology of Hysteria', in *The Standard Edition of the Complete Psychological Works of Sigmund Freud*, ed. and trans. James Strachey et al., 24 vols (London: Hogarth Press and Institute of Psycho-Analysis, 1953–74), III, pp. 189–221.

—, 'The Uncanny', in *Literary Theory: An Anthology*, ed. Julie Rivkin and Michael Ryan, 2nd edn (Oxford: Blackwell Publishing, [1998] 2004), pp. 418–30.

Friedberg, Anne, 'Borderline and the POOL films', in Donald, Friedberg and Marcus, eds, *Cinema and Modernism*, pp. 212–20.

Friedman, Susan Stanford, 'Definitional Excursions: The Meanings of Modern/Modernity/Modernism', *Modernism/Modernity*, 8.3 (2001), pp. 493–513.

—, *Psyche Reborn: The Emergence of H.D.* (Bloomington: Indiana University Press, 1981).

Fry, Roger, 'Acquisition by the National Gallery at Helsingfors', *Burlington Magazine*, 18 (1911), p. 293.

—, 'The Allied Artists', *Nation*, 2 August 1913, pp. 676–7, in Bullen, ed., *Post-Impressionists in England*, pp. 456–60.

—, 'An Essay in Aesthetics', in *Vision and Design* (London: Chatto & Windus, 1920), pp. 11–25.

—, 'Are we Compelled by the True & Apostolic Faith to Regard the Standard of Beauty as Relative?', autograph manuscript papers to the Cambridge Conversazione Society, October 1889, REF 1/10.

—, 'Art and Life', in *Vision and Design*, pp. 1–10.

—, 'Art and Socialism', in *Vision and Design*, pp. 36–51.

—, 'The Artist's Vision', in *Vision and Design*, pp. 31–5.

—, *Cézanne: A Study of his Development* (London: Hogarth Press, 1927).

—, 'Epicurus or Emerson', autograph manuscript papers to the Cambridge Conversazione Society, 11 February 1888, REF 1/10.

—, 'The French Group', *Catalogue of the Second Post-Impressionist Exhibition*, (1912), pp. 13–17, in Bullen, ed., *Post-Impressionists in England*, pp. 352–55.

—, 'Introduction', in *Catalogue of the Second Post-Impressionist Exhibition*, in Bullen, ed., *Post-Impressionists in England*, p. 348.

—, 'Introduction to Cézanne I, by Maurice Denis', in *Burlington Magazine*, 16 (1910), pp. 207–8.

—, 'The Last Phase of Impressionism', *Burlington Magazine*, 12 (1908), pp. 374–5.

—, *Letters of Roger Fry*, ed. Denys Sutton, 2 vols (London: Chatto & Windus, 1972).

—, 'Modern Mosaic and Mr. Boris Anrep', *Burlington Magazine*, 42.243 (1923), pp. 272–8.

—, 'Must Mahomet go to the Mountain?', autograph manuscript papers to the Cambridge Conversazione Society, June 1888, REF 1/10.

—, 'Ought we to be Hermaphrodite?', autograph manuscript papers to the Cambridge Conversazione Society, 1887–9, REF 1/10.

—, 'Post Impressionism', *Fortnightly Review*, 95 (May 1911), pp. 856–67, in Bullen, ed., *Post-Impressionists in England*, pp. 166–79.

—, 'A Postscript on Post-Impressionism', *Nation*, 24 December 1910, pp. 536–7, in Bullen, ed., *Post-Impressionists in England*, pp. 147–51.

—, Preface, in 'Works by Boris von Anrep', *Chenil Gallery Catalogue* (1913).

—, 'Retrospect', in *Vision and Design*, pp. 188–99.

—, 'Satirical Piece on Psychical Phenomena, untitled authored manuscript', 1885–9, REF 1/7.

—, 'Vitality', in *Last Lectures by Roger Fry: Slade Professor of Fine Arts in the University of Cambridge, 1933–1934*, ed. Kenneth Clark (Cambridge: Cambridge University Press, 1939), pp. 37–48.

Garafola, Lynn, *Diaghilev's Ballets Russes* (New York: Da Capo Press, 1989).

Garafola, Lynn and Nancy Van Norman Baer, eds, *The Ballets Russes and its World* (New Haven, CT: Yale University Press, 1999).

Garnett, Edward, 'A Literary Causerie: Dostoevsky', *The Academy*, 71 (1906), pp. 202–3.

—, 'Maxim Gorky', *The Speaker*, 11 March 1905, pp. 570–1.

—, 'Tolstoi's New Novel', *The Speaker*, 11 November 1899, pp. 145–6.

Garnett, Richard, *Constance Garnett: A Heroic Life* (London: Sinclair-Stevenson, 1991).

Garrity, Jane, *Step-daughters of England: British Women Modernists and the National Imaginary* (Manchester: Manchester University Press, 2003).

Garver, Lee, 'The Political Katherine Mansfield', *Modernism/Modernity*, 8.2 (2001), pp. 225–43.

Gathorne-Hardy, Robert, ed., *Ottoline: The Early Memoirs of Lady Ottoline Morrell* (London: Faber & Faber, 1963).

Gaudier-Brzeska, Henri, 'Allied Artists' Association Ltd', *The Egoist*, 1.12 (1914), 227–8.

Gauld, Alan, *The Founders of Psychical Research* (London: Routledge & Kegan Paul, 1968).

Gerrard, Deborah, 'Brown-ness, Trees, Rose Petals, and Chrysalises: The Influence of Edward Carpenter's Mystical Evolutionary Socialism on the Writing of Virginia Woolf, with Particular Reference to *The Years*', in *Woolfian Boundaries: Selected Papers from the Sixteenth Annual International Conference on Virginia Woolf*, ed. Anna Burrells et al. (Clemson: Clemson University Digital Press, 2007), pp. 15–21.

Gettmann, Royal A., *Turgenev in England and America* (Urbana: University of Illinois Press, 1941).

Gibbons, Tom, 'Cubism and "The Fourth Dimension" in the Context of the Late Nineteenth-Century and Early Twentieth-Century Revival of Occult Idealism', *Journal of the Warburg and Courtauld Institutes*, 44 (1981), pp. 130–47.

Gilbert, R. A., *Revelations of the Golden Dawn* (London: Quantum, 1997).

Gleason, John Howes, *The Genesis of Russophobia in Great Britain: A Study of the Interaction of Policy and Opinion* (Cambridge, MA: Harvard University Press, 1950).

Glew, Adrian, '"Blue Spiritual Sounds": Kandinsky and the Sadlers, 1911–16', *The Burlington Magazine*, 139.1134 (1997), pp. 600–15.

—, 'Introduction', in *Concerning the Spiritual in Art* (London: Tate Publishing, 2006), pp. vi–xxv.

Goldman, Jane, *The Feminist Aesthetics of Virginia Woolf: Modernism, Post-Impressionism and the Politics of the Visual* (Cambridge: Cambridge University Press, 1998).

—, *Modernism, 1910–1940: Image to Apocalypse* (London: Palgrave, 2004).

Goncharova, Natal'ia, (exhibition catalogue), Khudozhnikov Salon (Moscow: [n.pub.], 1913).

Goodrick-Clarke, Nicholas, *The Western Esoteric Traditions: A Historical Introduction* (Oxford: Oxford University Press, 2008).

Goodyear, Frederick, 'The New Thelema', *Rhythm*, 1.1 (1911), pp. 1–3.

Gorky, Maxim, 'The Kingdom of Shadows', in *Movies*, ed. Gilbert Adair (London: Penguin, 1999), pp. 10–13.

Gould Warwick, and Marjorie Reeves, *Joachim of Fiore and the Myth of the Eternal Evangel in the Nineteenth and Twentieth Centuries* (Oxford: Clarendon Press, 1987, revised edition 2001).

'The Grafton Galleries', *The Athenaeum*, 4446, 11 January 1913, p. 50.

Green, Christopher, ed., *Art Made Modern: Roger Fry's Vision of Art* (London: Merrell Holberton, 1999).

Griffin, Ernest, *John Middleton Murry* (New York: Twayne Publishers, 1969).

Grove, Allen, 'Röntgen's Ghosts: Photography, X-rays and the Victorian Imagination', *Literature and Medicine*, 16.2 (1997), pp. 141–73.

Gruetzner Robins, Anna, *Modern Art in Britain 1910–1914* (London: Merrell Holberton and Barbican Art Gallery, 1997).

Guest, Barbara, *Herself Defined: The Poet H.D. and her World* (London: Collins, 1985).

Gunning, Tom, 'Tracing the Individual Body: Photography, Detectives, and Early Cinema', in *Cinema and the Invention of Modern Life*, ed. Leo Charney and Vanessa Schwartz (Berkeley: University of California Press, 1995), pp. 15–45.

H.D., *Bid me to Live* (London: Virago, 1984).

—, '*Borderline*: A Pool Film with Paul Robeson' (1930), in Donald, Friedberg and Marcus, eds, *Cinema and Modernism*, pp. 221–36.

—, 'The Cinema and the Classics III: The Mask and the Movietone', *Close Up*, 1.5 (1927), in Donald, Friedberg and Marcus, eds, *Cinema and Modernism*, pp. 114–20.

—, 'Expiation', *Close Up*, 2.5 (1928), in Donald, Friedberg and Marcus, eds, *Cinema and Modernism*, pp. 125–30.

—, *The Gift*, ed. Jane Augustine (Gainesville: University Press of Florida, 1998).

—, 'Joan of Arc', *Close Up*, 3.1 (1928), in Donald, Friedberg and Marcus, eds, *Cinema and Modernism*, pp. 130–3.

—, *Notes on Thought and Vision and the Wise Sappho* (London: Peter Owen, 1982).

—, 'Russian Films', in Donald, Friedberg and Marcus, eds, *Cinema and Modernism*, pp. 134–9.

—, *The Sword Went out to Sea: Synthesis of a Dream*, ed. Cynthia Hoge and Julie Vandivere (Gainesville: University of Florida Press, 2007).

—, *Tribute to Freud; Writing on the Wall; Advent* (Manchester: Carcanet, [1970] 1985).

—, 'Turksib', *Close Up*, 5.6 (1929), pp. 488–92.

Hamer, Mary, 'Mary Butts, Mothers, and War', in *Women's Fiction and the Great War*, ed. Suzanne Raitt and Trudi Tate (Oxford: Oxford University Press, 1997), pp. 219–40.

Hanegraaff, Wouter et al., eds, *Dictionary of Gnosis and Western Esotericism* (Leiden: Brill, 2007).

Hardiman, Louise, 'Infantine Smudges of Paint . . . Infantine Rudeness of Soul': British Reception of Russian Art at the Exhibitions of the Allied Artists' Association 1908–1911', in Cross, ed., *A People Passing Rude*, pp. 133–47.

Harper, George Mills, *Yeats and the Occult* (London: Macmillan, 1976).

Harris, Frank, 'The Holy Man', *Rhythm*, 2.5 (1912).

Harrison, Charles, *English Art and Modernism* (London: Allen Lane Penguin, 1981).

Harrison, Jane, *Russia and the Russian Verb: A Contribution to the Psychology of the Russian People* (Cambridge: W. Heffer, 1915).

—, *Themis: A Study of the Social Origins of Greek Religion* (Cambridge: Cambridge University Press, 1912).

Hassall, Christopher, *Edward Marsh: Patron of the Arts: A Biography* (London: Longman's, 1959).

Hastings, Beatrice, 'Present-Day Criticism', *The New Age*, 10.22 (1912), p. 519.

'Heal & Son', Advertising Section, *Rhythm*, 2.2 (1912), p. ii.

Hellberg-Hirn, Elena, *Soil and Soul: The Symbolic World of Russianness* (Aldershot: Ashgate, 1998).

Hellmund-Waldow, E., Review of *The End of St Petersburg*, *Close Up*, 2.4 (1928), pp. 30–5.

Henderson, Linda Dalrymple, *The Fourth Dimension and Non-Euclidean Geometry in Modern Art* (Princeton: Princeton University Press, 1983, repr. Cambridge, MA: MIT Press, 2013).

—, 'Italian Futurism and "The Fourth Dimension"', *Art Journal*, 41.4 (1981), pp. 317–23.

—, 'Mysticism as the "Tie that Binds": The Case of Edward Carpenter and Modernism', *Art Journal*, 46.1 (1987), pp. 29–37.

—, 'A New Facet of Cubism: "The Fourth Dimension" and "Non-Euclidean Geometry" Reinterpreted', *Art Quarterly*, 34.4 (1971), pp. 410–33.

Henderson, Robert, 'The Free Russian Library in Whitechapel', in Beasley and Bullock, eds, *Russia in Britain*, pp. 71–86.

Henry, Holly, *Virginia Woolf and the Discourse of Science: The Aesthetics of Astronomy* (Cambridge: Cambridge University Press, 2003).

Herring, Robert, 'The Movies', *London Mercury*, 19.110 (1928), pp. 200–1.

—, 'A New Cinema, Magic and the Avant Garde', *Close Up*, 4.4 (1929), pp. 47–57.

—, 'Storm over London', *Close Up*, 4.3 (1929), pp. 34–44.

Hickman, Miranda *The Geometry of Modernism: The Vorticist Idiom in Lewis, Pound, H.D., and Yeats* (Austin: University of Texas Press, 2005).

Hind, C. Lewis, 'Ideals of Post Impressionism', *Daily Chronicle*, 5 October 1912, p. 6, in Bullen, ed., *Post-Impressionists in England*, pp. 365–8.

—, 'The Post Impressionists' (1911), in Bullen, ed., *Post-Impressionists in England*, pp. 187 91.

Hinojosa, Lynne Walhout, *The Renaissance, English Cultural Nationalism, and Modernism, 1860–1920* (New York: Palgrave Macmillan, 2009).

Hinton, Charles Howard, *The Fourth Dimension* (London: Swan Sonnenschein, 1904).

—, *A New Era of Thought* (London: Swan Sonnenschein, 1888).

—, 'A Plane World', *Scientific Romances*, 2 vols (London: Swan Sonnenschein, 1884–96), 1 (1886), pp. 9–159.

—, 'What is the Fourth Dimension?', *University Magazine* (Dublin), 1.1 (1880), pp. 15–34.

Hirschkop, Ken, 'Afterword', in Beasley and Bullock, eds, *Russia in Britain*, pp. 258–68.

Hoberman, Ruth, *Gendering Classicism: The Ancient World in Twentieth-Century*

Women's Historical Fiction (New York: State University of New York Press, 1997).

Hodgson, Richard, 'Account of Personal Investigations in Ida, and Discussion of the Authorship of the "Koot Hoomi" Letters', in *Proceedings of the Society for Psychical Research, 1885* (London: Trubner, Ludgate Hill, 1885), III, pp. 207–317.

Hoffman, Frederick, Charles Allen and Carolyn Ulrich, *The Little Magazine: A History and a Bibliography* (Princeton: Princeton University Press, 1946).

Holmes, Charles, 'Stray Thoughts on Rhythm in Painting', *Rhythm*, 1.3 (1911), pp. 1–3.

Hughes, Michael, *Beyond Holy Russia: The Life and Times of Stephen Graham* (Cambridge: OpenBook, 2014).

—, *Diplomacy before the Russian Revolution: Britain, Russia and the Old Diplomacy, 1894–1917* (Basingstoke: Macmillan, 2000).

Hulme, T. E., 'Bergson's Theory of Art' (1911 or 1912), in *The Collected Writings of T. E. Hulme*, ed. Karen Csengeri (Oxford: Oxford University Press, 1994), pp. 191–204.

—, 'Modern Art and its Philosophy' (1914), in *Collected Writings*, ed. Karen Csengeri, pp. 268–85.

—, 'The New Philosophy' (1909), in *Collected Writings*, ed. Karen Csengeri, pp. 85–8.

Humm, Maggie, *Modernist Women and Visual Cultures: Virginia Woolf, Vanessa Bell, Photography and Cinema* (New Brunswick, NJ: Rutgers University Press, 2003).

Hutchings, Steven, *Russian Modernism: The Transfiguration of the Everyday* (Cambridge: Cambridge University Press, 1997).

Huyssen, Andreas, *After the Great Divide: Modernism, Mass Culture, Postmodernism* (Bloomington: Indiana University Press, 1986).

Hynes, Samuel, *The Edwardian Turn of Mind* (London: Oxford University Press, 1968).

Ingold, Felix Philipp, *Rayonnism: Its History and Theory* (exhibition catalogue) (Zurich: Galerie Schlégl, 1986).

Jackson, Holbrook, *The Eighteen Nineties: A Review of Art and Ideas at the Close of the Nineteenth Century* (London: Grant Richards, 1913).

Jeans, James, *The Mysterious Universe* (Cambridge: Cambridge University Press, 1930).

—, *The Universe Around Us* (Cambridge: Cambridge University Press, 1929).

Jones, W. Gareth, ed., *Tolstoi and Britain* (Oxford: Berg, 1995).

Kandinsky, Wassily, *The Art of Spiritual Harmony*, trans. Michael T. H. Sadler (London: Constable, 1914).

—, *Concerning the Spiritual in Art*, trans. Michael T. H. Sadler (London: Tate, 2006).

—, 'Whither the "New" Art?' (1911), in *Kandinsky: Complete Writings on Art*, ed. Kenneth Lindsay and Peter Vergo, 2 vols (Boston, MA: G. K. Hall, 1982), I, pp. 98–104.

Kane, Julie,'Varieties of Mystical Experience in the Writings of Virginia Woolf', *Twentieth Century Literature*, 41.4 (1995), pp. 328–49.

Kareev, N. I., 'How Far Russia Knows England', trans. Adeline Lister Kaye, in *The Soul of Russia*, ed. Winifred Stephens, pp. 96–101.

Kasinec, Edward and Boris Kerdimun, 'Occult Literature in Russia', in *The Spiritual in Art*, ed. Maurice Tuchman, pp. 361–5.

Kaye, Peter, *Dostoevsky and English Modernism 1900–1930* (Cambridge: Cambridge University Press, 1999).

Kaznina, Olga, *Russkie v Anglii: Russkaia emigratsiia v kontekste Russko-Angliiskikh literaturnykh sviazei v pervoi polovine XX veka* [Russians in England: Russian Emigration in the Context of Russo-English Literary Connections in the First Half of the Twentieth Century] (Moscow: Nasledia, 1997).

Keats, John, *The Letters of John Keats: 1814–1821*, 2 vols (Cambridge: Cambridge University Press, 1958).

Kennaway, George, 'Lithuanian Art and Music Abroad: English Reception of the Work of M. K. Ciurlionis, 1912–39', *Slavonic and East European Review*, 83.2 (2005), pp. 234–53.

Kennedy, Janet, Review, '*Mikhail Larionov and the Russian Avant-Garde* by Anthony Parton' (1993), in *Slavic Review*, 54.1 (1995), pp. 250–1.

Kessler, Jascha, 'Mary Butts: Lost . . . and Found', *The Kenyan Review*, 17.3–4 (1995), pp. 206–18.

'The King and Queen', *The Times*, 12 December 1910, p. 13.

Konody, P. G., 'Art and Artists: English Post-Impressionists', *The Observer*, 27 October 1912, p. 10, in Bullen, ed., *Post-Impressionists in England*, pp. 386–9.

—, 'Art and Artists – More Post-Impressionism at the Grafton', *The Observer*, 6 October 1912, p. 6, in Bullen, ed., *Post-Impressionists in England*, pp. 368–72.

—, 'Art Notes: Allied Artists' Association at the Albert Hall', *The Observer*, 12 July 1908, p. 12.

Kuleshov on Film: Writings by Lev Kuleshov, ed. Ronald Levaco (Berkeley: University of California Press, 1974).

'Latest Intelligence: Coronation of the Tsar from Palace to Cathedral', *The Times*, 27 May 1896, p. 5.

Latham, Sean and Robert Scholes, 'The Rise of Periodical Studies', *PMLA*, 121 (2006), pp. 517–31.

Lavin, Maud, 'Roger Fry, Cézanne, and Mysticism', *Arts Magazine*, 58.1 (1983), pp. 98–101.

Lawrence, D. H., 'Reflections on the Death of a Porcupine', in *Reflections on the Death of a Porcupine and Other Essays*, ed. Michael Herbert (Cambridge: Cambridge University Press, 1988), pp. 349–63.

Lawton, Anna M., ed., *Words in Revolution: Russian Futurist Manifestos, 1912–1928* (Washington, DC: New Academia Publishing, 2005).

Leadbeater, Charles, *The Astral Plane: Its Scenery, Inhabitants and Phenomena* (London: Theosophical Publishing Society, first published 1895, third edition (revised) 1900).

—, *Clairvoyance* (London: Theosophical Publishing Society, 1899).

—, *Man Visible and Invisible* (London: Theosophical Publishing Society, 1902).

—, *The Other Side of Death* (London: Theosophical Publishing Society, 1904).

Leatherbarrow, W. J., ed., *Dostoevskii and Britain* (Oxford: Berg, 1995).

Lee, Hermione, *Virginia Woolf* (London: Chatto & Windus, 1996).

Lenauer, Jean, 'Vertoff: His Work and the Future', *Close Up*, 5.6 (1929), pp. 464–8.

Lethbridge, Marjorie, and Alan Lethbridge, *The Soul of the Russian* (London: John Lane, 1916).

Lewis, Wyndham, 'A Review of Contemporary Art', *Blast*, 2 (1915), pp. 38–47.

[—], 'Long Live the Vortex', *Blast*, 1 (1914), p. 7.

Leyda, Jay, *Kino, A History of the Russian and Soviet Film* (London: George Allen & Unwin, 1973).

Liven, Petr, *The Birth of the Ballets Russes*, trans. L. Zarine (London: Allen & Unwin, 1936).

Lodder, Christina, and Peter Hellyer, 'St Petersburg/Petrograd/Leningrad. From Aesthetics to Revolutionaries: *Mir Iskusstva (1898–1904); Apollon (1909–17); Studiya Impressionistov (1910); Soyuz Molodezhi (1912–13)*; and *Iskusstvo Kommuny (1918–19)*', in *The Oxford Critical and Cultural History of Modernist Magazines*, ed. Peter Brooker, Sascha Bru, Andrew Thacker and Christian Weikop, 3 vols (Oxford: Oxford University Press, 2013), II, pp. 1248–75.

'The London Salon', *The Times*, 13 July 1908, p. 10.

Lövgren, Hakan, 'Sergei Eisenstein's Gnostic Circle', in Rosenthal, ed., *The Occult in Russian and Soviet Culture*, pp. 273–97.

Lubbock, Percy, 'Dostoevsky', *The Times Literary Supplement*, 4 July 1912, pp. 269–70.

—, 'Georgian Stories', *The Times Literary Supplement*, 6 July 1922, p. 440.

—, 'New Novels', *The Times Literary Supplement*, 22 March 1923, p. 196.

Luckhurst, Roger, *The Invention of Telepathy: 1870–1901* (Oxford: Oxford University Press, 2002).

MacCabe, Colin, 'On Impurity: the Dialectics of Cinema and Literature', in *Literature and Visual Technologies: Writing After Cinema*, ed. Julian Murphet and Lydia Rainford (Basingstoke: Palgrave Macmillan, 2003), pp. 15–28.

MacCarthy, Desmond, 'The Art-Quake of 1910', *The Listener*, 1 February 1945, pp. 123–4.

—, 'The Post-Impressionists', Introduction to the catalogue of the exhibition, 'Manet and the Post-Impressionists' (1910), in Bullen, ed., *Post-Impressionists in England*, pp. 94–9.

MacColl, D. S., 'A Year of Post-Impressionism', *Nineteenth Century* (February 1912), pp. 285–302, in Bullen, ed., *Post-Impressionists in England*, pp. 263–84.

MacDonald, Nesta, *Diaghilev Observed: By Critics in England and the United States 1911–1929* (New York: Dance Horizons, 1975).

Macpherson, Kenneth, 'As Is', *Close Up*, 1.1 (1927), pp. 5–15.

—, 'As Is', *Close Up*, 2.1 (1928), pp. 5–12.

—, 'As Is', *Close Up*, 2.4 (1928), pp. 5–11.

—, 'As Is', *Close Up*, 3.3 (1928), pp. 5–13.

—, 'As Is', *Close Up*, 7.5 (1930), in Donald, Friedberg and Marcus, eds, *Cinema and Modernism*, pp. 236–8.

—, 'Introduction: The Fourth Dimension in the Kino', *Close Up*, 6.3 (1930), pp. 175–84.

Maddox, Brenda, *George's Ghosts: A New Life of W. B. Yeats* (London: Picador, 1999).

Maguire, Muireann, 'Crime and Publishing: How Dostoevskii Changed the British Murder', in Cross, ed., *A People Passing Rude*, pp. 149–61.

Majumdar, Saikat, 'Katherine Mansfield and the Fragility of Pakeha Boredom', *Modern Fiction Studies*, 55.1 (2009), pp. 119–41.

Mann, Thomas, *The Magic Mountain*, trans. H. T. Lowe-Porter, 2 vols (London: Martin Secker, 1927), I.

Manning, Henry, 'Introduction', in *The Fourth Dimension Simply Explained: A Collection of Essays Selected from those Submitted in the Scientific America's Prize Competition* (New York: Munn, 1910).

Mansfield, Katherine, 'Bliss' (1918), in *The Collected Short Stories of Katherine Mansfield* (London: Constable, 1948), pp. 91–105.

—, *The Collected Letters of Katherine Mansfield*, ed. Vincent O'Sullivan and Margaret Scott, 5 vols (Oxford: Clarendon Press, 1984–2000).

[—], 'The Earth Child in the Grass', *Rhythm*, 2.4 (1912), p. 125.

[—], 'Green Goggles', *The New Age*, 11.10 (1912), p. 237.

—, *Journal of Katherine Mansfield*, ed. John Middleton Murry (London: Constable, 1954).

—, *Katherine Mansfield Notebooks: Complete Edition*, ed. Margaret Scott (Minneapolis: University of Minnesota Press, 2002).

—, 'Prelude' (1918), in *Collected Short Stories of Katherine Mansfield*, pp. 11–60.

—, Review of *The Triumph of Pan* by Victor Neuburg, *Rhythm*, 2.2 (1912), p. 70.

[—], 'Tales of a Courtyard', *Rhythm*, 2.7 (1912), pp. 99–105.

[—], 'To God the Father', *Rhythm*, 2.10 (1912), p. 237.

[—], 'Two Poems of Boris Petrovsky', *Rhythm*, 1.4 (1912), p. 30.

Mao, Douglas, *Solid Objects: Modernism and the Test of Production* (Princeton: Princeton University Press, 1998).

Marcus, Laura, 'The European Dimensions of the Hogarth Press', in *The Reception of Virginia Woolf in Europe*, ed. Mary Ann Caws and Nicola Luckhurst (London: Continuum, 2002), pp. 328–56.

—, 'Introduction', in *Translations from the Russian by Virginia Woolf and S. S. Koteliansky*, ed. Stuart Clarke (Banks, Southport: Virginia Woolf Society of Great Britain, 2006), pp. vii–xxiv.

—, 'Playing the Sacred Game: The Neglect and Rediscovery of Mary Butts', *The Times Literary Supplement*, 24 August 2001, pp. 3–4.

—, 'The Tempo of Revolution: British Film Culture and Soviet Cinema in the 1920s', in Beasley and Bullock, eds, *Russia in Britain*, pp. 225–40.

—, *The Tenth Muse: Writing about Cinema in the Modernist Period* (Oxford: Oxford University Press, 2007).

Marks, Steven G., *How Russia Shaped the Modern World: From Art to Anti-Semitism, Ballet to Bolshevism* (Princeton: Princeton University Press, 2003).

Marsden, Dora, 'Views and Comments', *New Freewoman*, 1.2 (1913), p. 25.

Materer, Timothy, *Modernist Alchemy: Poetry and the Occult* (Ithaca, NY: Cornell University Press, 1995).

May, Rachel, *The Translator in the Text: On Reading Russian Literature in English* (Evanston, IL: Northwestern University Press, 1994).

McCabe, Susan, 'Borderline Modernism: Paul Robeson and the Femme Fatale', *Callaloo*, 25.2 (2002), pp. 639–53.

—, *Cinematic Modernism: Modernist Poetry and Film* (Cambridge: Cambridge University Press, 2005).

Meade, Marion, *Madame Blavatsky: The Woman Behind the Myth* (New York: G. P. Putnam's, 1980).

Minow-Pinkney, Makiko, 'Virginia Woolf and the Age of Motor Cars', in *Virginia Woolf in the Age of Mechanical Reproduction*, ed. Pamela L. Caughie (London: Garland Publishing, 2000), pp. 159–82.

Mirsky, D. S., *The Intelligentsia of Great Britain*, trans. Alec Brown (London: Gollancz, 1935).

Moore, Rachel, *Savage Theory: Cinema as Modern Magic* (London: Duke University Press, 2000).

Moréas, Jean, 'Manifeste du Symbolisme', *Le Figaro*, 18 September 1886, <www.ieeff.org/manifestesymbolisme> [accessed 20 May 2014].

Morris, Margaret, *The Art of John Duncan Fergusson: A Biased Biography* (London: Blackie, 1974).

Morrisson, Mark, *Modern Alchemy: Occultism and the Emergence of Atomic Theory* (Oxford: Oxford University Press, 2007).

Muchnic, Helen, *Dostoevsky's English Reputation (1881–1936), Smith College Studies in Modern Languages*, 20.3/4 (Northampton, MA: Smith College, 1939).

Mullin, Katherine, 'Typhoid Turnips and Crooked Cucumbers: Theosophy in Ulysses', *Modernism/Modernity*, 8.1 (2001), pp. 77–97.

Murry, John Middleton, 'Aims and Ideals', *Rhythm*, 1.1 (1911), p. 36.

—, 'Art and Philosophy', *Rhythm*, 1.1 (1911), pp. 9–12.

[—?], 'The Art of Spiritual Harmony', *The Athenaeum*, 4523 (1914), pp. 23–4.

—, *Between Two Worlds: An Autobiography* (London: Jonathan Cape, 1935).

—, 'The Function of Criticism', in *Aspects of Literature* (London: Collins, 1920), pp. 1–14.

—, *Fyodor Dostoevsky: A Critical Study* (London: Martin Secker, 1916).

—, 'The Honesty of Russia', in *Evolution of an Intellectual* (London: Richard Cobden Sanderson, 1920), pp. 16–29.

—, 'More About Romanticism', *Adelphi*, 1.7 (1923), pp. 557–69.

[—], 'Notes', *Rhythm*, 2.5 (1912), p. 36.

—, 'Poetry, Philosophy, and Religion', *The Adelphi*, 2.8 (1925), pp. 645–58.

—, *Still Life* (London: Constable, 1916).

[—], 'What We Have Tried To Do', *Rhythm*, 1.3 (1911), 36.

Murry, John Middleton, and Katherine Mansfield, 'The Meaning of Rhythm', *Rhythm*, 2.1 (1912), pp. 18–20.

—, and Katherine Mansfield, 'Seriousness in Art', *Rhythm*, 2.2 (1912), 46–9.

Nadelman, Elie, 'The Photo-Secession Gallery', *Camera Work*, 32 (1910), 41.

Nathanson, Carol, *The Expressive Fauvism of Anne Estelle Rice* (Dayton: Wright State University, 1997).

Nayman, Anatoly, *Remembering Anna Akhmatova*, trans. Wendy Rosslyn (London: Peter Halban, 1991).

Nesbet, Anne, *Savage Junctures: Sergei Eisenstein and the Shape of Thinking* (London: I. B. Tauris, 2007).

'New Books and Reprints', *The Times Literary Supplement*, 24 May 1928, p. 397.

New, W. H., *Reading Mansfield and Metaphors of Form* (Montreal: McGill-Queen's University Press, 1999).

Newmarch, Rosa, *The Russian Arts* (London: Herbert Jenkins, 1916).

Noguchi, Yone, 'From a Japanese Ink-Slab', *Rhythm*, 2.14 (1913), p. 450.

'Notes from Russia', *Athenaeum*, 4402 (1912), p. 279.

Officer of the Grand Fleet, *The Fourth Dimension: Essays in the Realm of Unconventional Thought* (London: C. W. Daniel, 1919).

Oppenheim, Janet, *The Other World: Spiritualism and Psychical Research in England, 1850–1914* (Cambridge: Cambridge University Press, 1985).

Ouspensky, Petr Demianovich, *Letters from Russia 1919* (London: Routledge & Kegan Paul, 1978).

—, *Tertium Organum: The Third Canon of Thought, a Key to the Enigmas of the World*, trans. Nikolai Bessarabov and Claude Bragdon, 2nd edn, rev. (London: Kegan Paul, 1923).

Owen, Alex, *The Darkened Room: Women, Power, and Spiritualism in Late Nineteenth Century England* (London: Virago Press, 1989).

—, *The Place of Enchantment: British Occultism and the Culture of the Modern* (Chicago: University of Chicago Press, 2004).

—, 'The "Religious Sense" in a Post-War Secular Age', *Past and Present: A Journal of Historical Studies*, 1, supplement (2006), pp. 159–77.

'Paint Run Mad: Post-Impressionists at Grafton Galleries', *Daily Express*, 9 November 1910, p. 8, in Bullen, ed., *Post-Impressionists in England*, pp. 105–6.

Parton, Anthony, *Goncharova: The Art and Design of Natalia Goncharova* (Woodbridge, Suffolk: Antique Collector's Club, 2010).

—, *Mikhail Larionov and the Russian Avant-Garde* (London: Thames & Hudson, 1993).

Partridge, Frances, 'Unpublished Memoir of Boris Anrep', NAL, Manuscript. MSL/1974/16160.

Patterson, Charles Brodie, *A New Heaven and a New Earth or The Way to Life Eternal: Thought Studies of the Fourth Dimension* (London: George Harap, 1909).

Patterson, Ian, 'The Plan Behind the Plan: Russians, Jews and Mythologies of Change: The Case of Mary Butts', in *Modernity, Culture and the Jew*, ed. Bryan Cheyette and Laura Marcus (Stanford: Stanford University Press, 1998), pp. 126–40.

—, 'The Translation of Soviet Literature: John Rodker and PresLit', in Beasley and Bullock, eds, *Russia in Britain*, pp. 188–208.

Pesmen, Dale, *Russia and Soul: An Exploration* (Ithaca: Cornell University Press, 2000).

Petrova, Yevgenia et al., *Natalia Goncharova: The Russian Years* (St Petersburg: Palace Editions, 2002).

Phelps, Gilbert, *The Russian Novel in English Fiction* (London: Hutchinson's University Library, 1956).

Polonsky, Rachel, 'Chekhov and the Buried Life of Katherine Mansfield', in Cross, ed., *A People Passing Rude*, pp. 201–14.

—, *English Literature and the Russian Aesthetic Renaissance* (Cambridge: Cambridge University Press, 1998).

'"Post-Impressionist" Painting', *The Times*, 7 November 1910, p. 12.

Prettejohn, Elizabeth, 'Out of the Nineteenth Century: Roger Fry's Early Art Criticism 1900–1906', in Green, ed., *Art Made Modern*, pp. 31–44.

Proctor, Dennis, ed., *The Autobiography of G. Lowes Dickinson and Other Unpublished Writings* (London: Duckworth, 1973).

Protopopova, Dar'ia, 'Dostoevsky, Chekhov, and the Ballets Russes: Images of Savagery and Spirituality in the British Response to Russian Culture, 1911–1929', *The New Collection*, 3 (Oxford: New College, 2008), pp. 28–41.

Przerwa-Tetmajer, Kazimierz, 'Song of the Night Mists', trans. Paul Selver, *The New Age*, 10.13 (1912), p. 292.

Pudovkin, Vsevolod, *Film Technique and Film Acting: The Cinema Writing of V. I. Pudovkin*, trans. Ivor Montagu (London: Vision Press, 1954).

Rainey, Lawrence, 'Good Things: Pederasty and Jazz and Opium and Research', *London Review of Books*, 16 July 1998, pp. 14–17.

Ray, Robert, *How a Film Theory Got Lost and Other Mysteries in Cultural Studies* (Bloomington: Indiana University Press, 2001).

Rayfield, Donald, 'False Teeth and Frozen Fish', *The Times Literary Supplement*, 28 March 2014, pp. 11–12.

Reed, Christopher, 'Revision and Design: The Later Essays', in Reed, ed., *A Roger Fry Reader* (Chicago: University of Chicago Press, 1996), pp. 305–25.

'Report of the Committee appointed to Investigate Phenomena connected with the Theosophical Society', in *Proceedings of the Society for Psychical Research, 1885* (London: Trubner, Ludgate Hill, 1885), III, pp. 201–7.

'Rhythm 1912–1913 Monthly', Advertising Section, *Rhythm*, 1.4 (1912), p. iv.

Rice, Anne Estelle, 'Les Ballets Russes', *Rhythm*, 2.3 (1912), pp. 106–10.

Richardson, John Adkins, *Modern Art and Scientific Thought* (Chicago: University of Illinois Press, 1971).

Ringbom, Sixten, *The Sounding Cosmos: A Study in the Spiritualism of Kandinsky and the Genesis of Abstract Painting* (Åbo: Åbo Akademi, 1970).

Rives, Rochelle, 'Problem Space: Mary Butts, Modernism, and the Etiquette of Placement', *Modernism/Modernity*, 12.4 (2005), pp. 607–27.

Rose, Jacqueline, *On Not Being Able to Sleep: Psychoanalysis and the Modern World* (London: Chatto & Windus, 2003).

Rosenthal, Bernice Glatzer, ed., *The Occult in Russian and Soviet Culture* (Ithaca, NY: Cornell University Press, 1997).

[Ross, Robert?], 'Cézanne and the Post-Impressionists', *The Times*, 8 January 1913, p. 10, in Bullen, ed., *Post-Impressionists in England*, pp. 410–12.

[—?], 'A Post-Impressionist Exhibition: Matisse and Picasso', *The Times*, 4 October 1912, p. 9, in *Post-Impressionists in England*, pp. 361–5.

—, 'The Post-Impressionists at the Grafton: The Twilight of the Idols', *The Morning Post*, 7 November 1910, p. 3, in *Post-Impressionists in England*, pp. 100–4.

[—?], 'The Post-Impressionists: Some French and English work', *The Times*, 21 October 1912, p. 10, in *Post-Impressionists in England*, pp. 378–82.

Ross, Stephen, 'Uncanny Modernism', in Pamela Caughie, ed., *Disciplining Modernism* (Basingstoke: Palgrave, 2009), pp. 33–52.

Rosslyn, Wendy, 'Boris Anrep and the Poems of Anna Akhmatova', *Modern Language Review*, 74.4 (1979), pp. 884–96.

Rubenstein, Roberta, *Virginia Woolf and the Russian Point of View* (Houndmills: Palgrave, 2009).

Ruby, Scott, 'The Crystal Palace Exhibition and Britain's Encounter with Russia', in Cross, ed., *A People Passing Rude*, pp. 89–96.

Russell, Bertrand, 'Mysticism and Logic' (1914), in *Mysticism and Logic and Other Essays* (London: Longmans, Green, 1918), pp. 1–32.

'Russian Art in London', *The Times*, 26 October 1910, p. 6.

'The Russian Ballet', *The Times*, 24 June 1911, p. 13.

Rutter, Frank, *Art in My Time* (London: Rich & Cowan, 1933).

—, *Revolution in Art: An Introduction to the Study of Cézanne, Gauguin, Van Gogh, and Other Modern Painters* (London: Art News Press, 1910).

—, *Since I was Twenty-Five* (London: Constable, 1927).

Sadleir, Michael, 'After Gauguin', *Rhythm*, 1.4 (1912), pp. 23–9.

—, 'Fauvism and a Fauve', *Rhythm*, 1.1 (1911), pp. 14–18.

—, 'Introduction', in Wassily Kandinsky, *The Art of Spiritual Harmony*, trans. M. T. H. Sadler (London: Constable, 1914).

—, 'Kandinsky's Book on Art', *Art News*, 9 March 1912, pp. 45–6.

—, 'The Letters of Vincent Van Gogh', *Rhythm*, 1.2 (1911), pp. 16–19.

—, *Michael Ernest Sadler 1861–1943: A Memoir by his Son* (London: Constable, 1949).

'The Salon D'Automne', *The Times*, 9 October 1906, p. 10.

Sarabianov, Dmitry, 'The Many Faces of the Russian Avant-Garde: Late 1900s to Early 1920s', in *Russia! Nine Hundred Years of Masterpieces and Master Collections*, (exhibition catalogue) (New York: Guggenheim Museum Publications, 2005), pp. 267–75.

Sargeant, Amy, *Vsevolod Pudovkin: Classic Films of the Soviet Avant-Garde* (London: I. B. Tauris, 2000).

Scarborough, Dorothy, *The Supernatural in Modern English Fiction* (London: C. P. Putnam's, 1917).

Schofield, A. T., *Another World: or The Fourth Dimension* (London: Swan Sonnenschein, 1888).

Schwartz, Sanford, *The Matrix of Modernism: Pound, Eliot and Early-Twentieth Century Thought* (Princeton: Princeton University Press, 1985).

Schwinn Smith, Marilyn, '"Bergsonian Poetics" and the Beast: Jane Harrison's Translations from the Russian', in Beasley and Bullock, eds, *Translating Russia*, pp. 314–33.

Scott, Bonnie Kime, ed., *The Gender of Modernism* (Bloomington: Indiana University Press, 1990).

—, 'The Journals of Mary Butts', *Modernism/Modernity*, 11.1 (2004), pp. 188–90.

Searle, Adrian, 'One Damn Masterpiece after Another', *Guardian*, 23 January 2008, p. 23.

Senelick, Laurence, *The Chekhov Theatre: A Century of the Plays in Performance* (Cambridge: Cambridge University Press, 1997).

—, '"For God, for Czar, for Fatherland": Russians on the British Stage from Napoleon to the Great War', in Beasley and Bullock, eds, *Russia in Britain*, pp. 19–34.

Seton, Marie, *Sergei M. Eisenstein: A Biography* (London: Dennis Dobson, [1952] 1978).

Shail, Andrew, *The Cinema and the Origins of Literary Modernism* (Abingdon: Routledge, 2012).

Sharp, Jane Ashton, *Russian Modernism between East and West: Natal'ia Goncharova and the Moscow Avant-Garde* (Cambridge: Cambridge University Press, 2006).

Shields, David, *Reality Hunger: A Manifesto* (London: Hamish Hamilton, 2010).

Shklovsky, Victor, 'Art as Technique' (1917), in *Russian Formalist Criticism*, ed. Lee Lemon and Marion Reiss (Lincoln, NE: University of Nebraska Press, 1965), pp. 5–24.

Shone, Richard, *The Art of Bloomsbury: Roger Fry, Vanessa Bell and Duncan Grant* (London: Tate Gallery Publishing, 1999).

Sidgwick, Mrs H., 'Note on the Evidence, Collected by the Society, for Phantasms of the Dead', in *Proceedings of the Society for Psychical Research* (London: Trubner, Ludgate Hill, 1885), III, pp. 69–150.

Simpson, Celia, 'The Cinema', *Spectator*, 9 February 1929, p. 191.

Sinclair, May, 'The Finding of the Absolute', in *May Sinclair's Uncanny Stories* (London: Hutchinson, 1923), pp. 243–71.

Smith, G. S., *D. S. Mirsky: A Russian-English Life, 1890–1939* (Oxford: Oxford University Press, 2000).

Smith, Helen, 'Edward Garnett: Interpreting the Russians', in Beasley and Bullock, eds, *Translating Russia*, pp. 301–13.

Soloviev, Evgeny, *Dostoievsky: His Life and Literary Activity a Biographical Sketch*, trans. C. J. Hogarth (London: George Allen & Unwin, 1916).

Spalding, Frances, *Roger Fry: Art and Life* (London: Granada Publishing, 1980).

Spence, Lewis, *An Encyclopaedia of Occultism: A Compendium of Information on The Occult Sciences, Occult Personalities, Psychic Science, Magic, Demonology, Spiritism and Mysticism* (London: George Routledge, 1920).

Stephens, Winifred, ed., *The Soul of Russia* (London: Macmillan, 1916).

Surette, Leon, *The Birth of Modernism: Ezra Pound, T. S. Eliot, W. B. Yeats and the Occult* (Montreal: McGill-Queen's University Press, 1993).

Swinnerton, Frank, *The Georgian Literary Scene: A Panorama* (London: Heinemann, 1935).

Sword, Helen, *Ghostwriting Modernism* (Ithaca, NY: Cornell University Press, 2002).

Taylor, Richard, *The Politics of the Soviet Cinema: 1917–1929* (Cambridge: Cambridge University Press, 1979).

Tedlock, E. W., 'D. H. Lawrence's Annotation of Ouspensky's *Tertium Organum*', *Texas Studies in Literature and Language*, 2.2 (1960), pp. 206–18.

Thacker, Andrew, *Moving Through Modernity: Space and Geography in Modernism* (Manchester: Manchester University Press, 2003).

Tillyard, S. K., *The Impact of Modernism 1900–1920: Early Modernism and the Arts and Crafts Movement in Edwardian England* (London: Routledge, 1988).

Tolstoy, Lev, 'The Three Hermits', in *Walk in the Light and Twenty-Three Tales*, trans. Louise and Aylmer Maude (Farmington, PA: Plough Publishing House, 1998).

Tomalin, Claire, *Katherine Mansfield: A Secret Life* (Harmondsworth: Penguin, 1987).

Trotter, David, *Cinema and Modernism* (Oxford: Blackwell, 2007).

Tryphonopoulos, Demetres, *The Celestial Tradition: A Study of Ezra Pound's 'The Cantos'* (Waterloo, ON: Wilfrid Laurier University Press, 1992).

Tsivian, Iurii, *Early Cinema in Russia and its Cultural Reception*, trans. Alan Bodger, ed. Richard Taylor (London: Routledge, 1991).

Tsuzuki, Chushichi, *Edward Carpenter 1844–1929: Prophet of Human Fellowship* (Cambridge: Cambridge University Press, 1980).

Tuchman, Maurice, 'Hidden Meanings in Abstract Art', in *The Spiritual in Art: Abstract Painting 1890–1985*, (exhibition catalogue), ed. Tuchman (New York: Abbeville, 1986), pp. 17–61.

Turner, Sarah, '"Spiritual Rhythm" and "Material Things": Art, Cultural Networks and Modernity in Britain, c.1900–1914' (unpublished doctoral thesis, University of London, Courtauld Institute of Art, 2008).

Turton, Glyn, *Turgenev and the Context of English Literature, 1850–1900* (London: Routledge, 1992).

Underhill, Evelyn, *Mysticism: A Study in the Nature and Development of Man's Spiritual Consciousness* (London: Methuen, 1911).

Vachell, Horace Annesley, *The Fourth Dimension* (London: John Murray, 1920).

Viacheslaf, Ivanof, 'The Theatre of the Future', trans. Stephen Graham, *The English Review*, 10 (1912), pp. 634–50.

Waddington, Patrick, ed., *Ivan Turgenev and Britain* (Oxford: Berg, 1995).

Wadsworth, Edward, 'Inner Necessity', *Blast*, 1 (1914), pp. 119–25.

Wagstaff, Christopher, ed., *A Sacred Quest: The Life and Writings of Mary Butts* (Kingston, NY: McPherson, 1995).

Waldman, Milton, 'The Movies', *London Mercury*, 13.76 (1926), pp. 425–7.

Walton, Jean, 'White Neurotics, Black Primitives, and the Queer Matrix of *Borderline*', in *Out Takes: Essays on Queer Theory and Film*, ed. Ellis Hanson (Durham, NC: Duke University Press, 1999), pp. 243–70.

Warren, Sarah, *Mikhail Larionov and the Cultural Politics of Late Imperial Russia* (Ashgate: Farnham, 2013).

Washton-Long, Rose Carol, 'Expressionism, Abstraction, and the Search for Utopia in Germany', in Tuchman, ed., *The Spiritual in Art*, pp. 201–17.

Waugh, Patricia, 'Science and the Aesthetics of English Modernism', *New Formations*, 49 (2003), pp. 32–47.

Webb, James, *The Harmonious Circle* (London: Thames & Hudson, 1980).

—, *The Occult Underground* (La Salle: Open Court, 1974).

Weber, Max, 'The Fourth Dimension From a Plastic Point of View', *Camera Work*, 31 (1910), p. 25.

Wells, H. G., 'The Case of Davidson's Eyes', in *The Complete Short Stories of H. G. Wells* (London: Ernest Benn, [1927] 1965), pp. 273–83.

—, 'The Plattner Story', in *The Complete Short Stories*, pp. 325–45.

Whitworth, Michael, *Einstein's Wake: Relativity, Metaphor and Modernist Literature* (Oxford: Oxford University Press, 2001).

Wilde, Oscar, 'The Canterville Ghost', in *The Canterville Ghost and Other Stories* (New York: Dover, 2001).

Williams, Jane, 'A Russian Interpretation of British Society in Mosaic', paper given at 'Russian in Britain 1880–1940: Reception, Translation and the Modernist Cultural Agenda' conference (Institute of English Studies, 2009).

Williams, Robert C., *Russia Imagined: Art, Culture, and National Identity, 1840–1955* (New York: Peter Lang, 1997).

Williams, William Carlos, 'A Sort of Song', *The Collected Poems of William Carlos Williams*, ed. Christopher MacGowan, 2 vols (Manchester: Carcanet Press, 1988), II, p. 55.

Wilson, Colin, *The Occult* (London: Hodder & Stoughton, 1971).

Wilson, Keith, *The Policy of the Entente: Essays on the Determinants of British Foreign Policy 1904–1914* (Cambridge: Cambridge University Press, 1985).

Wilson, Leigh, *Modernism and Magic: Experiments with Spiritualism, Theosophy and the Occult* (Edinburgh: Edinburgh University Press, 2013).

Wing Beat, Advertisement, *Close Up*, 1.1 (1927).

Woods, Joanna, *Katerina: The Russian World of Katherine Mansfield* (London: Penguin, 2001).

Woolf, Leonard, *Beginning Again: An Autobiography of the Years 1911–1918* (London: Hogarth Press, 1964).

Woolf, Virginia, 'Across the Border', *The Times Literary Supplement*, 31 January 1918, p. 55.

—, *Between the Acts* (1941) (London: Hogarth Press, 1990).

—, 'Character in Fiction' (1924), in *Essays*, IV (1994), pp. 420–38.

—, 'The Cinema' (1926), in *Essays*, IV (1994), pp. 348–54.

—, *The Diary of Virginia Woolf*, ed. Ann Olivier Bell and Andrew McNeillie, 5 vols (London: Hogarth Press, 1975–84).

—, *The Essays of Virginia Woolf*, ed. Andrew McNeillie, 5 vols (London: Hogarth Press, 1986–8).

—, *Jacob's Room* (1922) (Oxford: Oxford University Press, 1999).

—, *The Letters of Virginia Woolf*, ed. Nigel Nicolson and Joanne Trautmann, 6 vols (London: Hogarth Press, 1975–80).

—, 'Modern Fiction' (1925), in *Essays*, IV (1994), pp. 157–65.

—, 'More Dostoevsky', *The Times Literary Supplement*, 22 February 1917, p. 91.

—, *Mrs Dalloway* (London: Hogarth Press, 1925).

—, *Night and Day* (1919) (London: Hogarth Press, 1990).

—, 'On Being Ill' (1926), *Essays*, IV (1994), pp. 317–29.

—, *Orlando* (1928) (Ware: Wordsworth Editions, 2003).

—, *Roger Fry: A Biography* (London: Hogarth Press, 1940).

—, 'The Russian Background', *The Times Literary Supplement*, 14 August 1919, p. 435.

—, 'The Russian Point of View' (1925), *Essays*, IV (1994), pp. 181–90.

—, 'The Russian View', *The Times Literary Supplement*, 19 December 1918, p. 641.

—, 'Solid Objects' (1920), in *The Complete Shorter Fiction of Virginia Woolf*, ed. Susan Dick (New York: Harvest, 1985), pp. 102–7.

—, 'Street Music' (1905), *Essays*, I (1986), pp. 27–32.

—, 'Tchehov's Questions' (1918), *Essays*, II (1987), pp. 244–8.

—, *To the Lighthouse* (London: Hogarth Press, 1927).

—, 'A View of the Russian Revolution' (1918), in *Essays*, II (1987), pp. 338–40.

—, *Walter Sickert: A Conversation* (London: Hogarth Press, 1934).

—, *The Waves* (1931) (London: Penguin, 1992).

Wright, Patrick, *On Living in an Old Country: The National Past in Contemporary Britain* (Verso: London, 1985).

Žižek, Slavoj, *The Parallax View* (Boston, MA: MIT Press, 2006).

Index

Page numbers in italics refer to figures. The name 'McTaggart' is arranged within the alphabetical listing as if 'Mac'.